KEYS TO THE KINGDOM

Annie Dike

Keys to the Kingdom

© 2015 Annie Dike
First published in 2015 via CreateSpace and Kindle Direct Publishing

Printed in the United States of America. Except as permitted under the United States Copyright Act of 1976, no part of this publication may be reproduced or distributed in any form or by any means, or stored in a database or retrieval system, without the prior written permission of the publisher.

Table of Contents

Prologue 5
Chapter One   The Break 11
Chapter Two   What Goes Up 17
Chapter Three   The Treetop Phenomenon 29
Chapter Four   The First Stone 39
Chapter Five   Keen on the Keys 61
Chapter Six   The Black Abyss 77
Chapter Seven   The Iron Maiden 97
Chapter Eight   Telling Stuff 107
Chapter Nine   Ass-First 127
Chapter Ten   "Motorin'!" 153
Chapter Eleven   My Opening Statement 163
Chapter Twelve   Go to Danglin' 191
Chapter Thirteen   April Showers 205
Chapter Fourteen   When It Rains 213
Chapter Fifteen   The Stress Dial 221
Chapter Sixteen   Up Salt Creek Without a Shackle 239
Chapter Seventeen   Have Genny, Will Travel 247
Chapter Eighteen   Waste Not 259
Chapter Nineteen   Want Not 277
Chapter Twenty   "Annie, Are You Okay?" 299

Chapter Twenty-One	Life is Not	311
Chapter Twenty-Two	My Tunnel, My Time	321
Chapter Twenty-Three	This Is Me Roaring	333
Epilogue		343
About the Author		349

Prologue

I wake every morning and stand to be counted. I see, through bars, the others standing as well. If they move quickly, I move quickly, without reason. My feet shuffle me to the edge of my cell and I wait to hear it—that unmistakable click that tells me I have a place here. I am secure. I know I will get a tray and a spoon and a bowl of bland oatmeal every morning. I will get government-issued shoes and walk them around a tumbleweed track. I will wake up again tomorrow on the same cot, under the same stiff sheet and shuffle myself to the edge of my cell again, along with everyone around me, to be counted—included in a place I hate to be.

I've heard tapping every night the last couple of years and decided it was others like me. They're planning to go all *Shawshank Redemption* on the place and break free. I'm either crazy or sure of it. Either way, I've decided to join them. I hung my own Rita Hayworth equivalent and I, too, have been picking nightly at my personal wall. But tonight I broke through. The cool night air that blew in surprised me at first, as if I had forgotten my own goal. I had been making such tedious progress for years that the effort had almost become purposeless. The picking was easy. There was no real consequence and no real reward. Now I can feel a compromise in the structure, a chance that it really might crumble if only I were to stand and ram my body through it. Now it is real. *The moment is here.* I jump at the thought and back away from the hole, scramble to my rusty cot on the other side, pull my knees tightly to my chest and eye the poster over them.

Rita is flapping lightly against the cinder block, beckoning me but I cannot leave. The picking seemed so easy, so inconsequential. Now the choice is real. The perils of the great beyond taunt me: *Where will you go? What will you do? How will you get by?* As a prisoner accustomed to my daily regime, comfortable as a cog in the wheel, there is one fear of freedom that seizes me: *Who will count me? Who will I matter to?* I sit here and pick at my mattress, haunted by the hard things I may face beyond the wall, paralyzed by my own fear of the unknown. So I remain. In my cell, with my shelter and my routine.

It can be an elusive irony—security, comfort, predictability—particularly to those who begin to realize they never really wanted it. I didn't but it took me a while to come to that reckoning and even longer to actually do something about it. My decisions had put me there and I knew the break would be disruptive, hurtful, hard and would force me to give up the comforts that I knew. I heard the nightly tapping but at first I tuned it out, waking every day and rising to be counted, to get my oatmeal and walk my track. I lived for years in a prison of my own making. That's the way it began to feel to me, at least, spending every day in a place I didn't want to be, doing things I was required to do to achieve things I was supposed to want—a big house, a nice car, a degree, a husband, a handsome salary—security, basically, an assurance that I would be comfortable and my life would be easy.

But it wasn't. It was stressful and consuming and full of hostility and resentment. I had a lot of things, expensive things, and a lot of money—none of which I needed and none of which made me happy. They merely occupied me. My time was spent trying to earn more money to buy more superfluous things until I felt like I was locked in a prison of my own production. I had built the cell myself—block by block—by deciding every day to do the things I was supposed to do. I didn't feel happy though. I felt confined. What it seems they don't tell you about all of that sought-after security is that its purpose is predictability—a reassuring repetition that tells you tomorrow will be the same as today so you don't have to fear it. And many may find themselves just as happy as the formula predicted because they had acquired all of the things they were supposed to want and they're content. Fantastic.

I was not. I picked at the wall.

I began to see the things in my life (many I worked very hard to attain) as gray and unfulfilling as government-issued prison shoes. There were so many things I still wanted to do but I had neither the time nor the freedom to do them. It's a paralyzing revelation to find you have created a life you want desperately, daily to escape. I had no idea what I was going to do, where I was going to go or how I would get by. I just knew I wanted out. But it's easy to just think about it—to dream and plan and pick at it. There will come a moment, though, when you have to decide if you're actually going to break free or remain and it will seize your heart. You don't know what awaits you beyond the wall. There will be nothing repetitive or reassuring about it. It's likely going to be hard. It will hurt. It may break you but you know, as the breeze from the tunnel beckons, that the very last thing you want is to wake tomorrow, stand to be counted and remain dissatisfied but secure in your cell.

When I blinked through the breeze of that hole in my cell I saw myself doing a million different worldly things. I was hiking the Himalayas, cave diving in Bali, and birthing baby elephants in Africa. I heaved a boulder-sized backpack up the Pacific Crest Trail. Reese Witherspoon was right next to me. In my new life, we were best friends. I climbed mountains. I crossed oceans. Minus the miniature giraffe, I was the most interesting woman in the world! Most importantly, I was tan, toned and visibly happy. Almost sickeningly so. I'll bet if I sneezed, confetti would poof out. *My God, I looked good!* I was clutching every moment as if it were my last. I even saw myself drenched and fighting to cling to mud in a landslide, brace myself for the blow of a volcano and hold on to the rails of a boat as it battled through torrents of wind and rain. I watched as I was tossed and slapped around with surprising ease by an angry sea. I saw it all. I knew how insignificant I might be to the vast world and how life-threatening my new life might sometimes be but in the visions I was, at the very least, living a life worth threatening.

In near-death moments like that you tend to focus more on your *life* than your peril. You ask yourself what it is exactly, that you are gripping and gnashing and struggling to protect. When I almost lost mine I finally saw the chalky little cell I'd been living in. I was giving my own pitiful little tour: *This is my cell and this is my cot.* What I took away was despair—discontentment with my current situation and the decisions that had led me there. Death, I knew, was inevitable. Life, I learned, was not.

I knew I would rather go down in a pile of wet confetti on a boat than continue my slow rot in prison. I wanted to rip and claw at the seams of my very existence. I wanted to scream—to rip, shred and scream—no, not scream, roar. In that moment I knew I was going to do it, *really* do it. I was about to grab my life by the collar and roar. I shot off my cot and began clawing at the cinder, smashing blocks on the cell walls and the rails of my rickety cot. I even shredded the lovely Hayworth on the way out and let her flap, ripped and ragged behind me. And I didn't know where I was going to go or what I was going to do. I had just turned thirty and I was divorced, unemployed, without a home, income or a clue as to how I was going to get by, but I was no longer afraid. I was free. I mattered to me.

CHAPTER ONE

The Break

The truck hummed beneath me but I couldn't get myself to reach for the key in the ignition. I had put it in park but I couldn't turn it off. I didn't want to go inside. I didn't want to be in that house. Hell, I didn't want the house. I didn't want anything in it. I certainly didn't want the mortgage. I had so many things I didn't want—the big flat-screen T.V., the two-car garage, the fifteen-hundred dollar front-load washer, the Cox premium cable package. *Why did I have all of this crap? Who bought all of these things? Who signed those papers?*

I really felt like it was someone other than me, some morphed Stepford version of myself that walked around, told people things they wanted to hear and did things I didn't want to do without my consent. It was hard to explain but it was as if there were a series of a hundred decisions, one after the other, where I erred on the side of what I thought I was *supposed* to do, rather than what I really *wanted* to do. Over time those decisions slowly started to pile up like little pebbles around me until I was peeking out from a forged stone prison, sick with irritation for putting myself there.

It was a paralyzing thought: staring at everything I had built, everything I had worked so hard for, sacrificed so much time and money for, and knowing I wanted to tear it all down and start again. I was afraid of doing it, of course, but I was more afraid of what would happen if I didn't. I was afraid I would come to hate him—or worse, myself if I didn't. As I sat there watching him through the window I had a suspicion I already did.

He was hunched over his computer at the makeshift desk he had made in the corner of our guest bedroom, scrolling through Craigslist ads. I could tell all the way from the truck. And he was wearing his University of Alabama sweatpants because he was still in school. Eleven years an undergrad and I hated that. I could see all of my suits hanging neatly behind him in the closet and I hated them too. I could see every room of our house because there was a light on in each of them and I thought of the power bill, then the mortgage, then his tuition and I hated those more. Yet here I sat knowing that but lacking the courage to change it. I would have hated the mere fact that I hadn't—when things had come to a head and I had the ability and the motivation and yet I hadn't.

During that time in my life, I didn't need a life-threatening moment to tell me what I would take away from it. I already knew. It haunted me daily. Acknowledging my unhappiness was the easy part. The actual doing of something to change it was where I got stuck. I lingered in a wasteful purgatory, ambling through each day like I was on a conveyor belt, doing everything I was supposed to, clocking in and out, going to bed and waking up and doing it all over again. Pounds packed on.

I was overweight, pasty and soft—a cow being shuffled along to the slaughterhouse without even putting up a fight.

I simply pulled panty hose up over my squishy parts every day, stuffed them into a suit and sat them in an office. I was lethargic, sluggish. I didn't do fun, active things because I didn't feel like it and I didn't have time to. All I did was get back on the conveyor belt, day after day, distracting myself with the only things that could—work and liquor. And it was those two things that led me to that moment anyway, where I realized I could have just died, easily, like a bug being flicked off of a picnic table. All of the incredible things this world has to offer and I was so stupid I had almost given them all up because I was unhappy and overworked.

I stayed at the office late because I didn't want to go home. I drank with my colleagues afterward because I was supposed to network (still a form of working) and because I still didn't want to go home. The drinking wasn't exactly required but it was kind of necessary. An attorney who doesn't drink is just kind of weird, like a sailor who doesn't swim. You would just stand out and the most important part of networking is to show potential clients that, above all, you fit in. Besides, I liked it. I had good genes for it. Clinically I'm sure I drank too much (probably still do) but I certainly didn't drink more than anyone else. We all worked hard. We stayed out late. And we drank.

Stupidly I told myself this was okay because I was the provider, the breadwinner, and I was doing everything I was supposed to do to ensure my continued ability to fulfill that role, particularly in light of our continually growing loans, debt and consumer needs. The only potential harm I was causing was to myself, I argued internally. I wasn't sleeping around. I wasn't cheating on my husband. I was paying all of the bills, making my partners a lot of money. I was doing everything I was supposed to do—climbing that ladder. But all of those supposed-to decisions led me to drink myself into oblivion, get behind the wheel of a two-ton vehicle and drive it onto the interstate. That's how stupid I was. And what's worse is it wasn't the first time. I had done it so many times I was starting to have nightmares about it—seeing the view through my windshield as my truck skidded off the shoulder of the road and started to roll.

What really bothered me about those dreams was the fact that it was not painful. I felt no pain, no fear, no breaking of my own bones as I crashed cab-down onto a rocky slope. I saw everything but felt nothing because it was done. My life was over. There would be no more feeling, no more anything. I was just gone. And here I sat, on this night and I had done it again. Stupidly—inexplicably—I had done it again. Even after I had awoke from the last drunken, derailed death-dream and told myself I would never do it again, I had done it again. I almost couldn't believe myself. I was ashamed of my unjustifiable decisions and my pure dumb luck that they hadn't killed me or others. This time, *this night*, I couldn't even remember the drive home. I tried to blink it back but it was a black void in my mind. My truck was barreling at seventy miles per hour down the interstate and I was driving in a state of blind consciousness.

I could not remember the drive home.

Somehow I made it miraculously back to my house without killing myself or a family of three and here I sat, staring at our sprawling estate with the fancy motorized gate, the lighted walk, all of the pretty little things you buy and install and have people come repair. I was alive by some stroke of sheer luck. I wasn't behind bars with three life sentences stacked on for involuntary manslaughter. I was damn lucky and the realization of it struck me in that moment like a thousand watts of energy plugged right into my spine.

I was young, capable, healthy, driven. I was alive and I had almost thrown it all away. *Why?* I burned myself with the question. Because I was unhappy and didn't know what to do about it? Because I thought this was the way I was supposed to live and this was the only way I had found to cope with it? I made dumb, deadly decisions because I was afraid to hurt people's feelings by changing what I knew needed to change? I had become so weak. My own shame washed over me like liquid nitrogen, chilling every cell in my body.

But I was not weak. I had clawed and climbed my way from a little orange house in New Mexico to a coveted city view from my firm office. I went from garage sale t-shirts to tailored suits, cleaning houses for money to handling lawsuits worth millions all on my own. I had paid for my own education, a degree, a license to practice law, my very own two-story house with central heat and AC. I had acquired and accomplished all of those things. I was not weak. I was just unhappy and I was done—done risking my health and happiness because I was afraid to break free. Screw that. *No, fuck that.* I was enraged with myself.

There was no morphed version of me. There was no person that acted outside of my will. I had chosen all of this and I now knew I wanted to "unchoose" it. I was *going* to unchoose it. I didn't care how hard it was going to be or how much it might hurt other people. I was going to rot to death or end up a blood-stained streak on the interstate, three sad little picket crosses next to it, if I continued living my life this way. I had to do this for me. I had wanted to for a long time and now I had the motivation—that life-altering snap that makes you stand up and say the words you know will rip everything wide open. This was my moment. I was going to tear down the walls. I turned off my truck, walked into my two-story, too-big, too-expensive house and roared.

CHAPTER TWO

What Goes Up

"Aaaggghhhhh!" The sound seemed to emanate from the base of my spine and rattle every vertebra on its way out. It was a deep, guttural wail that thundered through my body but it was more than my voice coming out. It felt like a shockwave of energy that pulsed out of me and traveled my entire plane of existence like that old black-and-white footage of the atomic bomb. It shot out of me when I walked into my house that night and started this entire destructive, revitalizing journey. Now here I was three years later and it was radiating out of me again as I clung to the top of a sailboat mast.

Of all the places I thought this whole prison break vision quest might take me, fifty feet above a boat in the middle of the Gulf of Mexico wasn't one of them but that's where I found myself—filling my chest with crisp salt air, looking out on glistening sunlit chop and roaring once again. I felt like an African lioness, standing out on that big rock-throne from the *Lion King*, bellowing out over my kingdom—my own battle-cry rumbling and resonating in my chest. It shook the walls of my house that night and I could feel it again now—ringing in the aluminum against my legs, humming through the entire boat beneath me, my new home on the water. They were all echoing my cry.

It had been an arduous trek—the years I spent pushing myself out of the rubble heap I had created, crawling over blocks and boulders and finally climbing out—but I had done it. I felt I was now at the apex of my climb with my reward—an endless blue horizon—spread to infinity before me. This was my new kingdom—this boat, this beautiful body of blue water, this powerful body of mine that had pulled me from the wreckage and hoisted me to the top. My arms and legs now clung tightly to the mast which swayed me back and forth, in big, sweeping arcs, above the treacherous deck below. I had no safety net beneath me, no back-up plan, no guarantee for my security or even a safe descent yet I was the least worried, in my adult life, that I had ever been. I now had such fewer needs, such fewer things but so much more potential and possibility.

Three years of struggling, stripping many of the comforts of my former life, and I was now exactly where I wanted to be doing exactly what I wanted to be doing: sailing south in blue waters on an incredible boat with an incredible man. Now, where did I find said incredible man? Where all promising relationships are born: late one night in a run-down bar. But this man seemed to have his own gravitational pull. I was spinning wildly at the time—freshly freed, newly single—but he stopped the entirety of my inertia in one conversation about his dream to live aboard a sailboat and cruise around the world.

He was absolutely driven by adventure and I wanted nothing more than to be his companion on each and every one. This man intrigued me. He was well-traveled, well-spoken, a marine, a lawyer, a veteran, a dreamer, a doer. He was incredibly accomplished and yet he rode his bike to work. He kitesurfed. He sailed. He skied. He cooked. This man was everything I had never known. This man was Phillip. And while I never saw him—or any man for that matter—in my most-interesting-woman visions, he became my most rewarding exploit of all. From the moment we met, Phillip and I became and have remained unorthodox yet unapologetic "adventure companions"—a bond which to us means everything, to others means nothing, but it is ours.

Not one year after we met, Phillip and I began shopping for our own sailboat. Within months we found ourselves and another crew member sailing our Niagara 35 home across the Gulf of Mexico in four- to six-foot seas and sawing off our flailing, choking dinghy from the davits in order to save the boat. While the trip was harrowing and costly, it was also thrilling and inspiring. The same summer we brought her home, Phillip and I began planning our first blue water sailing trip together, just the two of us. And I knew—as eye-opening and awe-inspiring as this blue water trip might be—it would simply be the first of many, each one affording us a new batch of colorful, invigorating, inspiring experiences and lifelong memories.

As long as we could keep the boat going, we could go anywhere. There was such freedom in this simplicity. I no longer worried about a manicured lawn or a motorized gate, the power bill or the mortgage. All that was really required of us was to keep the boat on course which meant my only immediate and foreseeable need was to retrieve that stupid halyard! It seemed such a small necessity in comparison to the things I used to spend lots of money on and worry about, but out there on the water a line needed to raise a sail was a key component to our few necessities: seaworthiness, fair winds, food and health. While I never dreamed I would find myself at the top of our mast in the middle of the Gulf not one week into our big, trip-of-a-lifetime, it was the exact type of experience Phillip and I were both after—a fresh adventure born daily out of the simple needs of our new life. If the halyard goes up the mast, it must come back down. If it does not, one must go up after it. These were the refreshing challenges of my new domain. Hal went up, so I had to go after him.

Now halyards don't usually hang out at the top of the mast. It's fifty feet up in the air—not really a convenient place to keep them if you ever want to, I don't know, get them down and use them. Like me, it seems our halyard had his heart set on a life-changing journey. He had started down on the deck of our boat—level, safe, secure—then he too broke free and began running around for the first time unfettered and climbing to new heights. I wonder what he saw up there, if it inspired him or frightened him, if he wanted to stay or come back down. When I went up after him I saw everything I had been working toward. I saw endless freedom, a vast landscape to explore. I saw all of the possibilities. But I was only there, on our gallant Niagara 35 sailboat, making my way south for the first time to the Florida Keys—because I too had done it: broken free, crashed and banged around but kept climbing.

The moment it left my hand I felt it but I didn't believe it. I looked at my spread fingers, my empty palm, my pitiful, halyard-less hand—as if it was some foreign object connected to me but not controlled by me. *What the hell were you thinking Hand?* I can't explain why I did it. It's like dumping a cup of coffee on yourself when you turn your wrist to look at your watch. Your mind simply decides something else is more important. Did a wave rock the boat and was I about to fall if I didn't grab something more than a halyard quick? Yes, but that doesn't give my rogue hand the authority to do something stupid! No matter what happens, no matter how many rollers come through, you never let go of the halyard. Not ever. *I* knew that but apparently my wayward hand did not.

The minute I let go he took off like a giddy Golden Retriever running around in circles in the backyard. Choppy little two-footers were just what he needed to start swinging wildly back and forth from the top of our fifty-foot mast, whipping around the boom, winding around the backstay, unwinding and swinging out freely again. Having the time of his unleashed life pretty much. He was taunting us with the shackle, as if he had a pair of my lacy panties in his mouth and he knew we would chase him for it. We were playing along too, at first, hopping around on the deck, reaching out and jumping for him. If we thought it would work we probably would have patted our thighs and said: "Here boy!" But every time we got close to grabbing him, he would tear away again, ducking his tail so we couldn't get it, shaking the shackle-panties in his teeth and laughing at us. It was clear. Hal was off his leash.

It's comical looking back on it now but there we were, Phillip and I, smack dab in the middle of our big trip to the Florida Keys, an adventure we had been planning for over a year—and we found ourselves out in the Gulf, jumping around on deck, playing old-timey dog-catchers on the boat. After the hard-knocks passage we had endured bringing our boat home for the first time across the Gulf the previous year, we were eager to get back out in blue water, apply some of the lessons we had learned and learn some more. The previous year's trek had been my first offshore passage on a boat, only the second sail of my life and the first trip with a new boat and new crew: Phillip, me and our mouthy-but-lovable buddy Mitch. It was the perfect combination for almost laughable peril and let's just say Mother Nature didn't miss the opportunity. We were lucky to get the boat home, two months later, minus a dinghy and a transmission. Embarking on such a challenging and invigorating journey, though, right when I was trying to challenge and invigorate myself sealed my destiny as a sailor. When we finally did get the boat to its new home in Pensacola—just Phillip and I in a bit of a heroic engine fluid fiasco—we absolutely knew cruising is what we wanted to do.

This time, however, there would be no dinghy on davits, there would be no schedule and (sorry buddy) but there would be no Mitch. While we didn't anticipate Hal and his shackle panties, we knew we would screw up again and learn more lessons but that's what it's all about. During the inaugural passage both the boat and I had proven our durability and seaworthiness but, more importantly, Phillip and I learned not only that I wanted to do it but that we *could* do it together. Just the two of us could get on that boat and go south, go somewhere, go anywhere. We wanted to sail through blue waters, pull into a remote anchorage, drop the hook and explore and experience our surroundings all wide-eyed and wanderlust. We wanted to open ourselves to all the world had to offer and we wanted to do it by sailboat. We weren't looking to just make another passage. We were looking to spend the days of our prime doing, seeing and tasting things that would enthrall us. At the very heart of it Phillip and I knew the cruising lifestyle offered exactly what we both desired—to live more freely.

"Where should we sail to first?" I would ask, big doe deer eyes blinking at him. It was a topic that came up often in the months that preceded our decision to buy a sailboat but the conversation became real when we finally got our boat back to Pensacola and started cruising her around our local waters. I remember the first time we dropped the hook at Ft. McRee and the boat just sat—completely still, safe and serene, just bobbing in the water. I couldn't believe you could make such a comfortable home on a boat and then sail it to any exotic place in the world and live there for a day, or weeks or months or a year.

Then, whenever your wondering heart desired, you could just raise your anchor and sail your glorious little home to the next glorious little place. It was such a liberating concept to have and worry about so few things (basically the boat and the weather) while experiencing so much. Sitting in the cockpit of the boat that first evening on anchor near the fort, I remember looking out on a magenta sunset, a glass of wine shimmering in my hand and letting the vision of my new life take shape in my mind.

I was going to travel the world. I was going to cruise. I was going to write! I could see my future on the horizon through wavy heat lines like an oasis, but it was there. If I kept moving forward I would reach it. So I did. Each step I took was intentionally planted in its direction. Our trip to the Keys was going to be the first big step. For me this trip was going to be a monumental adventure, a small taste of what it would really be like to live on our boat and travel the world. And I told myself I had better like it. I needed this trip to justify all of the chaos and turmoil I had created in my life for it—all that ripping and roaring I had done. But, deep down, I knew I wouldn't just like it. I would love it. I would live it, with every fiber of my being. I was ready to let go of everything and sail the world! Apparently a little *too* ready because that's precisely what I did in letting go of the halyard. *Stupid Hand! Stupid Annie!*

There was really no need to point fingers though. This wasn't the first time we had let go of a halyard and it certainly wouldn't be the last. And it doesn't really matter who does it, you both somehow have to get it back if you want to hoist your main and do any more sailing. Back then every time we dropped the mainsail, we would unhook the halyard used to raise it and clip it to the deck to secure it. I know what you're thinking: *That's a dumb idea.* Yes, thank you. We know that now. And I wish I could say this particular lesson is the one that trained Phillip and me. But alas.

It took one more but this was at least an eye-opening step in the right direction because Hal was reckless and ruthless up there—bashing and crashing around like one of those spikey balls Medieval warriors used to swing around on a stick-and-chain. Phillip got out the boat hook and started batting at the shackle. For reasons that baffle us to this day, Hal—in all his clanging and banging—had somehow managed to snap the shackle shut and we thought we might be able to 'hook' it and ease him back into reach. Hal must have sensed our plan, though, because the next time the shackle came whipping around, he had managed to open it, thereby thwarting our hook-and-snatch plan. *Real cute, Hal.*

But what do we, as sailors, do when things get complicated? We get creative! I had the brilliant idea to duct tape the fish net to the boat hook to make this extended Frankenstein-like halyard-catching contraption (patent pending) so we could snag the shackle in the netting. We probably looked like those old timey 'dog police' running around with our big dog-catching net. Phillip was standing on the backrest in the cockpit on his tiptoes with me behind him bracing him as he swatted and poked in the air. It wasn't funny in the moment but I'm sure if a nearby vessel got a look at us with our Frankenstein net trying to catch all those imaginary butterflies, we would have given them a hearty laugh. As Phillip gave it one last swing a wave rocked us, forcing him to forego the net and leap down into the cockpit to save his footing. Our butterfly contraption clattered on the deck and slinked overboard.

Phillip and I shared a dumb, oh-gees-is-it-gone? look. "No, we'll circle back," Phillip said. "Find it!" First rule on the sailboat—and I *knew* this but knowing is different than actually *doing*—if anything goes overboard (particularly a person), someone on board needs to immediately find the thing-slash-person in the water and shine a light on it if necessary or at least keep a watchful eye on it. Do not look away, not even for a second. Because you can lose a thing-slash-person in an instant in the great big sea … or Gulf, whatever. *You idiot, Annie* I thought to myself. *Look overboard! Find it!* Thankfully Phillip had instructed me quickly and, by the time I spotted it, it wasn't too far from the boat. By some stroke of pure luck (or good marine design) it was also floating and had some kind of reflective tape on it so we could spot it easily with the flashlight. Phillip turned us around and pointed us toward it. I got out our gaff (a pole with a sharp hook on one end that we use to pull fish aboard) and headed up to the bow to snag the floating hook-net contraption.

"Nothing else is going overboard tonight," Phillip hollered out to me. "Hang on and be careful!" *You got it*, I thought to myself as I made my way to the bow. I had no desire to go swimming that night. I could see the reflective tape bobbing toward us in the water. Phillip put me on it and I stretched far over the lifelines to get it but the water was much further than I anticipated. Plus trying to reach it over the lifelines was like bending over railing. My gaff didn't even reach the surface of the water and the net was about to float by. I dropped to my knees, grabbed a cleat and shoved the majority of my body out under the lifelines, gaff in hand. I fished it around in the water a bit and finally snagged the netting of our duct tape contraption. While getting the four-foot gaff—which was now connected to a three-foot boat hook which was taped to a three-foot fish net—back on the boat was certainly awkward and I'm sure not the most graceful thing I have ever done, it was somehow doable and now done.

With all of our gear, limbs and bodies intact, Phillip and I plopped down in the cockpit for a disheartened rendezvous. It had been a hairy moment and we were both glad to have survived it without any broken ankles or lost gear. As we sat in the silence—our halyard wrapping and banging around on the back-stay as a reminder of failed efforts—it was clear the next 'thing' that might go over would be one of us if we kept up the tiptoe butterfly bit. We both glared at him as he clanged around above our heads. *It's not funny anymore, Hal.* Sensing our irritation Hal whipped himself three times around the backstay and stayed there, the equivalent of him slinging a shoulder around, crossing his arms and pouting.

Some very half-hearted suggestions were then thrown out about climbing the backstay, climbing the boom, but we knew we weren't going to pursue any of them—not at night. The decision was made to leave the halyard until dawn. It was wound tightly around the backstay and we figured it would stay there. We motored on through the night, taking our shifts, and we heard no further peep out of Hal. He was quiet because he was busy.

CHAPTER THREE

The Treetop Phenomenon

"I have some bad news," Phillip said. Three minutes after 6:00 a.m. is when he said it. It was kind of laughable. I knew we were out in the middle of the Gulf on a sailboat with no way to raise our mainsail. I also knew in order *to* sail we were going to have to find some way to climb up on the bimini and get our halyard off of the backstay. *But, wait, you have worse news? Okay, shoot.*

"It climbed its way up the mast," Phillip hollered down to me in the saloon. *Up the mast? Climbed? It?* I shook my head a few times and rubbed my eyes trying to piece together what he was telling me and clear my vision at the same time.

"The what did?" I asked, still a little groggy.

"The halyard," he said. "It's at the top of the mast."

Although his words made sense, I didn't really understand how it could have happened. The last time I saw our main halyard—that turd—he was wrapped a couple of times around the backstay, too high up to reach, but he seemed secure at the time. And I call him a 'he' because he is. He's a snot-nosed little brat. Don't let go of him for a second was the lesson we took away from all of this. By all appearances Hal was going to stay wound around the backstay, just a few feet over our heads, until the morning when we could fetch him back in broad daylight. That would have been great. That's not what happened. I had never suspected he would be anywhere else when the sun rose. *How could Hal have possibly snaked his way back up the mast?* Not that I didn't believe Phillip but I had to step up into the cockpit to see for myself. And there he was. Our main halyard—waaay up at the top of the mast—was giving us a friendly little wave from upon high. *You turd!*

Apparently the weight of the line from below was enough to counterbalance the length of line that was out, particularly when it was wound around the backstay. As a result the shackle eventually creeped its way all the way up the backstay to the top of the mast. You might have guessed this but, unfortunately, a *big* part of sailing is the ability to raise the sails. There was no way around it. Phillip and I weren't going to be doing any sailing until one of us climbed the mast to bring that halyard back down so we could raise the mainsail back up. We were still out in the Gulf, about five or six hours from Clearwater with favorable wind and we had already been motoring through the night. Sailing was really the best option.

We made some coffee and assessed the situation. The seas were relatively calm that morning. We had two- to three-foot swells rolling through every three to four seconds but they were quartering us nicely on the port bow so the boat was rocking gently over them. It was a moderately smooth sea state. Swaying gently below, however, is perceived far differently fifty feet up in the air. Think back on those days when, as a child, you climbed to the top of a tall tree—one that appeared to be standing still on the ground—and it surprised you how much it actually swayed from side to side in the wind once you made it to the very top.

The same principle applies to the mast of a sailboat. They are far more flexible than you think. As you have probably already guessed, I drew the short straw and was deemed the lucky deck-hand to climb the mast. *Oh happy day!* While I had ascended the mast several times at that point in my short sailing career, all of those times occurred when the boat was docked safely at the marina, not while we were underway and not while the boat was bobbing and swaying over two- to three-foot seas. But it was a simple, undeniable truth: he had gone up so I had to go after him.

I was ready though. To be honest, I was excited. I was about to climb the height of our beautiful boat and look out across an expanse of crystal blue waters in the Gulf. I was exactly where I wanted to be: one week into our much-anticipated inaugural trip to the Florida Keys, just Phillip and me on our incredible Niagara 35. From the moment we brought her home from Punta Gorda, Florida to Pensacola the previous year, we had been talking about planning and making another offshore trip. Now here we were back out in the Gulf making our way down to the Florida Keys, and it seemed nothing could dampen our mood.

So we let go of the main halyard? *Okay, "we" means "I" here.* But we knew we'd get it back. So we needed to climb the mast mid-sea to do it. We knew we, meaning I, could. When you're cruising around on a sailboat, you just kind of start to expect these things. They're not setbacks; they're normal occurrences that you just have to deal with. Things are going to break and need to be repaired. You're going to get caught in weather sometimes and get a little roughed up. Equipment is going to fail when you least expect, want or need it to. It's just going to happen. The more you're out there experiencing and learning from it, though, the better you will be at handling the next 'expected unexpected' catastrophe and the more you will enjoy it. It's hard. It's fun. It's frustrating but it's the ultimate reward. I can guarantee one thing—cruising is never boring. And it certainly wasn't going to be this day. I was about to scale a fifty-foot pole while sailing across the Gulf of Mexico. Here we go!

While the mast-climb mid-sea was, in and of itself, going to be a pretty daunting undertaking, we had yet another issue to deal with. You see the problem with having to ascend the mast to get your *main* halyard back down is that you can't *use* the main halyard (typically your strongest line for hoisting heavy objects) to do it. Bring in the B Team. After some examination of the mast it was determined we would have to use the spinnaker halyard because it was the only line coming out of the mast that would (in theory) allow me to actually get to the top. The others—the topping lift for the spinnaker, the inner forestay for the staysail and the halyard for the staysail—all stopped short a few feet shy of the top of the mast where the main halyard was gaily waving down at us. *We see you. You turd!* I had to be able to get all the way to the top to retrieve it.

The spinnaker halyard we believed (also in theory) would be plenty strong enough to raise me but we had yet to use ours on the boat. Phillip and I are far more leisure cruisers than racers; hence, there is no real need to hoist that big, huge billowing sail just to pick up a couple knots. Spinnakers are beautiful, yes, even iconic in sailing paintings and pictures.

They're also a huge chore. The thought of using the line designed to raise a lofty flowing sail for the first time to raise Yours Truly fifty feet into the air made both Phillip and I a little uneasy, but it was our only option. Plus I weigh less than Phillip which makes me the obvious choice for ascending. To be safe, though, Phillip decided to secure the halyard for the staysail to me as a backup safety line. That way if for whatever reason the spinnaker halyard failed, I would only tumble seven or eight feet before the backup line would catch and send me banging into the mast. That was better than a splat on the deck. The decision was made. It was time to get to it. We left some coffee warm in our mugs and started rigging me up.

After some discussion Phillip and I decided to latch our boat hook—yes, the same one I had rescued from dark waters the night before—to me. I wanted to use it to snag the halyard in case it was just a few feet or inches out of my reach at the top of the mast. It was a great plan in theory, an epic failure in execution. We tied a length of line, approximately three feet, to the end of the hook and latched that to my bosun's chair so it would be secured to me in a manner that I could hoist and use it while still having it secured to my bosun's chair. Think of it like a set of keys on a chain.

Once I was tied three ways to Sunday we started the ascension, starting from atop the boom, and Phillip working all of the lines from the cockpit. We had also been fighting nightly banging from our inner forestay during this trip, so we decided one other item to accomplish during this ascension would be to remove the inner forestay from the mast. We figured we could easily ascend again to re-mount it on the off-chance we would need it on this trip. And I hope you experienced sailors out there do appreciate this genius line of reasoning for what it's truly worth: "Let's climb the mast in light seas to take down a stay we will need to re-climb the mast to mount in rough seas." Why would we do this? Because it was banging. Apparently we like undertaking mid-sea mast ascensions in storm conditions more than banging. Clearly it was a decision we would frown upon later but that's the hilarity of hindsight. At the time we thought it was a splendidly brilliant idea and added it to my list of mid-mast chores.

Another downside of ascending using the spinnaker halyard is that it comes out on the fore(bow)-side of the mast so I had to climb on the front side of the mast where many blocks, pulleys, tracks and a steaming light reside. These caused some pain as I was scraped and pulled across them and proved decidedly fatal for our steaming light. As I was ascending I was watching the spinnaker halyard at the top of the mast, watching my back-up safety line as Phillip intermittently cranked it in and checking periodically to make sure the boat hook was still attached to me. Everything seemed to be cranking along as smoothly as could be expected until I saw a problem.

"STOP!" I thundered down to Phillip.

The knot for my backup line was riding just below the steaming light on the front of the mast and I knew he was about to crank right over it, dragging the knot and all of my 143 pounds behind it. *Okay, 145. We did have steak the night before.* But with my being approximately twenty-five feet up already, trying to shout through wind and waves to Phillip back in the cockpit, he couldn't hear me. The knot caught tight underneath the light and I watched as it pinched, puckered and shattered our steaming light when Phillip hoisted me up a few cranks. I hated to see it happen but, thankfully, it's not one of the more crucial lights on the mast. So ... *c'est la vie*.

It was about that time that what I like to call the "treetop" phenomenon started to kick in. It's startling how much the movement of the mast changes a mere thirty feet up and how flexible the mast really is. She really can sway. And because she was, it became far more crucial that I cling to her—with both legs and arms wrapped tightly around and clinched together on the other side. I was literally a mast-hugger. The mild two- to three-foot rollers we had felt below felt like four- to five-foot monsters at that height and I was struggling merely to keep my body wrapped around the mast, much less ascend it. I knew if I let go, I would be toast. I would swing out just as wildly as the main halyard had, bang every shroud in my ten-foot radius and—assuming I didn't get wrapped around one, which really would be worse— would come swinging back around and crash into the mast. All of this would occur with me unable to control which way I was turning, which limbs or body parts would hit where and whether or not I would even stay conscious for the whole thing, much less alive. The mast was swaying in a huge arc, forward and backward, but I could not let go. It was the only thing that could ensure my safe ascent down.

With the exaggerated rocking to and fro, and my hands otherwise occupied around the mast, it was about that time that the boat hook came unfastened from my bosun's chair and fell the three-foot length of line we had tied to it—like a pocket watch dangling at the end of its chain, although I do not now believe a boat hook can do anything near as dainty as 'dangle.' I watched as it began swinging and clanging wildly against the backs of my calves, my feet and the mast. There was nothing I could do about it, though, but hold firm when I knew it was whipping back to potentially strike me.

It made quite a ruckus banging around up there but, I'll tell you, the worst sound was the groaning and creaking of the spinnaker halyard. I could see Phillip cranking hard below—four, five, six times around with the winch—but the halyard would only seem to pull me up three inches, *maybe* four, while letting out a gut-wrenching wail of exhaustion. You would have thought I weighed four hundred pounds the way that thing was carrying on. Although I hope she can't hear me, I must admit there are times I doubted the spinnaker halyard could raise me any further. She was stretched so thin. I started to believe she must be right so I clung all four hundred of my seeming pounds tightly to the mast with a kung-fu death-grip to help her with the weight.

After a few clamorous bangs of the boat hook on the mast I finally heard a hollow, aluminum pop behind me but this time there was a light tug on my rear and then a bit of a weightless release. And there it went. *The boat hook.* I watched it fly freely, end over end, over the bimini, past the stern, twirling lightly through the air before it landed in the water a good thirty feet behind the boat. The thing is four feet, easily, and it looked like a toothpick being flicked into the wind. I suddenly felt so incredibly small, so frighteningly insubstantial.

I think that's when the real fear kicked in. I knew now I wasn't going to have any kind of magic extender to help me reach out to grab the halyard when I got to the top. Stretching to it would likely mean extracting my battered body from the safety of the bosun's chair—a proposition I was not yet willing to entertain as my thighs were tiring and I was still swinging wildly three feet one way and another three feet back from the waves. But I was already up there. It was now or never. Just a few more feet. Phillip and I both watched the boat hook hit the water and float away. We met eyes for a moment and simultaneously decided there was nothing that could be done. We couldn't stop everything to turn around and rescue it this time. It was gone. Phillip shrugged his shoulders and shouted, "You ready?" I hollered a mighty "Yes!" back that I hoped sounded braver than I felt.

The last few feet up the mast seemed to be the most straining on the spinnaker halyard. I watched Phillip crank, around and around, and felt myself inch up the mast at a snail's pace. Finally the knot on the spinnaker halyard reached the pulley at the top and I knew there was nothing more Phillip could do. I shouted for him to stop and set my sights on the halyard. It was probably about ten inches out of my reach with my weight resting safely in the seat of the bosun's chair—or as safely as possible fifty feet up, clinging to a swaying mast. I was so close.

I gripped my bare thighs around the aluminum. They were already scraped and red and bruised from all of the gripping I had done during the climb. They hurt but I didn't care. I squeezed tighter and they clung. I knew I was going to have to climb the last foot of the mast on my own, with no safety chair, just my bruised and battered appendages holding my tired body tight to the mast and inching it upwards. There was no other way. The boat heeled left, then right as a roller came through. As soon as it passed, I went for it, inching my way up with quivering thighs, the heat from the bosun's chair leaving me quickly and the wind chilling my backside, reminding me of the indifferent emptiness beneath me.

CHAPTER FOUR

The First Stone

My legs shook with the grave realization that I really could fall and really could die. It was one of those life-threatening moments that forces you to freeze time and ponder your life. Memories flooded me involuntarily. They washed through the gullies of my mind and began to fill behind my eyes, forming images, hazy then clear, until I felt I could no longer see the endless body of blue water over which I was rocking and swaying. I looked up to try and spot the halyard above me but it seemed to be glinting into an apparition.

"I see it! There, there!"

I was shouting to my brother below me through thick leaves and branches and bunches of green. But when I looked out and blinked into the sun I *could* see it—the building we had climbed the tree to see—our school, Highland Elementary. Little did I know that climb, as well, would almost kill me. I had only spent six years in this big, bright world when I embarked on a journey that almost took me from it. Like most of the dangerous things John and I did at home, it started on the roof of our house in New Mexico. We had one of those flat-top roofs covered with rocks. I'm not sure they even make those anymore but, for whatever reason, my brother and I grew up thinking people with pitched-roof houses were somehow privileged. Probably because they had central heat and air.

We had no AC and one furnace heater in the center hall that had a little half circle of soot formed in the shag carpet in front of it. John and I used to curl up in front of it after our bath to let it warm the towels on our backs. We loved that house and, looking back on it, I'm glad our roof was flat because it added an entire new space to play. It was the ultimate hiding place for backyard hide-and-seek. It also served as a universal launching pad for people, things, pets. We leapt off of it with Superman capes made out of sheets. We scooched the trampoline up to it so we could jump off the roof onto it and it wasn't long before we had the brilliant idea to try and jump from the trampoline back up *onto* the roof. God we were terrible children. We deserved every spanking we got but we didn't get half as many as we deserved. My brother, John, and I (and John in particular) were pretty good at covering our tracks.

On this particular day, John and I—standing atop the flat roof—somehow found ourselves in a hot debate over whether our elementary school had a flat roof too. Don't ask. We argued about stupid things all the time. I was in the flat camp while John was a proponent of pitched. We had to find out. The tallest tree was in our neighbor, Mr. Christian's, yard but from years of experienced trespassing in our neighborhood, John and I knew we could get *into* his tree from our flat-top roof. *I told you the roof was key.* Being smaller than John, I was able to tinker my way up to the higher, smaller branches to get the best view. It was during that climb that I first experienced what I call the treetop phenomenon, where the trunk of the tree standing on the ground looks solid as a stone pillar—completely unmoveable—but at the top it is swaying five feet in either direction. Trees, like masts, have much more flex than you realize.

I liked the swaying though. I thought it was fun. I just held tight and let it swing me around. I waited for a stiff breeze to pass before I traversed up further and soon I could see our elementary school in the distance. *There's Highland!* And I was right. It did have a flat-top roof. *I told you John!* It felt so weird, though, to look at it from a treetop view. It looked so small and insignificant but it was where I spent most of my days. It was where Mrs. Pipkin sat me in time-out when I didn't deserve it, but more often when I did. It was where I raced Scottie from the tetherball poles to the P.E. door. It housed so much and yet it sat like a speck on the horizon. So small. I started to step out to get a little better look but the branch I pushed down on was too bendy. In my little kid brain that's how I remember it. Being prudent I decided that branch wouldn't be a good choice so I stepped back but somehow I misjudged where my previous, un-bendy branch was and let my weight sink through a foot that had nothing underneath it. I knew the moment it started to happen that it was just going to happen. I couldn't stop it. Instantly I started snapping and crashing through every limb in the tree during my free-fall to the ground. I could hear it vividly but I don't remember seeing much other than swishes and flashes of green and sun. Then BOOM.

 I hit the ground like an elephant falling over. I imagine a little cloud of dust coming out from under me like a cartoon. That's what the little bendy branch I had tried to step on probably saw as she looked down at me now from a good forty or fifty feet up. It was the first time I'd had the wind knocked out of me and I remember what a strange and shocking feeling that was. Telling my lungs to pull air in but they wouldn't. I opened my mouth wider as if that would help and tried to force air in but still nothing. My lungs were in shock. *I* was in shock. My eyes adjusted in the moment and I saw John scrambling down the tree, almost slipping and falling himself a time or two, trying to get down in a hurry. Finally air rushed into my lungs like an avalanche. I heaved my chest so full it raised me from the ground, seemingly from the dead.

Now you would have thought this was where I said, "I thought I was going to die" and my little six-year-old life flashed before me—little frolicking Care Bears and all—but it wasn't. A mast climb, a tree climb: that's far too cliche. Many of you may agree but it's funny how, as a kid, you perceive your body differently because most of its functions are foreign to you. Even when you're in real danger, as long as it does things you understand—moves, breathes, bends, smells like it's supposed to—it doesn't scare you. But when it starts to go off the rails and emit strange discharges, fluids and odors or begins sprouting weird hair and lumps—*that's* when it becomes frightening. I still distinctly recall my thoughts of fatality when I developed my first case of the squirts. I thought organs were coming out. Falls were normal. Bodily fluids going awry were not. The fall honestly didn't scare me as much as the blood.

A few muffled coughs sputtered out of me as I sat and breathed myself back to life for a minute while John made his way down to me. He hadn't screamed when I fell and I knew why. It wasn't because he didn't care. It was because he did. Remember the tree we were climbing was Mr. Christian's. Falling to the bottom of it meant I had landed in Mr. Christian's yard. Somehow John had to get me up, out through Christian's side gate, across our front lawn and inside through *our* front door without Mr. Christian, or worse, *Mom* seeing us. We both knew if she found out we'd been climbing in Mr. Christian's tree again—like she specifically told us not to—and, particularly, if my dumb ass had fallen out of it while doing so—like she specifically said we probably would—her spanking and punishment would hurt far worse than a little tumble from a tree. John and I both knew we had to make out like this whole tree-fall thing never happened and quick.

I remember the look on John's face as he skidded up next to me in the dirt—a little bit of disbelief but, for the most part, he was a professional. He started lifting my arms and inspecting my torso like a field surgeon.

"You're okay," he said. It wasn't a question but it wasn't really a diagnosis either. It was more like a command. "You're fine, you got that?"

"Okay," I sputtered out, finding it a little hard to speak, swallow or turn my head to the right. But, for the most part, I did feel okay until I looked down at my little Care Bears t-shirt and saw blood streaks starting to soak through it. Then I started to get scared. John lifted it up so we could both see and while I definitely was a little red and seared, I think we both let out a sigh of relief. I was scraped to hell and back; thick swatches of red, raw skin littered my belly and underarms from the branches I had swiped as I fell, but they appeared to be only skin deep. There wasn't some sharp twig jutting out from my lower intestines or anything, no bones cracked and bent around in the wrong direction.

For the most part John was right. I was okay. I could breathe, speak and see—to the left at least. But I needed to get back to the house, cleaned up and covered up quick. John did a kind of army-style hunched-over sprint to Mr. Christian's gate and poked his head out to run reconnaissance and make sure the coast was clear. I don't know where my mom and stepdad were but John deemed it safe to make a run for it. He flagged me over to the gate and I hunch-sprinted to the best of my battered body's ability up behind him. We followed that flag-and-sprint pattern at every stopping point until somehow we ended up both in the bathroom at home unseen.

The water in the sink turned a murky brown as John swabbed at my bloody welts with a wet, wadded-up hunk of toilet paper. We knew not to use a rag because then there would be evidence. He soaked through three wads before chunking them in the toilet and flushing it. The blood was actually washing out of my Care Bears shirt pretty good. I guess because we got to it so quickly the crimson streaks were still fresh and wet, easy to massage out under the faucet. Plus most of my little kid clothes were the color of washed-out blood anyway. It probably wouldn't stand out. John rung it out in the sink and told me to start running the roll of toilet paper around my torso like we had done when we dressed up as mummies for Halloween last year. "I'll go get you a long-sleeve. Keep the door shut and don't flush again."

When he came back into the bathroom I'd made ten or twelve good rounds around my pot belly with the toilet paper. The worst gash was on my left side, just under the ribs, so I had covered it an extra few times hoping to stop the bleeding so it wouldn't get on the new shirt. John had brought me my Rainbow Brite long-sleeve. Man that was such a great shirt. I loved those little front print tees. We would pick them up at garage sales for a nickel apiece—a dime for long-sleeves—and the slick Rainbow graphic on this one was hardly worn off, when I got it at least. I kind of curled up my face at John for a second because I didn't want to soil that shirt with my nasty gashes but John cut me off. We didn't have time for me to be picky.

"Just put it on," he said as he helped me wiggle into it, keeping the toilet paper girdle in place as I pulled it down. I winced a bit as the sleeves dragged across the fresh scrapes on my arms but I got it on. John patted it around my midsection to make the toilet paper sit right and make sure it all looked legit, not like I was growing lumpy tumors around my ribs.

"You're okay," he said again, this time with a little smile. Despite the scrapes and whiplash I had to smile a little too. It seemed we were going to be able to pull this off. But the hardest part was yet to come. I remember the stern you-got-this look John gave me when mom called us to the kitchen that night for dinner. I walked in kind of Frankenstein-like trying to keep my toilet paper girdle in place. I wiggled up into my booster seat as Mom set our plastic plates with pork chops and peas in front of us. John and I started shoveling dinner down in hopes of getting in and out of the spotlight as fast as possible. I thought we were doing okay until John looked down at my left side and let his eyes pop white for a moment. I waited a moment later until mom and our stepdad, Pa, were busy with their own pork and peas then I looked down and saw it too. Blood had soaked through my toilet paper bandage, through my Rainbow Brite shirt and was making its way down to my little-kid jeans—a rich, bold river of red.

I was bleeding out.

That's when I got scared. I had never bled that much before. Never a pumping stream like that, all the way to my jeans. I didn't know how much blood I had in me. I started to think it was all going to drain out and leave me cold and purple-looking like that weird Count Something guy on Sesame Street. I didn't want to be cold. Or purple. That's when it happened. I couldn't help it. I liked my little pink, plump life. I mourned it already. Big fat tears began to form in my eyes and my lower lip trembled. John gave me a stop-it scowl but I couldn't. I thought I was dying. I just wanted it to stop. I imagined there was some kind of faucet valve hidden on me somewhere that Mom would know how to find and turn off to make the bleeding stop.

Much to John's dismay, I started bawling out of fear, which is a much louder bawl than from pain. Dinner turned to chaos when mom quickly found my bleed site and took me to the bathroom to doctor me up. I don't remember much of what happened after that. I know John and I both got our due whooping for climbing Mr. Christian's tree but Mom knew whose idea the mummy wrap was so John definitely bore the brunt of it. No wonder he said he hated me sometimes and shoved me in the dirt. I deserved it. I said I hated him too sometimes but only when I really meant it.

I was glad to have John around, though—glad he was there to help assess and patch me after most of my childhood falls and glad he was there to help me avoid most of the Mom-whoopings I should have received as a result. The Count Dracula catharsis was certainly a lesson. I never climbed Mr. Christian's tree again, well at least not that high. *I said we were terrible.* And I fell out of plenty more before my childhood years were said and done. But as I sat in my booster seat that night—chilling and changing purple—and I took stock of my little life, I can't say I had any real regrets at the time. I didn't want to die—no pink, plump six-year-old does—but I didn't want to make any drastic changes either. Life was pretty peachy. I climbed trees, jumped off cliffs and always beat Scottie from the tetherball poles to the gym. I was doing just about everything I wanted. Living life just as a six year old should, my days revolved around getting into trouble, getting out of it and eating cookies. I probably didn't have many regrets because I didn't have big choices to wrestle with. It was just the grungy Care Bears shirt or the grungy Star Bright one. Neither one was going to give me much remorse. The less I had to decide between the better things seemed.

As I watched the water in our cracked bathroom sink turn red while Mom washed me up I could feel myself warming. Mom had apparently found that faucet-valve thing on my back, shut off my river of red and finally I began to believe I was going to make it! I remembered feeling so grateful in that moment for an all-too-often presumed given: life. Memories swirled inside me like the water in the sink and a different red streak began to appear. It was a swipe on glass. I squinted now, trying to make out the image, still seeing nothing of the bustling blue waters around me at the top of the mast—only the mashed-up memories of my terrified mind which seemed set on frightening me with reflections of my own mortality.

As the image finished forming, I could see it was the windshield of my truck lying on its side, half buried in the gravel and dirt. There was a large red splatter above the steering wheel, the mark a painted-red basketball would make when hitting a window. A bold red streak trailed from the splat down to the dash and I could now see myself, a crumpled, broken heap lying on the passenger side door, my arms thankfully covering my blood-soaked hair and face because I did not want to see the wreckage beneath. It was the same image I had seen when I sat in my truck in the driveway, sick with the realization of what I had just done. This was me unhappy. This was me gone.

And yet I had so much to live for, compared to my childhood at least. At twenty-nine, I had a law degree, a lucrative career, a big, fancy house, a new truck, a laptop, a Blackberry. I could see it all spread out before me—my sprawling shrine of achievement. I also had a mortgage, a car note (or truck note, same thing), two actually, counting the hubby's. I also had student loans, credit cards, a huge life insurance policy. It seemed the more money I made the more things I needed to spend it on and the more decisions I had to make about it: Get the Cox premium cable package or keep the Netflix? Rent out the house up in Tuscaloosa another year or put her on the market now? Go with the $500,000 life insurance policy or spring for the mil? Funny how that works. The more money I had to spend with a seemingly endless supply of crap I believed I needed to spend it on, the more unhappy it seemed I was. And I kid you not. I had no kids, no dependents and I seriously felt the need to put a million dollars on my head. I can't explain it. It's what everyone else was doing. It all seemed so necessary.

Until it didn't. When I finally realized these were not the things I wanted to live for, I found myself sitting in my truck, repulsed by the realization that I had been striving and sacrificing for years toward a goal I did not want and paralyzed by my own fear of destroying all that I had built. This time, when I realized what a drunken, dangerous mess I was and that I could have just died—one sad set of tire streaks careening off the side of the interstate—I could not say in any way that I was content. I was restless, frustrated, pissed off and determined now to tear it all a-fucking-part. As I shut the door to my truck and started walking toward the house, I felt like that freaky Firestarter girl who could set the whole house ablaze with just my mind. I don't think I opened the door. The energy radiating out of me just blew it off the hinges when I walked into the house and told my husband of five years the very thing he did not want to hear.

"I want a divorce." The words came out of me like a sword out of its sheath, steely and sharp.

"What?" he said as he began frantically clicking windows on his screen closed, making sure he'd gotten them all before he turned around. As if it mattered. As if he was looking at porn. It was worse. He was shopping. He was always shopping. That was just one of one hundred reasons I was standing there, destroying us. "Wait, what?" he asked as he finally turned around even though he had heard me and I damn well knew it. But I also knew he was surprised. Our bond—a tether that was daily chafed—had been degrading for years. We both likely knew it would one day sever, but I doubt he thought I had the nerve to do it so suddenly. At the very least, he didn't see it coming on this night, in this moment, my first words when I walked through the door. His eyes shifted awkwardly around me, intentionally avoiding my face. I didn't say it again. It had taken a lot to say it once and I was afraid of what I would say after that might change or soften it.

I just stood there, my arms hanging flaccid at my side, my keys still in my hand from the truck I had driven in a black void to a place I didn't want to be. I didn't say anything else and he didn't ask me to repeat it. Not then. I just turned, walked out of the room and shut and locked every door between us—the door to the guest bedroom, the door to the hall, the door to our bedroom, the door to our bathroom—and let the weight of my body fall hard against the last. I felt like I had instantly sobered. Sweat dripped down my ribcage and soaked into the waistband of my skirt. Once my body began to cool I felt it hot and moist around my hairline as well, in my bra, between my breasts, in my palm around the keys and I remembered wondering when I had started sweating. Probably the minute I walked inside but I hadn't felt anything until I had shut and heaved myself against the door and I was alone with my churning thoughts.

I was kind of shocked I had finally said it. All of the months I had spent letting that seed take root and now it had grown like a solid oak, wrapping around every bone in my being and cracking through concrete. It didn't matter how many times I told myself I couldn't. I had made a promise. It wasn't fair. It would tear my life and others apart. It would be hard. The adversity seemed to only nourish it. A part of me even wanted it to be hard. I deserved that and I knew if I could survive that it would teach me never to make those supposed-to decisions again, never to compromise my own happiness because it might hurt or disappoint people. I knew I was going to hurt him and his family and I was angry at myself for having made a promise I could no longer allow myself to keep, a promise I made simply because it was protocol: You grow up. You meet someone. You marry. *Why?*

My relentless inquiry revealed a truth I was reluctant but forced to face: it was time to admit I had made a terrible, hurtful mistake. Once I did I knew I would then have to suffer the devastating consequences of disappointing people I cared about by choosing my happiness over my word but I knew I had to. I had to tear it all down and find a way to forgive myself for it so I could finally build a happier, healthier life. I told myself the process would, at the very least, prevent me from doing this to anyone else again. I was going to live my life differently, consciously and the decision to do that started it all for me—this entire journey. Not the divorce but the decision to do it.

It was my decision. Aside from the annoying college sweat pants, I won't say anything disparaging about my ex-husband here, because it's not in any way necessary and there's not much to say in that regard. Although he disappointed me in many ways—as I'm sure I disappointed him—he wasn't a bad person. He was just wrong for me at the time and exceedingly wrong for the person I was becoming. And he spent way too much time on Craigslist. (Okay, that's the last one I swear.) We just had different mindsets, different values and goals, and we needed things from one another neither was willing to give, at least not without compromising our own divergent moral cores. Looking back on it I actually now think it was a good thing we parted ways when we did because, for better or worse, we did not change one another. But, as a result of our differences, our individual needs and our equal resistance to bend to one another, we did grow to resent each other deeply over time.

After five years of relationship decay I knew the only reason I remained with him was because I was supposed to, because I had said a long time ago that I would. The thought that really sickened me was the shredding of a family—people and children that I spent weekends and holidays with and called nieces and nephews and said "I love you" to. That was all going to disappear. *But it has to, right?* I interrogated myself. *If I'm unhappy, drinking myself to derailment, it has to.*

Stupidly, one of the reasons I didn't do it sooner was because I didn't want to have to tell my partners at the law firm about it. I was worried what they might think of me or how it would reflect on the firm. I also loathed the thought of going back to my maiden name because it would impose on them the trouble and cost of reprinting all of their letterhead, business cards and marketing materials. I worried it also might make it awkward for them to have to introduce me in meetings or cocktail parties with a new last name and an embarrassing explanation. That's how much I cared about bothering other people with my needs back then. I was still married because I didn't want to increase the firm's printing costs.

It's kind of a shame though. I should have at least hyphenated my maiden and married names when I got married so I could've spent the rest of my years—married or not—as Annie Jo Dickey-Dike. *Lookout!* But—even without the hyphenation—the discovery, by new acquaintances and colleagues, that I went from Dickey to Dike still proved thoroughly entertaining and, professionally, the Dike name afforded me many memorable icebreakers and introductions. You can't imagine how many bad Dike jokes were made over the course of my short legal career. "Hi, I'm Annie, the only Dike in the Alabama Bar." *And the crowd goes wild!* While I dreaded the name change, I also knew if I was unhappy, it was a stupid reason to not get a divorce. But if you're afraid to do something, the tiniest hurdle can slow you down, if not stop you entirely.

Thankfully my mental fog eventually cleared and I could finally see how ridiculous it all was. I could also see that it had to be done. *It must be done.* My mind was made up. All that was left was the doing—the uttering of words that would shatter my current life and his. I would love to say I was brave enough to do it immediately. But I was not. I knew it needed to be done and I knew every day that I didn't do it was another day of my life I had pissed away in my supposed prison. I knew all of that and still I didn't do it. All I can really say is it's a hard thing to do. You know you're going to hurt people and your life is going to change drastically. It's not something you really jump out of bed eager to do. So, I waited. Scared and worried but knowing it had to be done, I told myself every day: "Soon, Annie. You'll find the right time."

The thought is laughable now. When is the right time to tell the person you promised to stay with forever that you've just changed your mind? Over coffee and toast? Or is it more of a candlelit dinner topic? Obviously, there is no right time. There is no Emily Post book of etiquette on how to properly announce your desire for a divorce. *I don't think.* It simply gets put off because it's hard to do. But while you wait—in that state of purgatory—you do stupid things because you're scared and unhappy. You might make a risky investment because you think it will soothe you. You might finally bang that bartender who has been flirting with you because you feel like you deserve it. You might get plastered and drive home. I had made the decision months ago but because I didn't have the courage at the time to just do it. Drop a bomb over coffee and toast—I needed one of those moments. Thankfully it came and thankfully I was not a bloody, crumpled heap by the highway. I was still alive. My own sweat was such sweet proof.

But just as quickly as the hot sweat had come, it started to cool on my body. As I slid down the bathroom door and let the cold tile chill my shins and hands on the floor, my body began to regulate itself again. My radiating heart eventually slowed and I'm sure my temporary Firestarter powers escaped me. I was once again just Annie—alone, messed-up, bewildered but brave. I laid my cheek on the floor next to my hands and huffed a hot breath on the tile. I had pulled the first stone from the wall and soon my former life would lay before me, a pile of chalky rubble. But I knew I could do it—crawl out of the demolition and survive, maybe even thrive. I just had to keep climbing.

The chill from the cold mast on my cheek brought me back to the present—back to the Gulf, back to my rocking, swaying state—and my mind finally began to clear. Care Bears and a toilet-paper mummy wrap, wooden crosses and a wrecked truck all seemed to explode into cinder dust around me and I could once again see the vast blue horizon. As I clinched my red rash thighs around the mast, swaying like I had in Mr. Christian's tree, I had to smile at the simplicity of it all. I was scared up there, yes, but in a different kind of way. It wasn't this deep-rooted sickening fear, like some big weighty life-long regret. It a crisp, almost invigorating fear—that temporary heart-pumping jolt you get on a roller coaster ride.

I knew I felt that way because I had changed everything. I was either going to get the halyard down or die trying. But after that my only decisions were: Where should we sail to next and how long should we stay? I had one boat and one body to maintain and it seemed my days revolved once again around getting into trouble, out of trouble and eating—cookies included. Somehow it was all simple and fulfilling again. But it hadn't always been that way and it certainly hadn't been easy. That night in my truck the realization of how lucky I was to be alive hit me just as hard as my six year-old body had hit the ground and afterward there was, once again, some serious bloodletting. But it was undeniably worth it because here I was breathing in crisp salt air over a body of shimmering water. I now had a sense of awareness, a fresh sense of feeling—every sensation, every fear, every accomplishment. It was as if my life had been fuzzy for years—each day a dull, hazy repetition of the one before—and it was finally now clicked into focus, everything in high-def.

My body heaved against the mast as another wave rolled through, snapping me out of my little life reflection. I could once again feel the cold aluminum on my skin and the bruises on my thighs from clinging to the mast. As soon as the rush started to subside my exhaustion filled the void. I had the halyard in hand but I was still fifty feet up with a harrowing, rocking, swaying, fifty feet between me and a safe touchdown on the deck of the boat below. My calf muscles were shaking and I knew something could just as easily go wrong on the way down. I needed to get the halyard down to Phillip and focus on my descent.

Phillip raised his hands in the air—a sign for me to lower the halyard to him. Looking back on it I'm not sure that was the best decision—to let that thing go swinging around again on the way down to him. Why not just clip it to me and let it come down with me? If anything it could have been a *third* backup line. Why didn't we do that? I can't really tell you, other than we were so focused on getting that halyard back down to the deck it's all we could think about. For both of us, it seemed to take precedence even over me coming down. Had we actually stopped to think about it, I'm hopeful we would have realized it was going to be harder to do it that way—trying to worm the halyard down through the shrouds and spreaders and stack-pack lines while the boat swayed and rocked around. But that's what we did. After some time I was relieved to finally see Phillip's hand clasp tightly on it. He clipped it to the boom and went back around to the cockpit to begin lowering me. As I watched him make his way aft, though, I was shocked to see the same scene unfold once again below me.

"The halyard!" I screamed down to Phillip.

"I know!" he shouted. "I've got to get the winch handle on!" he snapped. I will say it is easy to be focused on your own issues in stressful moments like that and to snap curtly even at your most trusted mates when you think they're telling you something you already know. He thought I was talking about the spinnaker halyard and that I was trying to tell him to get a move on and get me down. That would be like telling someone who is already clearly rushing to "Hurry up!" Such a comment probably would have irritated me too. *If* that's what I had been talking about. But I wasn't referring to the spinnaker halyard that was holding me. I was talking about the *main*—the one I had climbed the mast for, carefully eased down to Phillip and that he had just (I can only presume) carefully clipped to something. Yet there it was—flying wildly again! I couldn't believe I was actually seeing it. The same problem we had just faced the evening before—the whole cause of this death-defying circus act—and there it was swinging violently above the deck. Again. *You turd!*

"No, the MAIN!" I bellowed.

Phillip craned his head to where the main had been shackled only to find it flailing around again like a ribbon in the wind. I heard a crash and saw a flurry of arms and knees and elbows before Phillip emerged again from the cockpit. I hate to say it, but from way up there, he looked like a circus clown trying to put out a fire with a seltzer bottle. I swear I could hear carnival music playing in the background. Luckily the main halyard hadn't been able to swing that long and it was still low enough that Phillip could reach it. He snatched it again, clipped it again and stared at it for a stern second to make sure it didn't move. He gave me a swift look before heading back to the winch to make sure I was still swaying up at the top of the mast. *Yep, still up here. Still swaying.* Then he set back to readying the winch and letting out the spinnaker halyard so I could come down.

Funny thing, though, Phillip would forget on occasion about the back-up safety line—the staysail halyard he had hooked up to me. He would often let out a couple of feet on the spinnaker halyard, look up at me a little puzzled to find me in the exact same spot and holler "Let go!" *As if I would stay up here for fun.*

"The safety line!" I would holler back to him and then the light bulb would go off. He would then immediately jump to the secondary winch, let out some safety line and *then* I would come down a few feet. Phillip managed this back and forth all the way down and I can't tell you how comforting the rough deck felt under my feet. *Ahhh ... solid footing.* My leg muscles were still shaking from the anxiety and my inner thighs were mottled with rope burns and bruises but I didn't care. I was down and so was the halyard. *No more mast climbs this trip*, I thought. We both thought. But, that wouldn't be the case.

Fortunately this one—our first while underway—was accomplished safely with only two minor casualties: the boat hook and the steaming light, both of which we considered minor losses in light of the feat. We have a fishing gaff that we use to haul fish on-board which we figured would easily suffice as a boat hook and the steaming light isn't critical. Oh, but there was the little matter of the coffee. And the solar shower. When I finally made it back to the cockpit I was welcomed to the scene Phillip had been slushing around in during the last half of the ordeal. The crash that I had heard earlier was him bumping the cup holder and launching our coffee mugs. It looked like a mocha murder scene in the cockpit. And he'd managed—in all of his hopping and jumping—to step on the spigot for the solar shower that was sitting in the cockpit floor, crunching it into pieces. We continued to use it for most of the trip and it continued to work on occasion. Still, these seemed very minor losses, considering. In all, it was quite the accomplishment for the day. Another mast climb down, our main halyard once again securely in-hand and we were not (too much) worse for the wear. That kind of became a recurring theme, though, for the entire journey: another mistake made, another lesson learned. No one ever said it was going to be easy. If I had remained in my cell because I was afraid I might fail at times, then it would have been the right decision because I did, many times. And—even with this rather dangerous one behind us—I knew I was bound to make plenty more mistakes on our trip to the Keys not to mention my whole prison-break vision quest. But you know what I've learned about mistakes? They often make for one hell of a story. I was already working on titles for this one—*Hal Unleashed?*—as we hoisted the main, made a second pot of coffee and set our sights on Clearwater.

CHAPTER FIVE

Keen on the Keys

"I can't. I don't want to. I'm scared."

I had my hand on the trigger but I couldn't pull it. My teeth were pressed down hard against one another, my eyes clenched tight, my sweaty fingers gripped around it and yet I still couldn't do it.

"You don't think it's going to blow up in my face?" I inquired aloud through closed eyes.

"It might."

I peeked one eye open to look at him when he said that. Now I could tell he was just having fun at my expense. Not only was he laughing at my true and utter fear of face explosion, he was filming it! Phillip had his camera up, aimed at me and he was smiling and nodding. That's all it took. I was doing it now. *This is for the Keys.* I closed my eyes back tightly, gripped and gave her one good, hard yank.

While the mid-sea mast climb was way up there on the list of harrowing experiences we encountered during the trip, the entire journey to the Keys—from the tedious planning and provisioning to the pristine and challenging passages—was a kaleidoscope of adventure, ranging from breathtaking to frightening, frustrating to inspiring. But I knew. In every single moment I knew. I was exactly where I wanted to be, doing exactly what I wanted to be doing. You may wonder how I can say that. I would second your inquiry. It all sounds nauseatingly perfect. Cue the confetti again. But my best indicator is if I can't think of another place in the world I would rather be or another thing I would rather be doing, then I know I'm there: thriving in the moment, right where I want most to be. Even when it was hard—even when I was wet, salty and uncomfortable—I knew, at the very least, I was living in my own skin, every minute, every day. No more purgatory. No more predictability. No more drunken-death dreams and deep-rooted desire for change. I was free.

And now that I was, I wanted to go everywhere—the Bahamas, Bermuda, Tahiti. I felt like I could just spin that big Wheel-of-Fortune wheel with an endless supply of exotic places on it and I wouldn't care one bit which one it landed on. Spin. Click. *Awesome! Let's go there.* While there are many different means of travel and many activities and hobbies Phillip and I loved to do—skiing, kitesurfing, hiking, climbing—after some discussion, we decided the first big trip we wanted to make would be by sailboat. It was our true passion after all. And we wanted to venture further than we had the last time when we brought our boat back from Punta Gorda, Florida. So the Florida Keys was a natural choice. But we wanted to do it cruiser-style, picking our way among the little inlets and sleepy towns along Florida's west coast, about which we had heard awesome things. Also, starting out with shorter two- to three-day passages as opposed to one five-day jaunt from Pensacola straight to Key West seemed like a better dip-your-toes-in-first approach for us (primarily me) as admittedly newbie cruisers.

What thrilled us about the Keys trip, though, was that it was going to be our first true sailboat voyage together—just Phillip and me—and we were going to test every bit of our grit and gumption and sense of adventure and humor along the way. This trip was going to tell us both whether we were really suited for this live-aboard, cruise-the-world lifestyle and—for me personally—it was going to tell me whether all the ripping and gnawing and gnashing I had been doing in my life was the right thing to do.

It's easy to *say* you want to quit your current life and just sail away, and many probably would. But after a two-day passage, I'm sure many of those same people would say: "Okay, pull over. Get me off of this thing." Sadly, in a sailboat, you can't really 'pull over.' If you set off to really go, you better hope you truly want to be out there, on the water, traveling in a slow boat. So, how do you find out if you're suited to it? You toss the lines and go. It's the only way I know. I had faith in my quit-and-sail-away decisions but that's all I had. I didn't yet have experience to truly justify them. That's what this trip was for. I had been working toward it for years. That boat was the key to my new adventure. I wanted to leave tomorrow.

But, do you just pick a date and shove off? Is it ever that easy? Absolutely not. I've said it many times but it always bears repeating. Cruising is hard work. The boat itself—your most prized possession, your ticket to world travel—is not only your vessel but also one, big never-ending project. There is always—and I literally mean, every minute of every day, *always*—something that needs to be done. Every day there is some thing (or, more frequently, many things) that need to be polished, cleaned, checked, filled, scraped, painted, caulked, re-wired, lubed, oiled, dried.

And by the time you finish the entire list, whatever thing you did first will need to be done again and so the process starts over. Maintaining a sailboat—in the way it really should be maintained—is practically a full-time job. Good thing I was unemployed by then! But even if you spend a good bit of your day in an office or at a computer, a little manual labor, grease, sweat and sunshine are welcomed. Thankfully the captain and I are pretty diligent workers and actually enjoy working on the boat together. I know how rare it is to find a couple like that and, believe me, I'm incredibly grateful. But just because you don't mind doing it and you have a work buddy doesn't make it any less work. Preparing our boat for the trip to the Keys was a heck of a lot of work.

While months of preparation and planning went into it, the final weeks before shove-off seemed to zip by at a speed that had to have violated some rules of relativity. It was like we stepped onto the Enterprise and shifted into warp speed. We were knocking out projects left and right though—all very exciting boat stuff—but it needed to be done. We took down our headsail, the Genoa whom we lovingly call Genny (because it's short for Genoa and because she's a bit of a big, finicky broad) so we could have her UV cover re-stitched. One of your very worst enemies on the boat is the sun. Salt is a close second. They work quietly and constantly, eating away at your precious equipment on a daily basis. We had our rigger come out to give the boat a good bow-to-stern inspection for the trip and one of the things he noticed was some popping of the stitching on Genny's UV cover. He recommended we send it off to be re-sewn. So down she went.

This time, though, we left the halyard used to raise our Genny *down* and clipped securely to the deck. Why am I telling you this? The last time we had dropped the headsail we raised the halyard, with no sail attached, all the way back up to the top of the mast—you know, for safe-keeping—until we were ready to hoist the Genny back up. All I can say is it was our very first time to drop the Genny and our very first time to experience the very unfortunate and insurmountable physics of a halyard sent up the mast without a sail attached to it. We actually thought he would just drop right back down when we needed him, so much so that we cleated him off up there just in case he got a wild hair and decided to drop down for fun.

"No, no, halyard, you stay up there." And stay up there he did. If only there had been folks around to see us whipping and popping the line down below trying to coax our poor little halyard down, but he clung fast like a scared cat in a tree. That little mistake was the reason for my very first-ever mast climb. It was back in Carrabelle when our boat spent a few weeks there getting the transmission replaced after we'd run her dirt dry crossing the Gulf the first time. *Ahh ... so many lessons learned.* But, clearly, it wasn't the last time we would climb our mast to retrieve a halyard. Each climb, however, offered a unique and valuable lesson and turned out to be kind of a fun adventure in the process. Such is life when cruising.

Next on our Keys list was the rigging of a new inner forestay. *A what?* The inner forestay is just about what it sounds like—a stay just inside of the main forestay, which is used to fly a smaller sail. And "stays," while we're at it, are pretty self-explanatory too. They're wires or rods that come from the top of the mast down to the boat to make sure the mast *stays* in place (upright) and doesn't swing too far forward or backward. Think of it like ropes tied to a leaning tree to stabilize it. Some boats have one forestay, meaning it runs *fore*ward, to the bow of the boat—while others have two. Adding an inner forestay to a sloop model is like creating a convertible cutter rig. *Excuse me?* Yeah, I was scratching my head, too, when Phillip first explained it to me. But let's break out some Annie nautical terminology, shall we? Our Niagara 35 is a sloop which means it has a single forestay that flies one large headsail. I remember it like a slalom (single) ski. Sloop, slalom, it's close enough for me. A cutter rig, on the other hand, has two forestays and two headsails as if they took the one big headsail and "cut her" to make two headsails—a medium and a small. Isn't learning fun? Cue the PBS shooting star. *The more you know!*

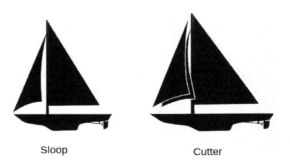

The cutter rig allows more sail plan options for, say, heavy winds in that you can do away with the bigger sail and just fly the "small" sail also known as a storm sail, which is much safer in howling winds. Our *single* forestay with the single *big* sail doesn't offer an optimal sail plan for heavy weather. It's kind of like holding a piece of plywood over your head in thirty-knot winds. Not the best approach. Of course we can make our big headsail smaller by reefing her (curling her up a bit), but that's not as comfortable for the boat as flying a sail specifically cut and made for heavy weather. An inner forestay we can rig up ourselves when a storm is approaching is simply a much better and safer option.

And the reason we were rigging up a *new* one is because our old inner old forestay blew out during our initial Gulf crossing when we first brought our boat home from Punta Gorda, FL. I'm not one to point fingers, but I think it might have been our third crew member, Mitch's, fault. Imagine that old Uncle Sam poster: "YOU!" Point. Regardless of fault, though, we needed to have a new one rigged up and ready for the trip in case we needed to fly a storm sail while making our way south. So we had our rigger fix us up a new one and mount it on the mast. Phillip and I hoped we wouldn't face a storm or need to fly a storm sail on this trip but hoping for things when you're sailing is just about as useful as throwing coins into a fountain. You can toss your whole purse in but it won't change anything. Sometimes you're going to get lucky and miss the storms and sometimes you're not. Hope and toss coins and do rain dances or whatever all you want, but be prepared.

Another project on the list was the lifelines which was quite the appropriate term because they're basically the guardrails around the perimeter of the deck that keep your scrawny hide on the boat during rough weather or the occasional stumble. Ours attached at the bow and stern with a simple knot-and-wrap method using Amsteel, which is exactly what it sounds like. It reminds me of ropesteel. The old Amsteel attachment points for our lifelines had become grayed and frayed from sun damage. I warned you about the sun! So we re-tied them with new line. When your body slings onto the lifelines as a last hope for remaining on the boat, you certainly want the attachment points to hold. I had no idea when I was tying them that they would get a legitimate save-my-ass test whack during our trip but I guess you check and maintain the lifelines for that very reason, no?

Knowing we might have to motor along for long stretches of time we also gave one of our most trusted and necessary systems on the boat—our beloved Westerbeke—a little TLC. Every engine loves a good oil change. It's like a soothing belly rub. We drained her and pumped her full of clean oil, checked the coolant systems and raw water strainer, inspected the hose clamps, checked our spares inventory to make sure we had the necessary back-up critical engine parts and deemed her ready for passage.

Last but not least (and perhaps most importantly) we inspected all of the safety gear. When we bought our boat back in 2013 it had two inflatable life jackets on it but we had no idea how old they were. They have a gas tube inside that is supposed to inflate instantly when you tug on the pull cord—like an airbag in a car—but ours looked pretty worn and ragged. So we decided to break them out one day and see if they still worked. You probably shouldn't wait until you're about to jump off the

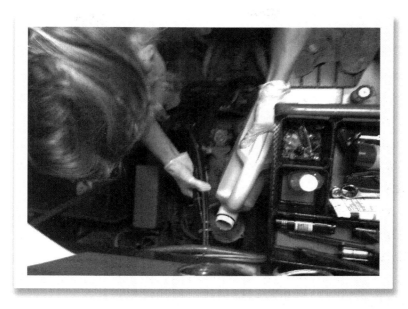

boat into a raging sea to check and make sure your life jacket inflates, am I right? We slipped them on at the dock and got ready to pull the cord.

I have to say, though, it took me a couple of false-jerks to really make it pop. I mean, the thing is wrapped around your neck, right up close to your face. Instinctively, you always want to protect the moneymaker. Some small voice in my head kept telling me it could burst right in my face and blind or maim me. It was possible. I always think the same thing can happen when I open a biscuit can and I hate opening them for the same reason—particularly when you've pulled all of the paper off and it still doesn't pop. Then what do you do? I usually throw it two or three feet away from me like a grenade and let it pop on the kitchen floor. If my brother ever came across a peeled-but-unpopped one when we were kids he'd usually throw it at me and let it bust somewhere on my little kid body. I hated when he did that! No wonder I was scared to death of biscuit cans. I thought it would look like an explosion of intestines when the can went off.

That's when the face-explosion fear kicked in and when Phillip clicked the camera on. He was getting a real kick out of my wincing, whining and false starts. I finally got brave enough, though (which translates to turning-away-and-squinting-hard enough), to pull the cord hard enough to engage the vest. The tube initially started to power open, blowing up from my midsection, up to my chest, shoulders, nearing the money maker (wince!) and then it pissed its way around the back of my neck with an anticlimactic finale.

I'm glad we checked them because they would have been about as useful as an empty biscuit canister out in the Gulf. Both vests leaked a steady stream of air near the manual blow-up valve. We would have been lucky to have floated for two minutes with those pissers. So the captain and I splurged (although I guess it doesn't really count as a splurge if your life depends on it) and got some new ones. We also upgraded to the hydrostatic models that automatically inflate when they are exposed to water, leaving no room for the wince-and-stall moment. Those suckers just blow up without you even thinking about it.

We also ordered some new jack lines—long nylon straps that run the length of the boat—to clip onto when we needed to go up on the deck at night or in rough weather. Those puppies are important. I'm pretty sure that's why all was not *yet* lost when Robert Redford went overboard in the movie but remained securely fastened to the boat. Unfortunately, he was dragged along underwater for a bit, but trust me you would prefer *that* as opposed to the boat leaving you behind in a churning black sea. While there are only three primary safety rules in sailing, staying on the boat is numero uno. As long as you 1) stay on the boat, 2) keep the boat afloat, and 3) don't run into anything there is about a 90% chance the boat will get you safely to your destination. With all of our stay-aboard, stay-afloat and stay-off-the-bottom systems checked all Phillip and I had left to do was inventory, pack and watch the weather.

We had been watching the weather for weeks trying to plan our departure date. Every time Phillip would click his phone to life and start scrolling through the NOAA reports I would sing that song. Sing it with me: "I can gather all the news I need from the weather report." Yes, every time. I'm lucky Phillip puts up with me. But I'm *kind of* the only first mate he's got. So. And, that song (Simon and Garfunkle, *The Only Living Boy in New York*) was a recurring hit on the trip. Our favorite line, aside from the weather mantra? "I've got nothing to do today but smile."

Finally, the date was decided. It was Thursday, April 3, 2014, barely a year to date after buying our boat, and we decided to leave mid- to late-afternoon in hopes of arriving at our destination port during the daytime. The weather in the Gulf looked pretty good to make the jump from Pensacola all the way to Clearwater.

We were expecting some potential storms on Friday and Saturday but the highest sea state prediction was three-to-five feet. Assuming that was more *three* than five it would make for pretty good weather on the trip. Friends and family were provided a detailed sail plan and all were forced to promise and pinkie swear that they could worry, panic or (most importantly) contact the Coast Guard if and *only if* they did not hear from us by Sunday evening. The run from Pensacola to Clearwater is about 275 nautical miles. Leaving Thursday afternoon, we planned to make it to Clearwater early Sunday morning. So if no one had heard from us by Sunday night, it was likely time to fret. But not a second before! A trigger-happy call to the Coast Guard from concerned loved ones was—believe it or not—one of our biggest concerns.

Phillip and I didn't seem to be near as worried or afraid as folks wanted us to be. We were cautious, sure—anxious and hopeful that we would be greeted with fair winds and forgiving weather and that nothing bad would happen to the boat or to either of us during the passage—but there was always going to be the possibility that it could. That's a given. If you're going to fear that, you're going to be afraid all the time. Something bad can happen at any time, whether you're crossing the Gulf in a sailboat or crossing the street. Crossing *anyway* is the adventure and that's what we were after. We were excited to get to the Keys but the destination was not the real goal—the journey was. If we wanted to really get out there and cruise to new, further-away places, we'd knew we needed to find out sooner rather than later if we truly enjoyed the actual cruising part. We were eager to test our strengths, our weaknesses and most importantly our theoretical desires. Phillip and I had both worked incredibly hard to get to this point. To get out there. To cross a body of blue water.

While we didn't finish everything on the list, Phillip and I began to learn during the process that we probably just never will. At any given moment—whether you're out there cruising the South Pacific or your boat's sitting at a dock in Pensacola—there will be a running list of things you want and need to do to the boat. The more work we did, the clearer it became to us that would always be the case. If we waited until we finished every little thing, we would never leave. We decided, rather, to make sure the more crucial projects (think safety and integrity of the vessel) were completed and then we watched for a good weather window to leave.

The same is true with the weather as well. It's very unlikely that you'll have a perfect stretch of weather that just pops up on the calendar for your trip. Any three-or-more day passage is going to bring with it some risk of bad weather. There may be the chance for some three- to four-foot seas the first day of your trip and then it's predicted to calm down after that or the forecast may provide for perfect winds the first couple of days and then turn unfavorable after that. In all, it's incredibly rare that you'll find a perfect pocket of weather for the entire passage. Much like completion of the boat projects, if you wait for that, you will never leave. You just have to be as cautious as you can and then you just have to go.

It was a crisp sunny Thursday. The projects were mostly done and the weather was mostly right when Phillip and I tossed the lines and sailed out into the Gulf.

CHAPTER SIX

The Black Abyss

"Another?" Phillip asked when he heard the click of my camera. "Yes, another, just one more. They're fun!" I squeaked, feeding happily on the excitement of being out there, the adrenaline and thrill of taking sailing selfies! *Look at me, I'm headed out to sea! Or the Gulf. Whatever.* Click.

I have to admit my teenage giddiness was probably a little embarrassing but this was it. Our big trip! We were really doing it. Heading back out into the Gulf, this time sailing *away* from home, on our first real cruising trip in the boat. It was a momentous occasion! In my opinion, sailing selfies weren't just allowed, they were warranted.

Clearwater by Sunday morning, though, was going to be a two-day, three-night haul—the longest Phillip and I had ever undertaken together—but we were excited about it, invigorated by the challenge and adventure. This was early in the trip however. We knew not what awaited us out there—darkness, danger, delight. We motor-sailed through the Pass at Pensacola to be sure to stay in the channel but once we were safely out, we cut the engine and clocked over on a nice southeast heading to Clearwater.

It was around dusk at that time and I learned another of my many important lessons in sailing. While the sea state (just as we imagined it would be knowing our luck) was far more five-foot waves than three, we were still doing fine. I wouldn't call it an uncomfortable passage but as I stared out on a blue horizon—feeling the boat rise and drop and ride the swells—I started to feel a little strange. Not nauseous, yet. Just a little off. I swallowed it back. *This is it Annie. The big trip. What's the matter with you?*

I was prepared to handle any wild, wanderlust adventure that lie in store for us out there in the great big sea. Or Gulf. Whatever. But I was not prepared to tolerate an inexplicable, unacceptable feeling of malaise. *No.* But my swallowing didn't change anything. The general malingering continued as I frowned out at the horizon. I was starting to feel a bit peckish and tried to convince myself it was not seasickness. *I've crossed the*

Gulf before, in four- to six-foot seas nonetheless. I don't get seasick. But I just felt weak, a little queasy, a little weird.

Then Phillip mentioned the idea of dinner and it sounded like some grand revelation. *Food? Why yes, yes. I think I would like this thing you call food.* And let me tell you, I ate my friends. I started inhaling and choking down my fair share and then-some of the tuna salad we had brought for dinner. Phillip eyed me suspiciously as I shoved heaping forkful after heaping forkful clumsily into my mouth, leaving messy swaths of dressing on my mouth and cheeks.

"You need to eat before you're hungry," he said. And Phillip was right. I should have stockpiled some energy hours ago. But I wasn't going to let this happen again. I kept eating! The bowl of tuna salad was followed by a handful of almonds, some trail mix, several chocolate-covered pretzels, some snap pea crisps, a couple heaping spoons of peanut butter and some more almonds before I finally just gave it up and inhaled a calorie-dense protein bar—much like the kind boxers scarf when they're trying to get to the next weight class. I'm sure I did in that half hour of indulgence. I was ravenous, carnivorous, *om*nivorous—eating everything in sight with unabashed abandon.

Within minutes, though, I felt better. *Much* better. *Food. Who knew?* So my lesson? Don't eat light when you're sailing. "Oh, I'll have the salad greens with the light vinaigrette, please." No. That's not going to cut it out there. We had been working on the boat all morning, packing up the last of the provisions, re-tying the Jerry cans and the anchor, running the solar lights, packing more provisions, filling the water tanks, all of that. There had been a lot of up and down the companionway stairs, hauling

heavy items here and there—in general, some hard work.

And all I'd had was a bowl of cereal and a little salad under my belt. Probably around six hundred calories. Total. And I'd probably burned about 2,469 calories (approximately) by that time. I was well underwater on the energy front, not ever a position you want to find yourself in when you're about to face who-the-hell knows out there in open water. If you're thirsty, you're likely already dehydrated. And if you're hungry, you're already a little late there too. And for the ladies (or men who like to wear bikinis, not that there's anything wrong with that)—it doesn't matter if you'll be slipping into a little string number later, if you're sailing, you're burning it off. Eat early and eat often. Like the captain said: eat before you're hungry.

Fat, full and happy after my binge, I finally snapped into the cruising routine. Every hour we were entering our coordinates, as well as our heading, speed, the sea state, weather and other note-worthy items, in the log book. Unfortunately the wind was right on our nose all evening and into the night. Of all the wind you can have when sailing—other than *no* wind I suppose—on the nose is the worst. Unfortunately, there is no way around it. You just can't sail directly into the wind. They call it "into the irons." And while I'm sure there is some meaningful, deeply-rooted-in-sailing history story from whence the iron phrase arises, I like to think of it as hacking your way through a throng of fighting soldiers—all bearing heavy shields—with only your flailing, swinging sword to take the lead. I would imagine swords of the olden days were made out of iron and beating through an army of shields is about what beating into the wind feels and sounds like—beating to windward.

There is virtually no sailboat—at least one that I am aware of, although I will admit I still consider myself a sailing novice and a lifetime blonde—that can sail directly into the wind. Even boats that reportedly "point well"—meaning they get as close to sailing into the wind as possible—still can only hold a course around twenty to thirty degrees off the wind. While I do believe our boat points fairly well, with wind directly on our nose this still forced us to take rather long tacks—thirty degrees off to the south, then thirty off to the east—in an attempt to go in a general southeast direction. It seemed to take *forever* to get anywhere. It's like zig-zagging rather than walking a straight line. You cover a lot more ground but it takes you a lot longer to get where you actually intend to go. If you want to sail though—not motor—sometimes seemingly ineffective tacking is the only option. As the sun dipped down Phillip and I donned our safety gear and settled in for a long night of "tacky" sailing.

Later in the night the wind picked up to fifteen knots—still on our nose—and we started pulling down canvas methodically. We put the first reef in the mainsail, followed by the second, followed by a reef in the Genny. We had just enough out to help stabilize the boat while trying to hide from the wind at the same time. The sea state was probably four- to five-foot waves throughout the night, which made for some rough landings and crashes on the boat. It really is shocking to see and feel your seemingly monstrous, unwieldly boat literally *jump* over a wave but it does. It really feels like that. The boat rears back, waiting for the next wave to get under its belly, then she lunges forward trying to clear the wave—a valiant equestrian leaping over her poles. It was somewhat frightening but also awe-inspiring to see how agile our little boat really is out there. Even in a moody Gulf that was trying to bob and tip and swat at us, she handled it so well. I know but it never hurts to be reminded: it's what she was built to do.

But what seems and sounds perfectly manageable topside in the cockpit, seems and sounds horrific down below. The groan of the hull as it slams into a wall of water can sometimes sound and feel like the boat has struck a solid object. You'll think the boat is breaking. You try to tell yourself it's just bending. It's hard to believe but the hull, the cabin, the hatches, they all flex a little in pounding seas. They do! That's why small leaks often appear during or after a rough passage. The boat is designed to flex—not break—but it's hard to differentiate the sound of one versus the other down below. When we started taking our two-hour shifts that night, it was hard to close our eyes and try to get some sleep when each wave-smack sounded like the hull was cracking in half. It's not—and some part of you deep down knows that—but another small part also asks: *Are you sure? Was that a crack? Maybe I should get up and check.*

Our first night on passage was, to say the least, a little challenging. The Gulf was certainly not cooperating. We rode waves up and down, crashing water over the bow and occasionally spraying us in the cockpit, and took turns getting fitful, restless pockets of sleep. I will say our autopilot really did put forth a solid effort. We call him "Otto" for short because our owner had him labeled as such on the DC panel below where we turn him on and off.

"Will you turn on Otto?" Phillip will holler down from the cockpit when we set off on a passage and he hasn't been flipped on yet. It's not *"the* auto-pilot." It's Otto. It's a he. And when we change shifts or hand over the helm and want to check how *he's* doing, it's: "How's Otto holding?" "Eh, he's hanging in there. It's been hard for him though." We speak of him as one of the crew—a tried and tested member of the team.

While I really do envision Otto like that grungy bus driver from *The Simpsons*, with headphones in his ears, talking in teen punk, he always steps up when needed, driving us along. It was hard for Otto to hold, though, in fifteen-knot winds and rolling five-foot seas, although he did hold much more than I ever thought he was capable of. When he would lose his ability to grip the wheel—which happened often—it would spin freely under his belt and his motor would screech out trying to stop it. Sometimes he would screech and groan and get it back. Other times, he knew he had lost it and Otto would let out a cackling cascade of beeps to let you know you were drifting off course. Those little beeps started to haunt both Phillip and I in our disjointed dreams. We both admitted to flinging ourselves awake on several occasions to imaginary Otto beeps.

But as much as you wanted to curse Otto when he began his annoying-beep bit, you really couldn't. Otto was doing the best he could. The problem was catching him in time once the beeps set in. If you weren't behind the wheel the moment he slipped, by the time you jumped back there, got your bearings and turned Otto off it was sometimes too late. He'd fallen too far off course and you were in a jam, having to turn the boat around in a large circle and catch the wind with a forceful pop around the backside. The thunderous clang of the rigging when this happened would often wake the other mate from whatever haunted Otto dreams he or she was having and cause said mate to come scrambling up to the cockpit to assess the situation.

You couldn't help it. What you **imagine down below when you hear a gut-wrenching clang is usually far worse than what you actually see** when you come topside. But you won't know until you pop your head up and confirm. After a raucous crash heard below, it's soothing to at least stick your head out and know everything's fine. But the jolt certainly wakes your heart up. You sit in the cockpit waiting for the boat to get its groove back and for your heart to beat normally again—an event that has to occur before you can even think about trying to go back to sleep again. Needless to say it was a long night and it was certainly hard on the boat. Phillip and I woke the next morning to find out just how hard.

"Well, we only suffered one casualty," Phillip shouted down to me from the cockpit above as he held the sunrise shift and I blinked myself awake. "Well, that I know of," he added.

My sleepy brain was a little slow to the draw. I was trying to figure out what the word 'casualty' would mean in that context. Some bird or fish on the boat perhaps? I thought the way Phillip had said it, it had to be *alive* to have *died*, but I should have known—every little block and tackle on the boat is alive to Phillip. When I came up the companionway stairs, I saw it—the sad remains of our starboard lazy jack lines for our *new* stack pack strewn haplessly across the deck. We'd had a stack pack put on a couple of months before our trip to the Keys to make raising and lowering the mainsail easier. It's like a big catcher's mitt that stands by—always waiting and ready to welcome the sail in the warmth of its slick, leather palm then zip her up safe, keeping her nice and protected from the sun.

In order to stay open, though—always waiting and ready—the stack pack has to be held up and in an open position, like arms holding open your trick-or-treat bag so folks can drop goodies in. We call the lines that do that "lazy jacks," probably because it means we're too lazy to catch, fold, strap and cover the mainsail ourselves. But that doesn't bother us. We like our bags nice and open for goodies to be dropped in. "Trick or treat! Give me a big fat sail to keep." Sadly, though, it seemed the forceful winds of the evening had caused our mainsail to put too *much* force on the lazy jack lines and the one on the starboard side finally gave out, ripping the eyelet on the starboard spreader that held her up clean off. And while the arm-and-treat-bag analogy is accurate, please don't imagine the bloody, mangled shoulder of a cute little pirate-dressed trick-or-treater here. Or perhaps do. That's probably what the boat felt like.

"Well, they're called *lazy* jacks for a reason," Phillip said, determined not to let anything discourage our big adventure. "People have been raising and lowering their sails for centuries without them, so … " We would just have to raise and lower our mainsail the not-so-lazy way for the rest of the trip. As long as we could secure the fallen line and get our sail up and back in the stack pack manually and zip her open and closed for UV protection, we were fine. But it was little bit of a morale blow.

It's like you know things on the boat are going to break when you undertake a passage like this but you hate to see it actually happen. For me, the boat tends to become an extension of me. It pains me to hear her groan and flex under strain. Seeing things on her rip, shear and break gives me a bit of a sinking, sickening feeling. I couldn't resist the urge to lovingly pat the dodger and say it: "Sorry girl." A hard passage sometimes just can't be avoided (that's kind of the whole point of going offshore) but damage to the boat is never easy to swallow, particularly on day one of the trip.

In all, though—considering the night we had—it seemed a pretty minor loss really. One day down and only one piece of lazy-slash-luxury equipment had been compromised. "Eh." Phillip and I shrugged our shoulders and continued south wondering what Day Two had in store for us. We were still on passage and needed to focus on the course, the weather and the hourly log entries. We secured the lazy jack lines and hunkered back in the cockpit, thankful at least, for the boat's maintained integrity, our survival of Night One and the much-anticipated daylight and visibility. This calls for another sailing selfie. Click!

After checking the chart and the weather and making some calculations we decided at the rate we were going with the southeast wind dead on us, we weren't going to make it to Clearwater—even on a straight haul—for another two and a half days. We had been sailing offshore a little over fifteen hours and had only put about forty-three nautical miles behind us. That's an average of less than three miles per hour. Imagine traveling fifteen hours in a car going only three miles per hour. Snails would probably pass you on the shoulder and give you the finger!

While three miles per hour is not super slow for a boat, it certainly wasn't near as fast as we wanted or needed to be going in the Gulf. Phillip and I were also both a little tired from the rough night. We had each slept maybe three hours total between our exchange of night shifts, hull slams, accidental turn-arounds and Otto beeps. Plus we were expecting a storm to come into Clearwater on Monday or Tuesday and, assuming we didn't *make* it to Clearwater by then, we did not want to be crossing the Gulf in that, or sitting in Clearwater waiting it out. We'd heard great things about Port St. Joe and had always wanted to check it out. The decision was made. We were going to pull out of the Gulf and take refuge there while we waited out the weather. Once the new course was set, we started cruising easy at 4.5 knots and had only fifty-three nautical miles to go.

It seemed Neptune wanted to reward our savvy sailing decision, too, because we had an awesome sail on Friday. It was nice wind and weather most of the day, with the southeast wind now crossing right over the middle of our boat (the beam) on the starboard side putting us on a darn-near-perfect beam reach. Plus Otto was doing all the work.

"Thank you Otto!"

"No sweat, lil' dudes."

Phillip and I took turns that day taking naps, reading, writing and munching on turkey and manchego sandwiches. It's hard to believe sometimes how different the sea state and winds feel when they're head-on as opposed to on the beam or stern. Just a ninety-degree turn makes all the difference.

We even had an eight- to ten-member dolphin group grace our boat that afternoon with their slick, sultry dance. It's incredible to see how fast dolphins can really swim. While you watch them flip and glide right along your boat, it's always mesmerizing to watch them zip away at light speed. It's like you forget how fast and athletic they really are and you feel a little humbled and gracious that they came along beside you to just frolic and play, if only for a moment. Their presence is truly a gift. I don't care how many times I've seen dolphins in my life, I will always get up to look again. I squealed pretty much the entire time they were there. Phillip and I plopped down in the cockpit breathing lofty sighs of contentment after they left and let our thoughts linger toward dinner.

Before we left Pensacola we had made two hearty meals that we had frozen in gallon Ziploc freezer bags for the passage—beef and pork Bolognese and chicken and sausage gumbo. The sea state, however, had been too rough the previous evening to try to heat up anything down below. With five-foot waves, any movement down below looks a bit like a timed foxtrot—one step forward, brace for a heel to starboard, three quick steps to the left, brace for a heel back to port. While cooking in this environment is totally possible (and on long trips, absolutely necessary as hot, hearty meals are a huge morale boost for the crew), for us—while the previous night was rough—it was our very first on the trip of a lifetime and morale was soaring on its own volition. So Phillip and I opted for an easy, ready-packed tuna salad followed by Cheez-its, sandwiches, crackers and the like, anything that could be grabbed and eaten by hand—toddler food, pretty much—but it did the trick and kept us going through the night.

By Friday afternoon, though, the sea had calmed down to about two- to three-foot waves and we decided it would be best to go ahead and heat up the first of our frozen bagged meals—the beef and pork Bolognese. The minimal work of plopping a freezer bag into boiling water was well worth it. It was like instant five-star gourmet dining—out of plastic bowls, sure, but the venue—a waterfront view to a vast blue horizon—was superb. A hot, hearty meal under our belts and morale continued to fly high!

It wasn't long before Phillip and I were taking nice leisurely naps in the evening light. While we still had another forty or so nautical miles to go and at the rate we were going (about four knots) that would put us in Port St. Joe early the next morning. Knowing we had another full night of two-hours shifts ahead, there was no need for apology or explanation. When one of us got sleepy, we told the other: "I'm going to shut my eyes for a bit." And that was that. Sleep-whenever-you-can was the rule. If you felt it coming on and the conditions were calm, sleep was the best thing you could do for your body.

We knew there were going to be some trying nights when we would have to hold the helm for hours on end, fighting waves and keeping a tiring, steady watch on the horizon. We had experienced several nights like that during our first Gulf crossing the previous year so we knew how truly exhausting they could be. Sleep was a good to be stockpiled on passage. You never knew when one of those nights or days—or an unfortunate series of them—would kick in and you would be forced to cash in all of your 'sleep chips' and take some out on loan.

And you never know what is going to be the curse-worthy cause of a sleepless stretch like that. While it is usually the weather, it can often be an unexpected equipment failure. Something that used to work great and needed no monitoring may now require constant monitoring, repair or jerry-rigging—all tasks which unfortunately make sleep a hazy dream of the past but are required simply to keep the boat moving. You never know what catastrophe is going to unfold. All you know is there will probably be one. And while you may curse being there at the time—when you're cold, wet, worried or hunched down in a steamy, greasy pocket of the boat trying to grab a wayward bolt with shaky fingers, you are also keenly aware of the moment and everything that's going on around you: the smells, the heat, the sounds. You're definitely living.

Out of all the things that I thought might keep us up at night on that boat, though, I never anticipated what was in store for us on night two of the Keys trip—particularly right after we had just suffered such a trying evening the night before. Personally I blame the captain. He was holding the helm when it creeped in. He let it come. Everything was fine when I turned in for my first two-hour snooze shift around 10:00 p.m. But when I woke at midnight, it was total darkness—not inside the cabin, but out. Visibility was zero.

While it does take your eyes a little time to adjust at night, once they do you can see far more of your surroundings on a sailboat than I ever thought possible before my first night sail. I still remember my first night out on our Niagara, when we were bringing her home across this same body of water and I was astounded at how truly visible everything was just from the twinkling stars and glowing moon. I could see the deck, the lifelines, the entire length of the boat, the sails, the waves, clouds on the horizon and dolphins that peeked out to say hello. But now, we could barely see the bow of the boat from the cockpit. A deep fog had set in, like a black curtain before our eyes. There was no horizon. There were no stars, no moon, nothing but a spotlight beam that was swallowed in the darkness.

Phillip told me it had set in about an hour before and had worsened as we moved along *You see? His fault.* There was no way to know how big this retarded blinding blob was or which was it was headed—assuming fog even moves—which meant trying to travel out of it was just as dangerous as trying to travel through it. So onward was the plan.

"Just stay on course," the Captain told me. "Shine the spotlight out every few minutes and blow the foghorn if you hear anything nearby."

While I tried to show complete confidence, I'm sure my face conveyed a bit of disbelief that he was actually going to leave me up there alone in that black haunted hell. But my scared face didn't stop him.

"You've got this," was all Phillip said as he headed down below for some much-needed shut-eye himself.

I watched him for a bit as he settled into the starboard settee and, at first, I thought I did, you know, *have it*. I had a beam of light and a loud, honking horn if anything came close. And it is a huge Gulf. I doubted anything was really out there, right next to us. *What are the odds?* But then I thought of Robert Redford again and that totally random shipping container that punched a five-foot hole in the side of his boat. Man, how I cursed that movie.

Then it started to sink in. I was steering our most prized possession—everything we toiled, sweated and bled for—into a wall of blackness. It was like driving blind, in a car that extends thirty feet out ahead of you. Such a wretched feeling. I couldn't stop shining the light, squinting at the horizon, listening with a hypersensitivity for the sound of some hull-puncturing object bobbing toward us in the water or an unlit boat blazing through the blackness, barreling toward us. Everything I imagined was headed right for us! We were the epicenter of the Gulf. Yet there was nothing to do but blink into the dark and trudge forward. I felt like I was passing through a busy intersection blindfolded, just waiting to hear the screech and crunch of glass and metal. We had slipped into an abyss with no way to see obstacles that might stand before us or what our path looked like. We just moved forward.

As I stood in the cockpit—my hands clenched on the dodger frame, cursing the blackness—I told myself I was fine. I repeated the captain's sentiment out loud. "You've got this." When I did it took me back to another night—just as black—when the darkness had once again swallowed me. I was standing in the stairwell to my new apartment in Mobile—my tiny, leaking, somewhat seedy new apartment.

It was my first night to stay there by myself and I was hauling only a single load up from the truck to my new home on the tenth floor by way of the stairs because the elevator was out. The elevator was always out in that rat hole. I often had to trudge loads of groceries and other crap up ten flights of stairs, often in heels. And they were now poised and ready—my calves clenching and convulsing trying to hold my body perfectly still in the dark until the danger passed or prepared to run if it didn't. My first night of physical freedom and I feared my body was about to suffer a kind of savagery only few women can comprehend.

CHAPTER SEVEN

The Iron Maiden

After I did it—launched this soul-searching journey by saying the first words that ripped my world apart, "I want a divorce"—things happened that I didn't expect to happen. Trust me, even when you think you have an entire life-changing plan figured out, you feel you've thought through all of the possible scenarios and are ready for the consequences, it will never turn out exactly as you planned. You will always be surprised, which is good I guess.

One thing I didn't anticipate was the living situation. I can't say I knew for sure exactly what was going to happen after I sheared our marital world in two. I just know I never saw myself leaving the house that soon. Rather, I saw myself sitting in it blissfully alone, eating M&Ms and peanut butter while I watched a scary movie marathon—finally with no arguments, no pointed words over coffee, no bitterness. That's what I had envisioned anyway—a blissful solitary sanctuary that I could come home to and do whatever the hell I wanted, without having to talk to, care for, feed or pick up after anyone. It actually looked a bit like Steve Carrel's apartment in the *40 Year Old Virgin*. I wouldn't say that guy was lame. He just had three too many hobbies. But he did have one kickass solitary sanctuary. He, at least, looked forward to going home.

I wanted that. I *needed* that. If you're going to be brave enough to tear down everything that once stood because you need to *want* to come home at night—even if it is to be alone—you should get that at the very least. Puzzled at my current state, I prodded myself with these questions: *Aren't you allowed to choose to be alone? If that's what you really want? Shouldn't the people who love you give you that? If that's what you really need?* I was baffled by my inexplicable quandary. I assumed when you said those words, when you ripped your marital relationship in two like a sheet of paper, the first thing that would happen would be a physical separation. That's the whole point, right? You get a divorce because you want to be apart. I assumed that would just automatically occur, but as I did with a lot of things, I assumed wrong. Even after I said the words, did the things that are supposed to work to kick a person out of a house—you know, stamp your foot on the ground, point at the door and shout—it didn't work. He wouldn't leave.

He would not leave.

I mean, I guess that was his right. While I had bought the house, paid the mortgage on it every month, furnished it and stocked it, he had put work into it too. He lived there too, and I guess it was still technically *the* marital estate. My lawyer-brain told me—theoretically, academically—he had a right to stay. But my pissed-off, wronged-wife self didn't understand why he would. Wasn't there supposed to be some deep-seated manly pride that would tell him it wasn't right to stay there while I paid the bills? Or was he supposed to perform some act of chivalry in leaving the poor divorcée with shelter, at least—like putting your jacket over a woman's shoulders in the rain? But I guess when you trudge stubbornly out into the downpour yourself, you really don't deserve the polite gesture.

Well when his didn't, mine did. My inner manly pride kicked in and I did the foot-stomping and the door-slamming. "Fine, I'll leave then." I *had* to leave. Even if it meant putting him up in the house while I paid for an apartment too, I was doing it dammit. And maybe he deserved that after what I had done. Maybe I deserved it too. Admittedly I was the one who had caused this whole mess. But—whether it was right, wrong or a financially-sound decision—I know it was what I needed. I *had* to leave. To save myself, fix myself, I had to *want* to come home.

I spent a total of two days searching apartment listings in Mobile—one day to find a seemingly suitable, low-rent space close to my office, the other to go look at it and sign the papers. I scheduled the movers for the following weekend but I left the sordid marital estate on that second night with an overnight bag and some very rudimentary household items: toilet paper, a pillow and blanket, an overnight bag, a suit for work the next day and a camping mattress. I know how pitiful it looked but I could not stay one night longer in the sprawling house with him, especially now with the way things were. Our eyes seared into one another as we passed silently in the hall or the kitchen. The air at the house was putrid; our relationship decay permeated every room. I don't care how many thousands of square feet the house was, it felt like we were locked in solitary together, bumping elbows and knees with every move. If he wouldn't, I would. I had to get out.

And there I stood—in the dark stairwell of my new apartment building, somewhere between the second and third floor—when the lights went out. I had a blow-up camping mattress under one arm and a blanket and a bag of toiletries under the other—a meager batch of stuff to let me stay just one night. I didn't have any food yet, or furniture, but I did have a place—a solitary, all-to-myself, place—and I was excited to spend my first night there. That was, until the lights went out. I felt like it was that moment after I had actually kicked down and broken through the prison wall and I was now blinking my way into the dark. I was alone, frightened and exposed to whatever danger laid in waiting for me there.

I started to really see myself—a vulnerable blonde, buried deep in the bowels of this derelict apartment building, trying to make her way in the dark up eight flights of stairs so she could what? Blow up a green Coleman mattress and sleep on the floor? I tried to remember what kind of lock was on the door to the apartment. *Was it a bolt? Was it enough?* The apartment building I had chosen wasn't too far from the upscale downtown Mobile beat but it was nestled behind a pretty sinister-looking city park, where grungy, seemingly homeless people often slept on the benches and eyed you strangely as you walked by. The houses and streets behind the building were filled with drug dealers and street roamers. I never planned to be caught in my new neighborhood alone at night but I honestly hadn't thought getting caught in the building alone would present such a frightening possibility.

I heard the door to the stairwell bang open a few flights above me. It was two or three guys talking about "going to T.J.'s." I stood there motionless, hoping they wouldn't hear my breathing—and praying that whoever this T.J. fellow was, that he had a place *above* the second floor where I clung, clenched to the dirty rail of the stairs. They clamored down a flight, banging, talking, their feet moving quickly on the stairs in the dark. I thought about making my way down even more quickly, back to the ground floor and sprinting back outside to the lit parking lot. Just as I turned around to start racing down the stairs, I heard the stairwell door open just a half flight above me and the T.J.-seeking crew clattered out. When the door banged shut, I was left, once again, in silence. The darkness around me was almost palpable, pressing on me from every angle. I could hear my heart beating but, more so, I could feel it pumping so hard it was raising and lowering the collar of my blouse.

Then a worse fear started to set in. This was going to be my new home? Dark, dangerous stairwells, sleeping alone on a blow-up mattress on the floor, wondering whether the lock on my door was 'enough?' This was what it felt like to be alone? I started to wonder whether I had made a huge mistake. I had given up the sanctuary, the safety, of my massive two-story estate for this? A blackened stairwell where I might be raped? *This is what you chose, Annie? This is what you want?* My heart continued to chug—coursing hot blood through my veins—as my own inner fear began to scare me more than the chatty T.J. guys had. Alone in the dark—unable to see the stairs in front of me, much less what my future in this new hell would look like—I started to do the thing I never thought I would do. I questioned myself.

Did I make a mistake?

But the minute I asked it, just internally, I knew instantly, I had not. The many months, years perhaps, I had spent nurturing that seed, telling myself I would find a way out, I would make my life my own, I would not be afraid—had strengthened me. That night in my truck, in particular, when I had almost lost it all and the drunken death dream, where I had felt nothing, they strengthened me. I was feeling everything now—my hand gripped on the oily metal railing, my legs poised one on each stair, calves clenched ready to run, my breathing, fast and intense. I made myself focus on it all—even the fear—because it told me, at the very least, that I was alive. I was scared of the dark stairwell and a pack of probably not-so-dangerous guys but I stood poised, ready to charge at them if necessary, ready to take this new life by the reins, roar and ride it out. I had not make a mistake. I was here because I wanted to be here—even if it was sometimes frightening and lonely. I was alive, my senses relishing in every feeling, every moment. I turned back around to face the stairs again and continue my ascension through the black abyss. I couldn't see what lay ahead of me, but I knew I was on the right course.

"You've got this," I told myself as I walked up each flight.

My grip on the dodger frame loosened just a bit when I thought back on that memory and the feeling of purpose and direction I had, trudging up that black stairwell, my little crumpled up plastic mattress in hand. I had certainly done it then, trudged forward despite my fear of the unknown, so I could certainly do it now. *Stay the course.* As I stood in the cockpit looking out on the blackness of my path, I was actually glad that dark memory had entered my mind, because it brought me back to the brightness too.

I finally did make it up those black flights of stairs. No one bothered or touched me that time. No T.J. guys cornered or assaulted me. While

I won't say I was safe, I did make it and when I finally did shut the door to my ratty little apartment (which by the way *did* have a bolt lock which proved to be more than enough), it was the exact dark, dreary scene I had pictured at the bottom of the stairwell. With just the yellowed light from a utility pole streaking in, the place looked kind of haunted. I could see the dust on the floor, the cracks in the window panes, the water stain crawling from the window to the center of the living room ceiling. I could see it for what it really was—an empty little cubby I had chosen to occupy. And, it could have been just that—sad, dreary, cracked and stained—but I refused to let that be the image of my first night of freedom. I had chosen this. I could make it what I wanted.

I clicked on every light in the apartment and let a high-powered feminine mantra wail out from my phone as I played air guitar in the empty living room. "I saw him dancing there by the record machaayne!" I was going to rock this new life! I didn't care if there wasn't a stick of furniture yet in it, I had a place all to myself—a clean slate to write whatever story I wanted on it. "I knew he must've been about seven*teen*!" Hard on the downstroke! I could deck the place out like a *Southern Living* spread, or I could go all beachy coastal with it, or I could even hang black lights and freaky Iron Maiden posters. I could do whatever the hell I wanted with it and *that* was the exciting part. It was a fresh start—a new, tiny space for me to fill with new things, new memories, new hobbies, new plans. *That* I knew I had chosen.

As I reflected back on that night in my apartment, my Iron-Maiden-half took over and I refused again to let the darkness of the unknown frighten me. My eyes had adjusted by now and I realized I could now see the bow of the boat—hazy but it was there. As I probed the darkness, the blackness of the fog seemed to change in front of me. What had at first seemed like a sinister curtain of doom now seemed only like a challenge. It couldn't deem it insurmountable if I hadn't yet tried to overcome it.

When I shined the spotlight out, I could probably see a good thirty foot radius around the boat—not exceptional visibility but not zero. I had my light, my foghorn and my wits about me. I just needed to stay alert, watch my radius and be ready with the horn. If I did, odds were, we would be fine. It was a fairly huge body of water we were traveling across. The likelihood that something would actually come into our thirty-foot radius was pretty low and then, even if the unlikely *did* occur, if I remained diligent, the odds that I would not be able to maneuver us out of its path or honk it off of ours before we collided were also … okay, those odds were pretty high, actually. Once I saw something within our thirty-foot radius, there might be ten seconds to react, if I was lucky. But that still meant there was a chance I would be able stop a collision, *if* I remained diligent. Looking at it that way, it wasn't insurmountable, it was merely challenging and I liked a challenge. Spotlight in one hand, foghorn in the other, I manned my shift, we trudged on in the dark and I sang a little. "I saw him dancing there by the record machaayne … "

Keys to The Kingdom • Annie Dike

CHAPTER EIGHT

Telling Stuff

"Turn around?" I asked, fighting and tugging my foul weather jacket on to take over the next shift. I didn't know what time it was yet, but if Phillip was waking me up, that would mean it was 4:00 a.m. I hadn't quite processed what he was saying, though—much less why. Was there a big barge ahead? An uncharted shoal? I almost laughed at myself at the thought of it: a random shoal out in the Gulf. I had plugged them in in my elementary nautical terminology days as big, broad "shoal-ders" that jut out from land. The key word there being *land*. Clearly a detached shoal in the middle of the Gulf wasn't my most brilliant moment but I was still confused. *What was he talking about 'turn around?'*

Phillip was holding the 2:00 a.m. to 4:00 a.m. shift on the black abyss night and he woke me about halfway through to let me know we needed to turn around. *Why?*

"We're going too fast," Phillip said, answering my thought-question.

That was laughable. All of this tedious, sluggish, slower-than-a-snail progress we had been making through the black veil and now we were going to turn around and undo it all. I think I read it on a cross-stitched pillow once. As cheesy as it sounds, it's just true: "Go where the wind takes you." Except in sailing, it's not this lofty, motivational goal, it's just fact. You can only go where the wind takes you. And while you shouldn't fight it, you shouldn't see yourself as constricted by it either. You're merely *guided* by it. While you're the one steering the boat, it's like these all-knowing mythical souls are helping you navigate your adventure, gently playing a role in where you and the boat end up.

Sometimes they force you into foul weather and it sucks but you often learn a valuable lesson. Other times they drift you gently to a new place. It may have been an area you didn't expect to visit. Rather, it was a place you chose when you thought the weather wasn't 'working with you' because it wouldn't allow you to get to your intended destination. But once you get to the new place—the wind-driven destination—you often decide it's where you should have wanted to go all along and you quietly thank the wind for its gentle input. You start to wonder whether the wind had it in mind all along. Trust me, she did. She's got all sorts of adventures in store for you, calamities too. *Why?* Because she's bored and it's fun.

The wind has a mischievous sense of humor. Not only did she congratulate us on the decision to turn toward Port St. Joe by putting us on a smooth, broad reach, but she sent us skimming along so fast, we were now going to reach Port St. Joe before sunrise. I'm sure many of you fellow cruisers follow the same rule. On the ole' *Rest* our goal is never to come into a new pass at night, so we actually had to turn around and sail *back out* into the Gulf for a bit to make sure we didn't beat the sun into the St. Joseph Bay inlet.

It was a strange feeling to have worked so hard to make such little headway for a day and a half, only to now turn around one hundred eighty degrees and sail for a few hours at five and a half knots in the opposite direction. Like I said, though, she thinks it's funny. I guess we were up for a little lighthearted teasing though. We only had to sail back out a couple of hours, then we turned back around and started heading into St. Joseph Bay right around sunrise. The fog was still so heavy we struggled to find even the flashing buoys. Markers you would typically see miles out would now only reveal themselves at about a hundred yards.

I sat up at the bow and squinted through the mist to try and find them. As the sun finally started to creep up and melt away some of the fog, we caught our first glimpse of the water in the morning light, spread out around us like a sheet of silk. I felt like I could just step off onto it and walk to shore, all biblical like.

Thankfully the inlet into St. Joseph Bay was an easy one and we made it into the marina and docked up without issue. Between you, me and the fencepost (and anyone who reads this book I suppose), I still get a little nervous every time we pull up to a dock because you just never know what's going to happen. I have failed to lasso a stern pole, jumped off the boat without a line and endured and performed many other docking mishaps that embarrass me to this day. I still get a little heartburn when we start pulling our big beauty out of the open blue and up next to treacherous pilings and other fiberglass beasts.

Much to Phillip's dismay, I still like to call ahead to any marina new to us and ask them to send out a dock-hand or three to help catch a line. I mean it's a big, expensive boat—our most prized possession. I'm not ashamed to ask for *eight* hands on deck to help save her. Luckily for me, the marina at Port St. Joe has a reputation for being the "friendliest marina in all of Florida" and I'll say I have to believe it. Without my even asking, they sent a competent young chap right out who proved to be an excellent line-catcher. He helped us get tied up nice and secure and gave us a quick tour of the facilities. I can't say enough good things about the folks at the Port St. Joe Marina. They all went above and beyond.

After a couple of rough days on passage we were definitely pleased to be safe in port—*this* port in particular which we later found afforded us great food, excellent facilities and a quaint little downtown strip perfect for ambling. While we love to be on passage, I think the wear of the passage—the uncomfortable conditions your body sometimes has to endure for hours on end—makes you truly appreciate the stillness, the security of being in port or on anchor. The simple act of washing my face after we were docked felt like a lavish spa experience. Well, I can't really say that. I have no idea what a "lavish spa experience" feels like because I've never experienced it. But just wiping the salt and muck off of my skin with a clean wet cloth was so soothing.

I lowered my face into a wet rag, pressed both hands against the pockets of my eyes and rubbed up and down. It felt good to not have an ounce of anything on my face—no makeup, no mascara, no lotions, sunscreen, nothing. It was all wiped clean. Whatever had caked on during our two days out on the open water was now washed away and the soft scratch of the terry cloth on my skin brought sheer pleasure. I wiped the back and front of my neck and swept my face one more time—my skin instantly tingling and cooling the minute the cloth left it. It was such a simple thing—a clean face—but what that face had weathered the past two days made a mere wipe with a wet rag feel like the best thing my face had ever experienced.

The passage did that. It's a funny phenomenon. It's like the more discomfort you endure the more comfort you find. One enables and enriches the other. The same is true about the boat. No matter how much you like to untie the lines, sail off into the sunset and head her south, into blue waters, you still take pleasure in seeing her still, safe, secure. While sailing is incredibly invigorating, it's also constantly worrisome. If your boat is moving, you must keep constant watch because you might hit something, you might break something, some system might fail. Sail long enough and that's practically a guarantee. And if you're not diligent in monitoring and checking on the boat, you may miss it and put your boat and crew in real danger. Once your passage is complete and you are able to dock her up or drop the anchor and see her sitting, safe and secure, there is a pleasure in that as well—an *Ahhh* ... factor that is only possible because of the passage.

Phillip and I were definitely in that blissful *Ahhh* ... state as we started packing our bags to each go take an indulgently-long shower at the marina.

"I see you smiling," he said,

That's all he needed to say. Phillip knew why I was so happy. It was the same reason he was so damn happy. He was smiling just as big as I was. We had just completed a passage—the first passage of our trip to the Keys nonetheless—just experienced another story-worthy adventure and were about to set out to explore our new, likely just as story-worthy, destination. Could there be any better feeling? Not in my opinion. As Phillip and I each packed a small bag with our shower stuff and a change of clothes and one bag of our dirty passage clothes to wash, a realization struck me. The clothes in those bags and on our backs constituted just about our entire wardrobe for the two-month trip. Everything on the boat could have constituted all of our worldly possessions and I would have felt we had more than enough.

It always seemed that way—the less stuff I had, the less space to fill and the fewer the things I needed to worry about—the happier I was. I liked when it was just the Care Bears shirt or the Star Brite one. It took me a while—and several life-altering downsizing purges—to realize it but unnecessary stuff festers. It soon buds its own set of obligations—maintenance, repair, monitoring, moving—that cake on like sandwich boards, so thick and heavy you can no longer move. *Who needs all that stuff?*

The revelation first struck me the night I was sitting in my truck, staring at our super-sized McMansion. I was focused on those little solar-powered lights that ran along either side of the walkway up to the front door. They cost me $260.00 and I remembered thinking when I bought them that it was a lot of money to spend to see a walkway I rarely used and had never had any trouble seeing when I did. It was just a random fleeting thought, though, playing softly in the background.

My forethoughts were telling me: "You're supposed to have a big, nice house. You're supposed to fill it with big, nice stuff." And, if that's your mentality, it's only natural to then tell yourself you should light the walkway so everyone can see your big, nice house with all the big, nice stuff in it. That's why we all worked so damn hard wasn't it? *Wasn't it?* I asked myself that same question when I tried to reach for my keys in the ignition that fateful night. I was supposed to want this big mansion spread out before me, with the motorized gate and manicured lawn. I was supposed to want this marriage, this thirty-year plan, this life. But, I knew I didn't. I feared it.

Since that night I felt like I had been downsizing everything about myself, stripping my life down to the essential core ingredients. Each time I let go of something I didn't really need, the lighter I felt. The old adage has proven itself true time and again for me—less truly is more. Hell, one of the best moves I ever made—and probably the most significant—was from that 1.5 acre, 2,700 square foot sprawling estate with the solar-lit walkway to the single-bedroom apartment with the poorly-lit stairwell. And I did it alone, in one weekend.

I had yet to tell my partners at the firm about any of it, but I doubt they sensed anything. Marital squabbles were just not something you brought to the office, ever, so I kept mine where it belonged—at home—which was fine with me. It's not like I wanted to sit down and talk about my marital feelings with Senior Partner Bob. *No.* I wanted the divorce to be finalized—signed, sealed and stamped—before I told anyone professionally. That way they wouldn't have to fear any long, drawn-out dramatic scene. I could just mention it, say it was a done deed and that it never needed to be discussed again and that would be that. You see? A huge, life-changing transition for me, and all I could think about was whose reputation it might affect and how my colleagues might react to it. I told you. I was a different person back then.

Some people may call me selfish now—always putting my needs first—but I think there is an equally-detrimental selflessness at the opposite end of that extreme. True to my firm-first form at the time, I decided when I finally did go through with the divorce to keep my married name so they wouldn't have to re-print all the fancy brochures and letterheads and, mostly, so it wouldn't have to be a noticed event in everyone's shared social circles. It could just happen quietly and most of my colleagues would never even have to know. While I'm still kicking myself over the missed Dickey-Dike opportunity, my primary goal in keeping the married name, was to keep as much as I could on the surface the same so no one would know everything in my life had changed.

Only my assistant, Michelle, knew about it at the time. She was incredible—a hard-worker, diligent, punctual, funny, smart. My partners often told me, half-kidding, mostly-not that: "Associates are a dime a dozen, but a good legal assistant, well … " But they were right. Even though I was an associate myself, as were the majority of my colleagues, it was easy to see *we* were far more expendable than the secretary Senior Partner Bob had held on to for twenty years. If you found a good one, you kept her around. (And, yes, I say *her* because the only ones I knew were. It's not sexist if it's fact).

Michelle, though, was not just good, she was exceptional. Case in point she saved me from letting the whole divorce scandal break out before I was procedurally or emotionally ready. It was the Monday after my weekend move to the apartment. The ex was kind enough to leave for the weekend so I could vacate and I had two guys and a truck, literally, come to the house bright and early Saturday morning to move my stuff. Why didn't I have friends come help, you might ask. *Because I didn't have any,* you might think. Funny. Not too far from the truth though. While I had plenty of 'acquaintances' back then, my close, personal friends could probably all fit at one dinner table. And while I know any one of them would have easily dropped everything to come help me move that weekend, I didn't want to impose that on them. I felt like I could—and deserved to—do it myself. I had decided I wanted this. I had said the words. I would move myself.

Aside from my suits and work clothes, a few books, bedding, bath and some kitchen stuff, the only real pieces I took were a hand-me-down bedroom set from my dad's mom, Big Mom, that had occupied our guest bedroom in the McMansion, a couch, a TV and a pool table. Yes, a pool table. It was a crappy little particle-board miniature we had found on Craigslist and kept out on the back porch and I kind of took it for spite. I mean, if I had to move into the ratty little apartment in downtown Mobile, I at least wanted a pool table to make it feel a little cooler! While it did technically "fit" in the little side-room/study of my 900-square-foot apartment, you could only shoot from one long end to the other. The walls wouldn't let the cue back far enough to shoot anything across the middle. But, again, I didn't care. It was like a symbol of my new-found bachelorette status. I wanted the pool table so I took it. I actually found it far more useful down the road for other extraneous activities. We'll get there.

As for Michelle and the Monday scene, while I busted my hump all weekend hauling loads—most of them up the stairs at the apartment complex when the elevator went out (again!) on Sunday—I had one final load left to bring on Monday morning: the last of my work suits and some miscellaneous bedding, linens and pots and pans. It doesn't sound like much but my truck cab didn't offer much, so it was quickly stuffed to the brim. I loaded it up late Sunday night at the house—knowing the ex would be coming back Monday and I wanted to be gone, gone, gone—slept my last night in the McMansion and drove straight to the office Monday morning like I normally did in the dark.

I liked to arrive at the office right around sunrise and use the first interruption-free hours to get the real work I needed to do that day done. If I didn't get it done then, that usually meant it wouldn't get done that day and would then stack on to an already jam-packed tomorrow. The practice of law is constantly, incessantly consuming in that regard. It never slows down. It never stops. Having arrived in the dark, I guess I just didn't notice it. To be so educated, I can often be so dumb sometimes. Lucky for me, Michelle likes to come in pretty early, too, and it was just a shade after 7:30 a.m. when she popped her head into my office, slipped in, shut the door behind her and proceeded to save me.

"Annie, my dear," she started in. "Are you serious?"

"Serious?" I asked, confused, caught-off guard. I figured I had totally botched some pleading or had her file something completely inappropriate with the court and she was now coming to let me know how royally I had screwed up and how hard, if not impossible, it was going to be to fix. I hated how much I feared screwing up. My heart would pound against my chest and my armpits would instantly begin sweating just at the thought of it. The practice of law was, for me, incredibly frightening in that regard.

Michelle looked at me deadpan for a second before walking over to my window, pushing the blinds apart and pointing down at my truck. "Are you serious?" she asked again.

My God, I was so stupid! Now, in the bright rays of morning light, I could see it. Shirt sleeves, pillows, a little Rubbermaid drawer set, some extension cords and a skillet were all pressed flat against the back window pane and every window of my cab. There was even a jean leg sticking out the passenger door. I must have caught it when I had heaved the truck door shut the night before, again in the dark, and had let it flap and flail all the way down the interstate to the office. My punctual, polished, suit-clad exterior may have worked well to hide my personal catastrophe, but my packed-out Beverly Hillbillies truck screamed domestic dispute!

I was such an idiot. In fifteen minutes, half the partners in the firm would walk by my truck and know something at the Dike household had gone awry. My 'stuff' was very telling. Questions would ensue. I would struggle to lie. And, having spent the weekend stripping myself from a life that had once seemed solid to set up anew, alone, in a strange place, I might have caved if they asked the right questions, if they probed in just the right places. I was strong but I was just so unsteady at the moment. I hadn't yet formulated answers to those types of questions and I feared what my fumbling self might say or do if I was confronted with it, now, when my wounds were still raw and searing and I stood in a pool of shame near my packed-out truck in the parking lot. Michelle was right. I was such an idiot!

"Go," she said, snapping me to. "Drop that crap off at your new place and get back here quick. I'll tell them you had a … a doctor's appointment or something." Michelle had already picked up my briefcase and was hustling me out the door. I scrambled down the stairs to the parking lot, sprinted to my truck and squealed the tires on the way down the parking lot ramp to make the eight-block run to my downtown apartment so I could hide all of my telling "crap" and come back clean, polished and protected from having to face the inquisition that day. Like I said, Michelle was not just good; she was exceptional.

With only three days and the move accomplished, it was definitely one of the quicker, easier moves I had made in my lifetime. My initial move from New Mexico to Alabama for college was one of the harder ones—mostly because it was my first. For me, that meant for the first time I was leaving my friends, family, a boyfriend, my childhood home, everything I had *known* behind. I wasn't as good then, as I am now, at venturing off and starting anew. Thankfully my dad drove all seventeen hours from Alabama out west just to turn around and make the seventeen-hour drive back with me in my little packed-down red Ford Escort. Yes, this would be the car that I started for years with a screwdriver. It just hadn't evolved to its infamous screwdriver status quite yet but—looking back on it now—I'm surprised I fit my entire eighteen-year-old world into the back half of a Ford Escort but somehow I did. While I promised Dad that I would drive "half the way, at least," I started blubbering and sniffling so hard at the Clovis city limits that Dad had to take over and he just drove the rest of the way from there. Having spent countless hours on the road as a long-haul truck driver, he was pretty used to it.

Dad and I always laugh, though, at this stupid "Annie" picture I insisted *had* to make the big college move with me. It was just a cheap, framed print, with my name in big letters across it, but because it was a gift from said left-behind boyfriend I thought it had some great sentimental value that I was going to need with me in college. Again, my stuff was telling. Although it was bulky and virtually useless, I felt it was a symbol of some part of me I didn't want to let go—a little crutch for my bruised heart or something.

At four feet long and a foot and a half tall, though, it was literally the size of one. The frame stretched the length of the entire car from the dash to the back seat and sat between dad and I the entire trip, like a tall fence between neighbors. It was so annoying to have to coordinate around, pass food and drink over and try to canoodle and sleep around during the entire seventeen-hour drive. It's embarrassing sometimes looking back at the stuff you hold onto, *cling to* as if it's the only thing that can stand in remembrance of something you hold dear. But the thought contradicts itself. *If it's so memorable, won't you just remember it?* After having babied and avoided it all that time, when we went to unpack the Escort at my grandma, Big Mom's, farm in Cullman, Alabama Dad scooched the passenger seat back to reach a box and somehow it caught the corner of a crate and punched it right through the second 'n' of my name in the picture.

"Awww hell," Dad said when he saw the damage. He was kind of pissed about it but I could tell he was worried more about my reaction. I'm sure he thought I was going to roll out my blubbering and sniffling bit again at his doing. "Babes, I'm sorry," he started in but I couldn't help it. I just started laughing. The irony of it was too much. We had maneuvered and coordinated around that stupid thing so carefully the entire seventeen-hour drive and for what? So we could pull into Big Mom's driveway and punch a hole right in the center? There was nothing to do but laugh. Once Dad saw me doubled over, he didn't hold back.

"I'da cracked the damn thing over my knee back in New Mexico if I'd known that was going to happen," Dad said, snickering himself. It was kind of a bummer but it was probably just what I needed at the time. If there was only one lesson I could thank my dad for, it would probably be that. The one thing that will really get you through this life is a sense of humor. It's going to be hard at times. You're going to lose things you're not ready to let go of. Sometimes the best and only thing you can do is find a way to laugh about it.

As soon as Dad said it, I knew I wanted to do it. I snatched that crappy picture out through the backseat and cracked it clean in half over my knee. *God that felt good!* Sometimes it takes losing something for you to see you never really needed to hold onto it in the first place. I didn't need a crutch. My heart was fine. I was going to be fine. If I didn't need it, holding onto it would only hinder my journey. At the very least, I now had less to carry. After it was gone, I felt like I stepped away lighter, anew.

I certainly didn't take any four foot long photo with me when I made the move down to Tuscaloosa the next month to start college at the University of Alabama. I just hauled another Beverly Hillbillies truck-cab full down to the college dorm Tutwiler—fourteen floors of whores they called it. And boy was that true. Coming from New Mexico, I simply had no idea what to make of these Southern belle broads. They wore makeup and pearls to the gym. Their hair never moved in the wind. More than half had boob jobs and most smoked but claimed "they didn't inhale." They were strange.

And they all came that day—the big "move-in day" at Tutwiler—with their entire nuclear and extended family, complete Vera Bradley luggage sets, zebra print dorm decor and, oh, everything monogrammed—pillow cases, toiletry bags, shower robes, towels, you name it—everything! I'm sure they didn't know what to make of me either, having pulled up alone in my dad's rusted out Dodge ram, the entirety of my *non*-monogrammed crap shoved in the cab or strung down in the bed with hay bailing twine. It was nice that it used to all fit in one truck. That wasn't the case when I made the move from Tuscaloosa to the McMansion just outside of Mobile. It required the largest U-Haul one could rent two truck-loads and a trailer and it still wasn't enough to fill the house.

I can't really say when exactly I started to accumulate so much stuff. I guess it was just the natural progression. You get a couple hand-me-down pieces of furniture in college. You start buying a couple paintings or decorative items you like. Then when you graduate, get a job and get married, you get a big house and start filling it with more stuff until you don't really even question the need any more. You just whip out a credit card and lay down $260.00 for some lights on a string. Now here I was, carrying one bag of clothes that could easily constitute my entire wardrobe and living for the next couple of months in a 150 square-foot cubby. Aside from the womb, it was the smallest place I had ever occupied and I was just about the happiest I had ever been. I had chosen all of this. I kept smiling as Phillip and I walked away from the boat for the first time in two days and headed to the showers—our three little bags in tow. It was the wind that had brought us there and I was sure we could get by for a month if need be on $260.00 and two bags of clothes.

"I'm glad we brought the wetsuits," Phillip said as we were walking to the showers.

I swear that man can hear everything I thought-say. Okay, two bags of clothes *and* a few pieces of key cruising gear. Despite our lack of unnecessary stuff on the boat, we do make allowances for the priorities—foul weather gear and wet gear. A wetsuit is easily a must when you have to get into some of Florida's still-cold-from-winter waters. While Phillip and I don't take polar bear plunges just for kicks, there's always the off-chance you will have to dive in to inspect the hull or a potentially-fouled prop. And we never turn down an opportunity to kitesurf when the conditions are right—even if the water temp is not. I can assure you: in April in north Florida, it's not.

On our way to the shower we spotted this awesome shallow cove in Port St. Joe that looked perfect for kitesurfing. If you're going to skim across a brisk, chilly body of water in April, powered solely by a massive, popping kite in the sky, chances are you're going to get wet—particularly in my case where there is a heightened risk for a face-plant, ass-plant, nose-plant and wide assortment of other random-body-part-plants along the way—which makes the wetsuit key.

After our indulgently-long showers, the necessary washing of ourselves, our clothes and the boat, we were excited to go poking around this quaint little old Florida town and see what Port St. Joe had in store for us. A closer inspection of the cove we had spotted on our way to the showers proved our instincts were right: it was going to be perfect for kitesurfing.

Coves are great because they allow you to kite in a wide range of wind directions and this one appeared to be shallow a good ways out, which was good news for me as somewhat of a still-new kiter because it meant I could stand if need be to rescue my board, myself, my kite, you name it. All we needed now was wind but we knew it was coming. One of the main reasons we had pulled into Port St. Joe was to avoid

a storm we knew was brewing in the Gulf. So all we had to do was bide our time while it built up. That's easy to do in Port St. Joe. We had a great time meandering around the little downtown strip, sipping wine at the Thirsty Goat and Haughty Heron and eating our fill at Joe Mama's Pizza and, particularly, Peppers. Having grown up in New Mexico, I was pretty familiar with your traditional Mexican restaurant and the usual chips-and-salsa routine, but Peppers blew my belt off.

"Seat Yourself" a little plastic sign on a rickety podium read when we walked in the door. *Don't mind if we do*, Phillip and I thought as we moseyed past some sombreros stapled to the wall to a little tucked-away table in the back with plastic covered booths. The minute our asses touched down a piping hot bowl of chips and salsa was placed on the table.

"Wow, thank you," I said, my eyes dancing over the hot, greasy chips. "De nada," the petite little Latino server replied and walked away. She wasn't our waitress but I watched her often as she eyed the room and was always standing at the ready with a fresh bowl of chips and salsa to plop down whenever new customers came in or current customers' bowls were getting low. Even though I tried to keep an eye on her, she always seem to pop up out of nowhere with a fresh new bowl for Phillip and I when we started reaching for crumbs. The *first* time she set a refill down we said "thanks" and eagerly dug in. The *second* time—before our meal had even come—we tried to wave her off, but it was no use. "No, thank you. That's okay," we would say shaking our heads. But plop went the bowl on the table and "de nada" she would say as she walked away. I have to say, I'll bet that little Latino can speak nearly perfect English but the no-hablo-espanol bit makes it easier for her to peddle chips.

Having already stuffed ourselves quite full on chips and salsa, Phillip and I ordered a burrito to split and that thing was huge! It had to be six inches in diameter and ten inches long, at least. And it was chalk full of this awesome cheesy, beef, bean, rice concoction. It was so good. Just when we were shoveling, almost miserably, the last bites in—Plop! A fresh hot bowl of chips came down again. Phillip and I both waved our hands and pushed it away, protesting vigorously, almost aggressively. I was so full the thought of eating just one more chip almost made me nauseous. But, "de nada," was all she said as she walked away. I can't say I know how it happened but somehow, between the time we got the check and paid for it, that fourth bowl of chips disappeared too. I'm sure it was Phillip. The Peppers experience was certainly entertaining and easily one of the most filling meals of the trip. The cheapest too. Do you want to know the grand total? A whopping $11.38. For the two of us. We love Port St. Joe.

Two days of peppers and pizza and just as predicted—which it seems bad weather always comes—the storm finally rolled in. When we woke on the third morning, the flags in the Port St. Joe marina were taut and flapping. The wind had filled in to a nice solid south, southeast, blowing twenty-five with gusts of thirty. Perfect for a session in the cove.

"It's pumping now!" Phillip shouted with a thunderous clap that probably woke up our boat neighbors in the marina. It was around seven in the morning but we didn't care. It was finally time to bust out the kites! We get a little pumped up about pumping them up, no pun intended. While I was somewhat of a competent kiter at the time—meaning I could get up and somewhat go in the direction I somewhat intended—I was far less experienced than Phillip. He had just started teaching me about a year prior to the Keys trip. It was definitely a steep learning curve but one of the most exciting sports I have ever tried. Some days I would get out there and spend my entire session tangling and untangling myself, crashing my kite and trying to re-launch it only to crash it again. It's just part of it. But, like many of the other "new" things I was experiencing with during that tumultuous time of my life, I was more than willing to get my ass out there (literally) and try it.

"Let's get on it then!" I said as we packed up our gear.

CHAPTER NINE

Ass-First

"**S**mooth is fast," Phillip told me as I was grunting and tugging and trying to curse my way into my wetsuit. *Yes I know that.* But there is nothing that can possibly be smooth or fast about trying to pull neoprene over sticky, sweaty skin. It's like trying to put on a pair of tight jeans when you're still wet from the shower. Everything sticks. Toes jam in the knee bend, the crotch section gets hung up around your thighs. There's a lot of hopping, pulling and grunting involved. Smooth is the last thing I would call it. And while I'm sure my sweating didn't help, it's not like I could just think dry thoughts and make it stop.

But the wetsuit is a necessary evil. The water was still a little chilly that time of year and while putting on that rubbery contraption is a bit of a minor annoyance, being cold is far worse. So I tugged and groaned my way through it as we packed up our gear. The wind was calling. It was finally time to fly the kite! Phillip and I hoisted our kiting gear and headed out to the cove in Port St. Joe.

Out of all the new "sports" I tried after the divorce, kitesurfing has definitely been the most frustrating, frightening, exhilarating and rewarding. As you stand on the shore and watch kiters zip by you, skimming on top of the water, kicking up a wake of champagne, their kites popping and playing in the air, you think: *I want to do that.* You're motivated by the sight alone. It's mesmerizing. Which is a good thing—because if it didn't look so damn fun you wouldn't bust your hump for months, even years, trying to learn. Unless you're an experienced windsurfer, wakeboarder or—for some reason (don't ask me why, maybe they're just somehow more dialed into wind-born vehicles and aerodynamics) a pilot—the learning curve can be very steep. But the fact that you are willing to spend two hours getting set up, pumped up, launched, crashed, tangled and untangled all for perhaps three glorious minutes where you were barely riding says it all, really. Just a glimpse of the feeling and you're addicted.

When you start out, though, many sessions can play out like that—ten minutes of fun for two hours of headache, assuming you even get the ten minutes. It just takes a while to get savvy enough with the kite and board to keep yourself out of a mess. But, what is it they say? "If it were easy, everyone would do it." That's why most don't. Most watch from the shore saying they want to do that. Some try for a bit but then eventually give up. Few actually continue to kite because it is so challenging. But if it were quickly conquerable, that wouldn't be any fun. The continued challenge is what brings you back.

And those three measly minutes when you were barely holding everything together, wiggling across the water, butt sticking way out, death grip on the control bar—basically doing everything completely and utterly wrong but somehow still somewhat miraculously doing it—makes it totally and completely worth it. The feeling when the kite pulls you up out of the water and you're skimming along, cutting through waves, moving solely by the sheer power of the wind, is a unique and invigorating experience. It cannot be matched. I guess that's what sailboats feel like, with their canvas up, slicing through the water.

But I'll have to admit when Phillip first mentioned this silly kitesurfing stuff to me, to be honest, I kind of pictured a sweet little image of a father and his son, frolicking in a golden wheat field, flying a rainbow kite. At least that was the first "kite" image that came to mind—Hallmark kiting. But what Phillip was talking about and what he was about to expose (and addict) me to was totally different—far from gay frolics in a wheat field. It was a total badass water sport. We would need one of those bumper stickers that says: "My kite beat up your honor student kite." I'll never forget the first time I saw Phillip do it.

"Make sure you stand upwind while I launch," Phillip said.

"Up where?" I asked, standing kind of dumb-founded near him as he was about to self-launch his kite. I think I understood the fact that he had *said* "upwind," but to tell you the truth, I was so bamboozled by the whole scene—this huge kite laying on the ground, Phillip tethered to it with this rather serious-looking harness around his waist—I couldn't have told you what direction the wind was even blowing at that moment, much less which direction was *up* from that. I was hoping Phillip would just point where he wanted me to go and thankfully he did.

"That way," he said as he shooed me in the direction that I can only assume was upwind. "Go stand over there."

I jogged about ten paces that way and watched in amazement as Phillip scooted this massive kite along the ground, popped a corner of it up and then launched it thirty feet over his head. It was so big it blocked the sun and I could see him smiling down below in its shadow. Phillip steered it left then right then gave it a big yank and came flying three feet off the ground. He ran a few steps when his feet touched down on the sand and he shouted out at me.

"The wind is good," he said. "I'm gonna go out and make some runs. I'll be back!" He had this sort of childish smile on his face, like a little kid who has just been handed a glistening ice cream cone. He looked ten years younger.

"Okay!" I shouted back at him, his child-smile infecting me too. "Be careful!"

He nodded as he headed out backwards toward the surf, carrying his board in one hand and flying the kite with the other. Phillip and I had been "companioning" for about six months but this was the first time

I had ever come out to watch him kitesurf and I was enamored by the whole process. He looked so graceful and regal doing it.

I couldn't wait to try it too. I had dabbled in my fair share of adventure sports in my time—gymnastics and barrel racing, tree climbing (which included the occasional tree-falling), rock-climbing, scuba-diving, even jello-wrestling back in college. And don't knock the wrestling. That was one of the toughest sports of all. Everything is so slippery! With that rudimentary "sports" background, I thought I would pick this kiting stuff up pretty quick and impress the snot out of Phillip with my impeccable kite skills. That would have been awesome. That's not what happened. The first time he hooked me up to the kite, I felt like he'd strapped me to an elephant and made me step on a skateboard.

While I'm sure my particular mental hang-ups had something to do with my slow progression, I have since met several people who reported the same steep learning curve. Kiting is simply not a hobby for the impatient. It can takes months, sometimes, before you ever learn to just get up on the board, much less go anywhere. Plus it's hard to line up the weather, the wind and the opportunity to drop everything and run to an ideal location for a session. Sometimes months would pass between my sessions and, by then, whatever rust I had knocked off the previous time had indeed caked back on and collected anew in other areas. Kiting is just so counter-intuitive and requires such a new and awkward set of muscle memory skills that it takes a while to learn, scold and train them. You spend most of your initial sessions beating back your auto-response and instilling a new set of muscle memories that enable you to fly the kite.

For instance, when the kite starts acting up, dragging you across the sand, trying to fly in circles, you know what you're supposed to do? Let go of the controls. Yes, I'm serious. When all hell breaks loose, you just let the kite fly. Now, what do you *actually* do, because you're panicked and freaking? You yank on the controls! Naturally. It's kind of like when you hydroplane and you're supposed to ease off the brakes and just let your car go until it finally grips. That's what you're supposed to do. But what do you often do? Slam on the brakes and get yourself in some real trouble. Those types of instinctive reactions are hard to train. But the basic "instinct" accomplishments merely enable you to fly the kite safely. Actually flying the kite in a manner than can propel you across the water is an entirely new and equally frustrating yet rewarding series of lessons.

As Phillip explained it to me, kiting is a lot like wake-boarding, except you're both riding the board behind the boat and driving the boat at the same time. For one who had done neither, that may explain a bit about my particularly slow progression. The kite, however, requires far more time and training than the board. The board skills are kind of just like the icing on the cake. Flying the kite is the most important part.

Even when you're getting smacked in the face with waves, you're being dragged across the ground—you've lost your board, your shades, your bathing suit, your dignity and all hope—you must still, at all times, fly the kite. And cursing the kite for not doing what you want it to do is also a futile endeavor. It is always operator error. As much as it may pain you to admit it, when the kite has crashed into the water, the brush, the woods or, God forbid, people, it was *you* who was controlling it at the time. There's no one else to blame when you fly the kite like a moron (which is easier to do than you think—recall the counter-intuitiveness). You are in control.

Despite the wave-smacking, dignity-lacking aspects of kiting, the thing I really love about kitesurfing is it is virtually unconquerable, which makes it perpetually challenging. No matter how skilled you get, you can always push yourself to learn a new trick, a new flip, a new *something* that challenges you all over again, not to mention different locations, churned-up surf, chest-high waves, on and on. This only speaks, however, to the challenges. The variety of experiences, the beauty of different kiting locations, the diversity of reefs and marine wildlife you might see while you're skimming across the water will also keep you coming back for more. Flips and tricks aside, there is nothing in the world that can replicate the feeling of kitesurfing. It's like you're skimming across a sea of champagne. If the conditions are right, kiting is the one thing in the world Phillip and I would rather do than sail. Plus the gear is light. It's just a board and a backpack, which makes it perfect for cruising. We usually take the kites with us on the boat wherever we go.

My kite-learning days were quite the entertaining adventure. "Waterstart" sessions seemed to last forever. I couldn't find just the right amount of 'gas' to get me up and going. I would either dip the kite just enough to lift only my ass out of the water, or I would slam the pedal down and pull myself over the board, resulting in a wicked face plant, after which my first thought always was: *Where's my kite? Fly the kite. Do not crash the kite.*

Needless to say it was pretty intense and I experienced my fair share of harrowing moments. Keeping such a close eye on the kite caused a strange phenomenon for me that Phillip said he had never quite seen. We call it "running out of water." I would be so focused on flying the kite and making sure it was in position and powered up, I would occasionally kitesurf myself right onto shore. The first time I did it, I was dragged across the marsh grass and sand a good ten or so feet on my belly while I scrambled to get the kite over my head and right myself. I didn't think (key word being *think*) Phillip had seen it so when he asked me later what had happened. "Nothing," I replied and shrugged my shoulders. "Why do you ask?"

"Really Annie?" Phillip asked as he pointed to my belly. Sadly when I looked down I could see that my full-frontal grass and grit streak told a different tale. I looked like a kid who ran out of Slip-N-Slide and scooted halfway across the yard on wet grass or, better yet, like Swamp Thing half-suited up. I shrugged my shoulders and gave Phillip the only answer I knew.

"I ran out of water."

Learning to kite, now those were good times. My post-divorce days in general—while they were kind of bewildering and uprooting—were also good times. As I mentioned I was a little overweight at the time—not grotesquely so, but shamefully so for my build. I had always been an active, athletic person, very fit and capable, and I found myself at that time carrying an extra fifteen frumpy pounds around my midsection and likely incapable of jogging a single mile. I was in sad shape in my mind. So I cleaned up my diet, started cooking better meals for myself at home and bringing them to the office for lunch. I started jogging, taking free Pilates classes at the downtown Mobile Y, stretching in the evenings. Within weeks I felt infinitely better.

And I know what you might be thinking: I could have done all of those things while I was still married. My only answer is that it seemed to require a state of mind, a new slate, a better outlook. I was not staying out late anymore because I didn't want to go home. I wasn't drinking nearly as much. Although, to this day, I do not believe I had a drinking problem, I believe I had a life problem that I tried to ignore by drinking, because as soon as I started to change the things I didn't like about my life, the drinking became once again just an occasional hobby, not a need. Most importantly, though, I never (ever!) drove home on the blackened brink of death again. Because I was happier I was healthier. I was finally doing things I had wanted to do for years.

The eating and exercise were first, the "playing" came next. Yes, I mean what you think I mean. But because I was at the time still worried about protecting the legal career, I did have the decency to at least play out of town. I made a few friends during that time that lived, worked and did their playing in Pensacola, Florida, a mere forty-five minutes away from Mobile. So, a quick under-an-hour drive after work and suddenly I was in a whole new realm, no longer acting as "Attorney Dike" but this new, fiery character who could do anything and anyone she wanted.

I should have had a super-hero outfit that I ~~dawned~~ *donned* under my work suit and stripped off during the drive over. I can tell you the "S" wouldn't stand for "Super." I was pleased to find Pensacola was filled to the brim with big, hunky navy boys just looking for a good time. *How fortuitous.* They could be easily bagged in Pensacola or shuttled back to my party pad in Mobile—my professional colleagues and partners being none the wiser. Thankfully, it was just a few months and while I did get a little wild and reckless it was—as a good friend of mine called it—"just a phase." At the very least it justified the ill-fitting pool table in the new apartment.

At first I merely danced around the idea, my eyes glittering over a sea of big biceps and buzz cuts. But when I finally slipped into that realm, it was an all-out landslide. Now, I didn't say I was good at playing initially, but I've never been known to be a quitter. The first one was an absolute fucking fiasco but highly indicative of my erratic state of mind at the time. I met this fiesty little redhead around the time of my move to the downtown apartment in Mobile who was the perfect transition companion for me. She was an incredibly spirited, funny, rambunctious gal who—being a little reckless herself—served as the perfect comrade for my brief stint of wild escapades.

We'll call her Justine because, well, that name just seems to fit. When you imagine a Justine, don't you picture a redhead, big Dallas hair, a cigarette hanging out of her mouth and tight hot pants paired with heels? I do. I picture a pistol, and that's about what Justine was. It may have been reckless, but I had just about the best damn time of my life bar-hopping in Pensacola with her. She had her own party pad in Pensacola that I was offered free reign to frequent. Over the course of our friendship, I'm sure I put a few bedpost holes in the wall of her upstairs loft, just as she put a few high heel gashes in my pool table in Mobile. Thank goodness it *was* just a phase.

One night in particular Justine and I were hanging out at a bar in Pensacola Beach and I had managed, once again, to lure a cute guy into my web. I had been flirting and talking a big game for a few months but the divorce was now "final" and I guess I decided it was time to stop playing eeny-meenie-miney-moe among the buzzcuts and just get this party started. You're only young and cute once, right? Better bang some twenty-one year-olds while you still can. For whatever reason, I decided this was going to be the night, which meant this was going to be the guy. And I do believe I picked the night, not the guy. The options every night were usually about the same in Pensacola, just swap out and insert very military-sounding last names: Decker, Reinhardt, Hightower. There was nothing incredibly special about this particular guy, I was just ready to saddle up.

So the cute guy and I sauntered out to my car where the topic of location finally came up. Turned out he was a marine. (I guess you can say I'm attracted to them by instinct.) He was out on liberty for the weekend and just staying with some friends on their couch so *that* was no good. As Justine tended to do, she had made a whole pack of new friends at the bar and was planning to herd them back to her place in Pensacola for a little house party, so *that* locale was nixed as well. Partying on the beach meant I was a drunk-drive hour away from my pool table shag-pad in Mobile and—as crazy as I may have seemed at the time—I did not do that anymore, never, not ever again. So that left just him, me, my car and my credit card. I figured I was a big, hot-shot attorney, so I could lay down some dough for a hotel room. Why not?

It's actually kind of embarrassing when I look back on it. I reeked of desperation. I know now the house party at Justine's would have cost me less, in both cash and pride, but I had already made up my mind. Here's how it played out. I got us a hotel room—real fancy-like at the Super 6 just down the road. Cute Guy and I decided the hotel pool would be a fun place to start, but it wasn't long before we decided behind-the-pool-house would be a fun place to finish. Now, what was behind the pool house? Hotel security? Hardly. A big flood light that revealed our "fun" to everyone? No. It was something much worse. And I can't possibly tell you why we didn't realize what was back there when we were back there. Sure there was a good bit of alcohol involved—not to mention our combined adrenaline, lust and hormones—but should that have clouded our ability to perceive piercing pain and venom in our most sensitive nether regions? One would think not but that's what happened.

After our pool-house fun, we stumbled back to the hotel room and crumpled into a heap on the bed. I woke up just after sunrise with a burning, itching sensation eating through the flesh of my right ass cheek. I reached down to feel my skin and my fingers touched down on the mottled, crater surface of the moon. I kind of freaked out in my mind, thinking: *Of course! Of-fucking-course!* The first time I decide to venture down this road and I pick the guy who gives me instant ass herpes? I really did think initially it had to have come from him. Cute Guy must have given me some supersonic spreading rash or something. I snuck off my side of the bed and tiptoed to the bathroom only to find three hundred bites on one cheek which exploded out like a red pimply fire bomb to my other cheek and down the backs of my thighs. It was almost comical in its hideousness. And it hurt like hell!

Then I freaked out completely. *What have I done?* I sacrificed my cute little apple ass for what? A desperate little romp behind the pool house? He wasn't even *that* cute. Okay who am I kidding? He was smoking hot and like eight years younger than me. I did have a certain "type" during my just-a-phase. In my silly single mind I had hit the jackpot with this guy but apparently the pot comes with a pimply, eat-up ass. I just had to get away. I didn't want to actually talk to him or see him the next morning. It was my first time to ever do something like this and I could already tell I was retarded at it.

I decided to leave him there—with some cash. Not like prostitution or anything, just some money so he could get home. He would need to call a cab or something I suspected. And, thinking I never wanted to re-live the embarrassment of this night again, I decided to delete my name and number from his phone. We had exchanged digits early in the evening and exchanged a text or two not knowing initially where things were headed, so I clicked his phone to life and deleted my contact. I deleted him from my phone as well—not really sure why. I then left a twenty dollar bill on the nightstand, slipped into my clothes and slipped the hell out of there.

It was like 6:00 a.m. but I called Justine anyway during the drive back to her place. She woke long enough to let out a good hearty laugh at me and to tell me to bring some Starbucks when I came so we could re-live the whole saga over lattes. Justine had about the same dry-heave reaction to my mottled ass that I did. It looked like the first stage of leprosy. We decided to slather it with Neosporin and swaddle it in a little beach sarong for the day. My skin was so irritated by all the venom it actually radiated heat. I was literally a hot mess.

As if that wasn't enough, here's the real kicker. Around 3:00 p.m. that day, Justine and I were driving somewhere—probably to another beach bar or something, I can't quite recall—but I got a text on my phone. There wasn't a name programmed in—just an ominous number. I didn't recognize the number so I clicked it open.

"Fire ants," it said.

That was it. Just "fire ants." I threw the phone in the floorboard like it was a pinless grenade. *How in the world?* I was totally stunned. Justine tried to hide her smile when I showed her the text. She was getting way too much pleasure out of this.

"But, how did he … " I stumbled around the thought for a bit. I had deleted my number from his phone. I deleted his number from mine. *How did he?* To be honest I was a little scared but a little flattered too. Perhaps he was like CIA or something and he had used his secret government powers to hunt down the little blonde from the bar. That's kind of sexy.

"The text stream," my phone read and I stared at it, still baffled but still not responding.

"You deleted your contact but not the text stream. And leave me with a $20? Really? What kind of crazy are you?" he texted.

Justine and I were doubled over with laughter at this point, wiping tears, snorting, the whole bit. This was unreal. Perhaps it was a dumb thing to do but it wasn't all that dangerous, not near as much anyway as getting plastered and barreling down the interstate. I was flattered, intrigued, excited. And, yes, okay, maybe my ass was a mound of hot, greasy ground beef but I was sure it would heal. If not, the scars would make for one hell of a story. At the very least, I was certainly living in the moment, in my hot rippled skin. *What kind of crazy was I?*

"The best kind," I texted back.

Cute Guy No. 1 and I actually spent the better part of the next month engaged in one of the most stimulating, witty text exchanges I have ever participated in. And I say "No. 1" because there were a handful of other twenty-two year-olds—mostly marine-build—that I had some fun with during my phase. It was really just a new hobby though—something

I was sort of trying out to see what, or should I say *who*, my new self liked to do. While I couldn't actually shoot a legitimate game on the pool table at the apartment, I found many other great uses for it.

But during my wild year with Justine and all the "toddlers" (Justin's word, because they were so much younger than me), I have to say Cute Guy No. 1 remained my favorite. He turned out to be very clever, wickedly funny and just a lot of fun. We hooked up a few more times before parting ways and always got a royal laugh from re-living our first fire ant-filled rendezvous. I think I came out better, though, as he was eat up with them all over the front—even amongst the family jewels—while I only suffered their savagery on the backside. Apparently it put him out of commission for a few weeks. You just can't explain that away.

I don't really know why, but many of the new things I tried during that time seemed to have a detrimental effect on my ass. Hell, it had just barely healed about the time I met Phillip. I had no idea when I plopped my slightly-mottled ass down next to him at the bar that fateful night that he would captivate me with talk of an upcoming trip to the Grenadines and his eventual plans to live aboard a sailboat and travel the world. Right when I thought no one or thing could ever captivate me again, Phillip unveiled an entirely new world of adventure. He showed and taught me things I couldn't have then even imagined—sailing, yes, but also skiing, wakeboarding, scuba diving and kitesurfing as well.

The kiting was still a bit new to me when we were in Port St. Joe and during that particular session I stayed true to my ass-first form. The cove was shallow—which is perfect for an intermediate kite surfer such as I was—but the winds were really howling. The kite would often pull me up, stretched and taut, like Gumby before trying to drag me face-first over the board. My go-to at the time, when I got a bit over-powered, was to plant my ass in the water as brakes. It's not a bad tactic if you're about to get pulled over your board but in some heavy winds and choppy seas it can feel a bit like a salt-water enema. After a three-time repeat of the stretch-and-squat routine, Phillip took the kite back from me to make some more runs. It was clear the winds had kicked up beyond my capabilities at the time to hold down our largest twelve-meter shared kite.

Benched and bummed, but knowing Phillip was right, I stood by on the shore like a faithful kite groupie, snapping pics and footage. Some lookie-loos had started working their way towards us while we were pumping up and launching. Kiting is a pretty spectator-worthy sport, particularly for those who have never seen it before. Odd-looking people sporting big, hulky backpacks and carrying wakeboards begin congregating on shore, holding their fingers up or their arms out feeling the wind. They open their backpacks and start whipping out these huge colorful canvases, popping them like fresh sheets on a bed. Then they begin ... pumping? If you're new to the sport, watching it all unfold from backpack to high-flying apparatus can be intriguing.

The kite begins to grow and uncurl as the bladder fills. Then there are all these lines. Folks tangling, untangling, running and re-running them. You hear the rough shriek of Velcro as they swaddle their midsections with some serious looking harnesses. As they step back, holding a bar in one hand and giving instruction to the fellow kiter holding their kite upright a good seemingly twenty, maybe thirty feet away, you think it's about to happen. *They're going to launch!* It's exciting. You can't help but watch. A couple of deft maneuvers on the bar and then it soars—a kite so big it blocks the sun. The pilot will usually fly it back and forth a few times and give it a good hard yank to test the power, which usually sends him flying two or three feet across the sand, only to come sprinting back down, sporting a smile so big you can see his teeth from where you're standing. If you haven't said it to yourself yet, this will likely be the time: *I want to do that.*

And, if you say that to yourself after just the launch, when you see them actually surfing, you say it out loud. Phillip was putting on quite the show that day in the cove. Probably because there was an audience, but can you blame him? If you've worked hard to hone your skills for

a sport you really love, isn't showing off half the reward? He would rip across the cove, leaned all the way back, his feet drilling into the board, edging and spraying a huge rooster's tail behind him. I can tell now by watching him—how he's arching back, powering up the kite and how low he's flying it near the water—when Phillip is about to let it rip. He'll zip the kite back over his head, pull hard and then he's soaring—a good five, ten, sometimes fifteen feet above the water. He'll usually grab his board behind him for a minute, get all extreme-watersports with it, before he flies the kite back down, just kisses the water and continues on. And that's just a jump. To watch him turn toe-side, lean down and skim his finger through the water like silk is just as mesmerizing. He makes it all look so effortless. It really is something to see.

Folks watching just can't help it. Like fire ants, their curiosity eats them alive. And while I get it. They're intrigued. They want to know more. Sometimes they just bug the living snot out of me—like fire ants too I suppose. Clearly I'm doing something difficult, that takes concentration and focus and they want to tap me on the shoulder while I'm flying a kite and ask mind-numbing questions like this?

Onlooker says: "Man, I can't believe you guys are doing that in this wind!"

We think: *You kind of* need *wind to kite. What do you think is keeping that kite up there? Magic?*

Onlooker says: "I'll bet you wish it was blowing a little less, huh?"

We think: *No. Never. Unless it's blowing like twenty-five miles per hour, we pretty much always want it to blow more. Always. More wind means more power which means more control.*

Onlooker says: "Do you have to be super strong to hold onto the kite?"

We think: *Nope. It's attached to you. Strong or not, you're going where it's going. It really doesn't take much muscle to fly the kite, just know-how and experience.*

It's just ignorance, I know. And I should be more patient. I know too. But I can't help it. I don't mind lookie-loos. I just don't want them asking me any questions. This one guy—and I swear he was one of those bulky bicep, buzzcut types that I *used* to like before I discovered myself, Phillip and thereafter my truer, richer sense of adventure—asked me if I needed help. I was kiting back in Pensacola one afternoon and I had lost my board—an annoying occurrence but it happens. And what sucks about it is the board is really your only method of brakes in the water. It is the only foothold you can push against to try and prevent the kite from pulling you too far downwind.

Even while holding the kite in its most de-powered position—straight above your head at high noon—if you're just a body in the water, she's still a big canvas in the sky that is going to drag you downwind no matter what you do, how hard you kick or how loud you curse her. And where does your board typically stay? Afloat behind you as you scooch further and further away. While there are ways to maneuver the kite in order to "body-drag" (feels exactly as pleasurable as it sounds) back upwind to your board, sometimes you're too far gone and the best solution—if you're close enough—is to body-drag back to shore, walk upwind well beyond your board, then body-drag back out, downwind toward your board. Thankfully Phillip had taught me several self-rescue tricks such as this, and I was daftly performing one when Mr. Biceps felt the need to save this apparent damsel in distress as I was walking along the shore to get back to my board.

"No, really," he said, bouncing his pecs. "I can hold the kite for you while you get your board."

I'm sure I let out an audible snort. Allowing him to do that would be akin to me saying, "Here, hold my pet tiger for a minute. I swear, he won't bite." *What a dumbass. My kite would kill you and you don't even have a harness.* Like he could just stand there and hold it. Why did he think I had all of that gear on? Because I was handicapped? I almost thought about giving it to him just for fun. But, I didn't. I was good.

"No, that's alright. Thanks though," I said as I shook my head and continued my trek upwind.

I know people are just curious—and some are just egotistic—but I have little patience. Sorry, it's just the truth of the matter. "Ask my friend, Chatty Kathy, over here. She'll be happy to tell you *all* about kiting." *While I'm out there ripping it up. Stand back!*

Luckily Phillip and I drew a good hand that day with our wild, high-flying antics, because the peanut gallery in Port St. Joe was pretty tolerable. Meaning, they asked mostly legitimate questions. And that's what most people do. Stand on the shore, ask questions and say to themselves: *I want to do that.* But they never actually do it. Even if they take a few lessons and try a few times, once they realize how hard it is and how long it might take for them to actually be out there enjoying it, they give up and they go back to shore. If my fire ant fiasco wasn't proof enough, when you first get out on the field to play, you're going to screw up. It might hurt. And it might be at times embarrassing and frightening.

But you just have to keep at it. The courageous do. If it were easy to be out there doing it, then everyone would.

The crowd seemed to dissipate a bit when Phillip decided to let me have another crack at it, which was probably a good thing. It was still a bit windy and I was still using the squat-brake method to avoid getting pulled over my board. Like I said, this is not a bad tactic if the alternative is a face-plant, but it's also not a great one if there are rocks, rubbish or—in my case—oyster beds on the bottom. One swift stomp-squat on my ass-brakes and I managed to tear a nice chunk out of the ass of my wetsuit when my bottom crashed on an oyster bed. I felt cool water immediately seep in and I knew I'd punctured it. An inspection later revealed I had not only punched a hole in the wetsuit but I had also managed to put a little puncture in my actual Annie-ass as well.

I guess it's like the sacrificial lamb. If I want to find out if I like something or not, my first tactic is to get out there, ass-first, and try it. And, as I also mentioned, when it comes to trying a new sport—even one that leads to the occasional mortifying blunder—I was never a quitter. In addition to the aforementioned hole in the ass of my wetsuit, I also managed to break a foot strap on the board, drag myself through all kinds of muck and debris, tumble three times and faceplant twice that day in Port St. Joe. But I am proud to say I did not crash the kite. I figured as long as I didn't put my ass in too much danger, I deserved to have a little fun with the new hobbies.

The kitesurfing also made me a much better sailor. Once I understood the mechanics of the board—which is essentially your keel and rudder on the boat—and how the board and kite (or keel and canvas)

work together to create a force that can be harnessed and used to *steer*, my sailing senses were heightened. I found, on the boat, I was much more in tune with the wind direction and strength, coming wind lines, gusts and how the canvas would react to them. Sailing and kitesurfing really go hand-in-hand.

It requires a lot more wind, however, to kitesurf than to sail. And the eighteen knots we were zipping and playing around in with the kite in the protected cove at Port St. Joe were not going be so much fun on the boat out in a churned-up Gulf, which is why we were biding our time in the safety of port. Turns out, though, it wasn't much fun at the dock either. Howling winds on the beam and a wedged-in-tight vessel make for the only thing I hate almost as much as a docking debacle: a de-docking one. The lesson I would not-yet-learn from this one however? (Do recall I am stubborn. It takes a time or two for things to sink through my thick skull.) Never sacrifice your body for the boat.

CHAPTER TEN

"Motorin'!"

"**M**otorin! Blinded by the light!" I was belting out that old classic pretty much all morning as we motored along, my face warming over a hot bowl of oatmeal. "What's your price for flight?"

I'm not even sure those are the right lyrics, but that didn't stop my bellowing. While the winds were great for kiting in Port St. Joe, they would not be so great for us to pop out for another offshore passage over to Clearwater. So we decided to wait one more day and motor the Gulf Intracoastal Waterway, known to locals and cruisers as "the ditch," from Port St. Joe over to Apalachicola the following day. While we had come into Port St. Joe seeking mere refuge from the rough Gulf, what we found was a quaint little Florida town frequented by a variety of interesting and diverse cruisers.

Our dock neighbors—"Skipper Bob" and his wife, Pat, aboard *s/v Maverick* and David and Mary on the *s/v Liza*—were particularly fun. We all quickly became dock buddies and decided to meet up boat-side our last night in Port St. Joe so we could walk to town to have dinner together. Bob regaled us with tales from his and Pat's time in the Bahamas. He apparently bumped and skipped his way into, and surprisingly *out of,* so many shallow, yet picturesque anchorages that he earned himself the title "Skipper Bob." David and Mary were bright, enthusiastic and hilarious in a way that you would almost miss if you weren't paying attention. Before dinner, we were planning to get a cocktail at the Thirsty Goat and they had a sign out front saying it was their "trivia night." David's immediate response? "I don't know much about goats." Funny guy, that David. You have to watch him. I love the people you meet while cruising.

Bob, Pat, David, Mary, Phillip and I were all hunkered down in Port St. Joe waiting for the storm in the Gulf to pass. It seemed the only thing that wind was good for was kitesurfing in the bay because it made for a pretty awful night on the boat our last night in Port St. Joe.

Eighteen knots of wind had us plastered to the dock like a wayward, wind-blown poster on a chain link fence. We bashed into the dock all night, the fenders squealing, the dock lines stretching and yelping. There wasn't much rest to be had aboard *Plaintiff's Rest* that evening.

Just as we were getting ready to shove off at dawn the next morning, Skipper Bob came out to lend a hand. It's a good thing too, because I'm not sure we could have done it without him. The wind was still blowing hard off the starboard bow and we were wedged in fairly tight between *Maverick* and *Liza*. With Bob's help, we decided to let the bow off and back out around *Liza* then turn our nose out and hopefully move forward outside of *Maverick*—a great plan, in theory, an epic failure in eighteen knots of wind.

Phillip started to back out and tried to push his stern out far enough to clear *Liza* behind him, but the wind wasn't having it. He went back and forth a couple of times (the beginnings of an eighty-two-point turn) and finally just scooched outside of *Liza* but when he started to move forward, the wind pushed hard on the boat broadside and sent her stern back toward the pilings. Bob and I looked like a pair of dancing monkeys—me on the boat and him on the dock—running the length of the boat and shoving it off pilings. It was a mighty struggle.

I stuck a foot out through the stern railing at the end, gave one last mighty push off the dock allowing our stern to clear a piling by just inches. Phillip was revving hard to avoid hitting Bob and Pat's stern in front of us and we missed that by just inches too, if not centimeters. Bob was a huge help, though, and a good sport. As we just squeezed by his dinghy, he hollered out: "You should've swiped her! We need a new one!

Safe travels you guys!" It was a heart-pounding moment and certainly not the way you want to start a leisurely morning.

When I finally made it back to the cockpit—heaving and sweating, my heart still thumping mightily in my chest—Phillip scolded me for trying to sacrifice my body for the boat. "The boat's tougher than you are, trust me. Between the two of you, save yourself." *Oh, all right!* I knew he was right (but I hate being scolded). It was a good lesson just not one I would really learn until later, but that's well on down the line. For the moment we were finally off the dock, our adrenaline subsiding and we enjoyed a magenta-streaked sunrise as we headed out into the bay.

The view was amazing when we came under the bridge to Port St. Joe. Slick, shimmering water, the slightest bit of fog steaming up and pelicans everywhere, just skimming the water. Well, most were skimming. One wasn't so lucky. As we turned in under the bridge to Port St. Joe we heard a mighty thump up at the bow. I had been staring off the starboard side—watching some pelicans glide above the water—and I was shocked to now see one, not ten feet away, flapping and wrestling around on our foredeck. A pelican! Flopping around on the boat!

For whatever reason—perhaps he'd had one too many Sailor Jerry's at the old Pelican's Perch the night before or he was just the local pelican idiot—he had flown right into our Genny sheet and the more he squirmed and flung those big, clumsy wings of his around, the more tangled up he got. At one point, the sheet was wrapped around his neck. I thought I might have to go rescue him and actually got a little excited about the prospect. *Man-handling a real, live pelican? Can you say adventure?*

Phillip and I watched him a moment or two longer in astonishment, exchanging a few lame guesses as to what in the hell had driven him right into our boat. I remember Phillip asking: "Is he retarded?" Good question. How do you know if a pelican is? I don't think they wear a little medical bracelet or anything. He finally flapped himself free of the Genny line, though, and then waddled and snaggled his way through the lifelines before taking off from the starboard bow. I watched him fly for just a bit and then he quickly plopped down in the water, shook his head a hard time or two and just sat there for a minute. Trying to get his bearings I would imagine. Big dumb bird. That was wild.

Once we'd shaken that image out of our mind, we sat back and enjoyed watching the sun come up over the edge of the foggy water. Cruising down the ditch at sunrise makes you feel like you've been transported back in time—big, rusty shrimp boats lining the docks, fog dissipating on the horizon, jagged tree stumps poking through along the shore. We could have been making our way right down the ole' Mississipp' with Huck Finn passing by on his rickety raft at any moment. It was such a surreal feeling.

We made a pot of piping oatmeal and savored our serene morning in the ditch. Well, minus the occasional belt-out by Yours Truly of course: "Motorin'!" Lake Wimico was gorgeous, too, and we made a nice, easy day of it motoring over to Apalachicola. We needed to fuel up for the planned Gulf crossing the following day, so we stopped into the fuel dock just before Apalachicola Bridge and suffered our second docking debacle of the day. *I seriously think I've got some kind of horrendous docking curse.* The current was really working against us, pushing us fast

right past the dock, so it was crucial (nay, critical!) that we get a line on a cleat or piling or in the hands of a sure-footed dock-hand—and fast.

I called ahead to let the fuel guys know we were coming. Like I said, I'm not in any way ashamed to ask for an extra hand to save our boat. But this goober? He's standing there on the dock—all open-arms and waiting. I throw the bow line to him as we come in and it lands right at his feet. *His feet!* Sadly, though, this fellow—perhaps cut from the same cloth as Griffith back in the days of Mayberry—did not move at the pace *I* do when we're docking: that of a rabid jackrabbit. I watched in horror as the man bent ever-so-slowly down toward it. He could have whistled the whole first verse of the Griffith theme song on the way down while I watched—in horror—as the line snaked away from his old-man Velcro shoes and slipped into the water.

I'm sure I snorted or performed some other body-exhale-equivalent to an expletive. But perhaps I should have taken a lesson from the goober. Phillip always says: "Smooth is fast." Yet I remain on jackrabbit speed. As I scrambled wildly to pull the bow line back up before it made its way back to the propeller and simultaneously throw Griffith a secondary, springer line, I slipped nicely on the wet foredeck and found the only thing that saved me from going overboard was the fat welp I had just created on my chin when it wedged against the lifeline. *Smooth Annie.*

At least we knew the lifelines we had re-tied during our Keys preparations were working. They certainly kept my sorry self on the boat that day and it wouldn't be the last time we would test them on this trip. After that tussle, we finally got the boat secure at the fuel dock and set about fueling her up. If I haven't expressed it quite clearly enough:

I hate docking! Something always seems to go awry and put our boat in grave danger. It's like watching your dog cross a busy street alone. It's just unnerving.

Thankfully though, conditions that made it hard to dock in Apalachicola made it very easy to leave. We untied the bow first—letting her nose drift out—and as soon as we untied the stern she just glided away from the dock. *Whew!* We hauled the lines in—including the soggy one at the bow—and made our way out into Apalachicola Bay. It was a gorgeous day and we had favorable wind. While our morning "Motorin'!" was fun, we have a sailboat for a reason. *We like to sail!* I didn't hesitate to jump up on the deck and ready our sails.

The wind picked up that afternoon—a steady northeast around fourteen knots—and we did some of the best sailing yet on our trip. We were heeled over, averaging six and a half, sometimes seven knots most of the way. That was the fastest we had gone the entire trip and it felt great! I was curled up and leaning out of the cockpit on the windward side—pretty much the equivalent of a dog sticking his head out of the car window, watching the hull cut through the water. We were sailing baby! Traveling at dog-out-the-window speed, we made it over to Dog Island around dusk. We got ready to drop the hook, proud of ourselves for covering a good bit of ground that day and excited about finally getting back offshore and out into the Gulf the following morning.

While we planned it merely as the most convenient spot near the East Pass, Dog Island turned out to be a fantastic anchorage. Pristine actually. Beautiful white sand, an exquisite view of both the Gulf on one side and St. George Sound on the other, with a few picturesque wooden

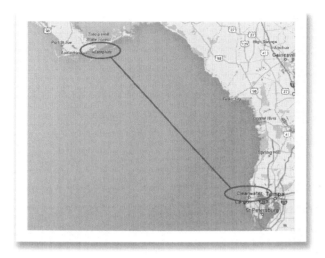

houses propped up on stilts overlooking both sides. The sunset there was absolutely stunning. Part of me couldn't quite believe I was really here. On this gallant boat with an incredible man, making our way down to the Florida Keys. It was already such a thrilling journey. I tingled at the thought of what was to come.

We made some cocktails, toasted the sunset and savored the evening. If things went well—and from our past record "well" wasn't usually how things progressed for us when crossing the Gulf—but if they did, we were looking at a thirty-hour passage from the East Pass to Clearwater. Well or otherwise, we were eager to see if the Gulf would smile upon us this time.

Clever foreshadowing be damned, she did not. Instead, she picked us up by the throat and slapped us. This would be the passage that would send us running around like old-timey dog-catchers and that would send this little mate-who-could up the mast mid-sea in two- to three-foot rollers to retrieve our halyard. *Good times.* But, while you know what happened when Hal came unleashed, what you don't yet know is how all of that mess began. It all started when I did something we have decided I am now never allowed to do again: declare it "Movie Night" on *Plaintiff's Rest*.

CHAPTER ELEVEN

My Opening Statement

"Otto's slipping!" Phillip woke with a snort. We were both a little disoriented on the boat the next morning. Having slept so soundly on anchor at Dog Island and waking to the cackling beeps of the alarm in pitch black, it was a little hard to tell if we were still dreaming or awake, moving or still. But we finally eased up after a few alarm snoozes to start readying the boat for passage and preparing to pull the anchor. I slipped on my *new* Gorton's pants—some, super trendy clown-pant Frogg Toggs we'd picked up in Port St. Joe—to try them out for the first time.

During our first passage across the Gulf, when we were bringing the boat home from Punta Gorda, Florida to Pensacola, the crew was thrilled to find the boat's previous owner, Jack, had left a whole Gorton's fisherman set on the boat. Head-to-toe, big yellow hat down to the boots. Phillip, Mitch and I all swapped and shared the collection during our inaugural passage. That yellow rubbery goodness really saved morale when we were out there the year prior, beating our way through a cold April Gulf.

Sadly, though, it was a super old set. Every time someone wore them in the cockpit it would leave behind a trail of little orange triangle-shaped rubber pieces behind. It took us forever—during our first Gulf crossing—to figure out what they were. I thought Mitch had eaten some Doritos and we were seeing their sad little remains from his multiple heaves. For this reason, I didn't inspect them for the longest time. I chose to not see them. Hocked-up food bits were—in my mind—worth ignoring. But we finally discovered they were little broken off rubber bits from the Gorton's suit and they were causing a real mess.

The Gorton's gear was also super bulky and hot. While I won't say standing at the bow, spraying cold water into the wind while raising our anchor is a necessarily *warm* place to be, it doesn't always require high-performance Arctic gear. While in Port St. Joe, Phillip and I decided it was time to get some thinner, newer foul weather gear to keep on the boat, along with the Gorton's set (that is still there today). I mean, it felt kind of like Gorton himself had been there watching over us on our first crossing, bellowing out old sailing terms in thick Irish (*in my mind he's Irish*): "Batten down 'em hatches men!"

We didn't want to discard or offend his spirit. So the Gorton's set stayed—bagged and tucked away in the bowels of our hanging locker for good luck and measure. While the new Frogg Toggs were just about as flattering as they sound, they are still waterproof which is key so I slipped them on and got into my wader boots and foul weather jacket knowing I'd be doing some serious chain spraying. Being early April, it was still a little chilly outside and a 6:00 a.m. deck wash calls for some good wet gear.

We had one hundred fifty feet of links lying out there in the mud that needed raising. Before I even got down to one hundred feet of chain, big chunks of gray clumpy mud were coming up in the links, and I knew this was not going to be a quick chore. "I've got mud at one hundred feet," I hollered back to Phillip to let him know he could settle in. We were going to be there a while! We spent the next twenty minutes raising and rinsing the chain but thank goodness we have a deck wash that pumps raw water up and makes the job a bit easier. I can't imagine what that chore is like via a single bucket. We finally got her all up, though, and kicked back to enjoy some coffee as we motored out of the East Pass, watching the sun just start to peek up—an electric pink sliver on the horizon. It certainly felt good to be back underway.

Unfortunately, the wind was light in the early hours and we had to motor a bit, but we were enjoying watching land disappear on the horizon and seeing nothing but blue ahead. The wind finally came around mid-morning and we got on a nice run—holding steady at four knots—toward Clearwater. Phillip and I curled up on the deck with a couple of page-turners and took turns napping in the sun.

We brought the solar shower up onto the deck so she could heat up and give us each a nice shower that afternoon. After two days underway, we would certainly be in need of it. In all, it was a beautiful day out on the water. Our arrival time for Clearwater popped up about midday: 11:37 a.m. the following morning. It only registers our ETA twenty-four hours out. Anything over twenty-four hours is designated only with bars—like a flatline heart monitor—so it's kind of exciting to see the arrival time appear, like the little heart of your trip has been revived! *Thump, thump.*

Only twenty-four hours now baby! We weren't in too much of a hurry though. The water had grown a deep, crystal blue around us and there wasn't a single blip on the horizon. Phillip and I were still averaging four knots and enjoying the soft, soothing swells that we were rocking over.

We heated up another frozen meal we had made for the passage for dinner: chicken and sausage gumbo. It was the perfect, hearty treat while underway. After dinner, we freshened up with a soothing warm solar shower in the cockpit. It was our first time using the solar shower. We had found it on the boat when inventorying during our Keys preparations and we were excited to try it out. Other than the finicky spout, which would occasionally pop off—spouting water like a fire hose and causing a soapy mad scramble to get her back on—it was one of the best showers we've ever had.

Of course, anyone would probably say that after two salty days at sea while enjoying free warm water from the sun. Something about the fact that it's been heated naturally makes it hard to beat. And there's something about getting clean on the boat that makes you feel that much more rejuvenated. It's hard to explain. I guess because at home you often already feel clean and comfortable so a shower doesn't really have a powerful refreshing effect. It's more perfunctory than anything. So habitual you just take it for granted.

But, on the boat, you're often a little hot or cold, you're sweaty and covered in sunscreen, salt or worse. You're not uncomfortable the entire time but you're not at your cleanest I will say that. So the shower seems to take on this revivifying property. You appreciate the squeaky fresh feel of your skin, the crispness of your clean hairs prickling in the wind and, all of a sudden, you can't wait to cake on another two days of passage muck. Boat showers are the best.

Around dusk, we had some dolphins come by to congratulate us on the excellent passage we were making—they seem to always be the ambassadors of good news—and bring us one of the most exquisite sunsets we've seen on passage. The water rippled like smooth silk, with deep tones of purple, magenta and gold. It felt like you could reach out and touch it and you wouldn't get wet at all. It would just slip around your fingers like satin.

It wasn't long after the sunset, though, that the wind started to die out. We tried to keep her going under sail, but Genny immediately made her displeasure known—luffing and whining and carrying on—and our speed kept dropping. The arrival time on the Garmin flat lined again, which was a sure sign. We were slowing down and our ETA needed a little reviving. So we decided to crank up the motor and motor-sail for a bit. The batteries needed a little charging anyway.

Since we were all powered up, putting some juice in, it seemed a good time to power up some electronics too. We quickly decided to rig up a little theater in our cockpit/movie room and declare it "Movie Day" on *Plaintiff's Rest*. And maybe I should say "I decided" because I was carrying on with the whole "Uh-oh, guess what day it is?" movie-day-camel bit. I even tried to do this little awkward camel walk. I'm not sure how you're supposed to try to *pretend* to have a hump on your back, but I was doing it. Phillip loves having me around. Movie *night* as opposed to day, however, would be more accurate as it was around 9:00 p.m. We booted up the laptop, hooked it into the cockpit speakers and nestled in for a little *Black Swan*.

But it was doomed from the start. Natalie, or whatever her movie-name is, was just started to get those freakish feathers poking out of her shoulder blades when the mainsail started flagging. The wind was right on our stern and it kept shifting the boom from one side to the other—a real interference with Movie Night. We took a brief intermission to drop the main, thinking it would be an easy chore. *Nothing to it in these light winds?*

Guess again crew. Cue Hal and his annoyingly-cute shackle panties bit. This was the fateful night where Hal would unsuspectingly climb our backstay and force me to ascend the mast mid-sea the following morning while we made our way into Clearwater to bring the halyard back down. While it was a pretty horrendous effort to undertake out in the Gulf, it was also an invigorating and fulfilling accomplishment once my feet touched back down on the deck the next morning. After I made it back down, I helped Phillip clean up his coffee-slasher scene in the cockpit—when he had bumped the cupholders while running around like a circus clown cranking me up—and get the boat squared back away for the day's sail.

It was a great feeling finally having our main halyard back in hand. Although I still felt it appropriate to call him a turd! I clipped him to the head of the mainsail and gave the halyard a good, hard tug before raising it just to make sure he was really secure. *Stay put Hal!* It was a little hard at first to let go of the halyard and send him back up again after the monstrous chore we had just undertaken in getting him down. What if he decided to pull one of his crazy clip/un-clip routines and just let go of the mainsail out of spite? Or what if he broke somehow, shot out wildly again, wrapping around stays and leaving the mainsail to flutter alone back to the boom? These were legitimate concerns, but they were always concerns. I hated feeling afraid of things I knew needed to be done. *If you're not going to sail your boat because you're afraid it might break,* I scolded myself, *then why have a sailboat at all?* I then let go of Hal and started raising him back up the mast.

Once the mainsail was flying, all worries were washed away because I knew we had truly done it: solved our problem, fixed our boat and got her going again. We were now sailing once again, day two of our second offshore passage of the trip, and just four or five hours out from Clearwater. As I sat up on the foredeck, second cup of coffee in hand, I relished in the feeling.

I knew I was learning more about the boat and this lifestyle as we traveled along than I could truly appreciate or realize. It's like on-the-job training. You don't really notice you're learning until the time comes when you have to step up and perform and you instinctively do what you've seen others do. All of sudden, you're just doing it. The training wheels are off and somehow you're cruising along. And here we were headed south, with just the boat and ourselves to maintain and an endless supply of things to see and do and places to go. That alone was a pretty cool feeling. As long as we can fix the boat and get her going again, we can go anywhere.

The realization resonated within me. *We can go anywhere.*

At the time, we were headed to Clearwater, but after that it would be destinations farther south, until we finally reached, on this trip, the Florida Keys. But next time—who knew—we could go to the Bahamas, Cuba, Isla Mujeres, the South Pacific. On this boat, the possibilities were endless. As I sat curled up in a deck chair on the foredeck watching her bow bob over crystal blue waters, I recalled the first time I had sat up on this deck and watched this boat under sail. I remembered the first time the Genny unfurled and popped full before me, like a magic sheet of silk. I was enchanted by her. I knew I wanted to go wherever she would take me.

I also knew at the time—not one year prior—that I couldn't. That was the day of our survey sea trial, before we even owned the boat. Before we had ever dropped her anchor and before I even knew how much this cruising lifestyle was going to mean to me. It was April 14, 2013—the first time I ever sailed on our boat—and I was excited, exhilarated and stressed beyond belief. I had gone up to the deck during the sea trial—not to enjoy the beauty of the boat under sail from the bow, but because I was fielding phone calls all day.

We were prepping a witness for a deposition the following week—an expert in a medical malpractice case—and he kept emailing me with questions about the medical records we had sent him. My partner was copied on the string so I had to—or let me say I *felt* I had to—stay on top of it, researching and answering every question as soon as it cropped

up before, finally, just calling the guy to spend a half hour—*during* our survey/sea trial—to flush out all the issues. This also required another half-hour follow-up phone call with the partner to re-hash and ensure the flushing of said issues.

Now why hadn't I just taken the necessary time off for the survey/sea trial so I wouldn't have to face these interruptions? Because I was a pansy. I never took off. I had taken three, maybe four days off total in five years. I was afraid of what my partners might think if I asked for too much time off. I was afraid they would assign work to others if they saw me as unreliable. I was so afraid that I lied. I told my partners I had a doctor's appointment out of town that day and I told myself it was kind of true because being on a boat would be a form of therapy. You see? A pansy.

I was so humbled, initially, by the fact that they had simply hired me, took a chance on me—*me?*—the rough-and-tumble garage sale t-shirt gal from New Mexico. Fueled by my gratitude and pride, I shot off the blocks. I had just spent seven years in school, studied my ass off to pass the bar, interviewed with hundreds of firms to land this one job with this one firm that was willing to take a chance on me. I was so grateful. I going to rock this legal career! Hell I had to. I owed tens of thousands in student loans and had just signed the next thirty years of my life away to buy a house near Mobile, Alabama and made the costly move into it. So rock it I did. I jumped in knee deep, always bit off more than I could chew, said yes to everyone and every request and worked my ass—which was already pretty much worn away from the bar exam—off again.

While I knew I wasn't really cut from the same piece of cloth as the rest of the guys in my firm—many of them were Alabama, if not Mobile, natives and just good, Southern gentlemen—I tried incredibly hard to fit in. Being only one of two females at the firm—yet the only female litigator and only female associate—I was already kind of a round peg for a square hole from the start but the guys at the firm were very welcoming and forgiving of my raised-out-west oddities. I was thankful they took me into the fold, paid me far more money than I can ever believe I'm worth and trained me to be a sharp, competent, capable litigator. In exchange I busted my ass for them, billed the snot out of every day and accomplished every task early and to the best of my ability.

Up until the day I left, I tried my absolute best to impress them and make them proud of me. Know that this entire career upheaval was all my doing and through no fault of theirs. As the saying goes: "It's not you, it's me." It was definitely me and my decision to pursue both a profession and a place in society that did not suit me. No matter how hard I tried to fit in, though—to mold myself to their world and want the things they wanted—I couldn't change my background, my experiences or my aspirations. As much as I tried to hide her, occasionally my inner-Annie came shining through. Case in point: the tree-stand story.

Every Friday we would have a firm luncheon. Me and twelve-or-so of the twenty attorneys at the firm would shuffle across the street to this place called Oliver's to occupy our same table and fill our plates with the same butter-saturated vegetables and unidentifiable chicken casserole dish they served every week. The conversation over lunch usually centered on politics, some particularly tough or oddball cases one of the attorneys was dealing with or recent community developments. But a close second was always talk of the men's hobbies, the same hobbies of most of the men I worked with: hunting, golf and fishing. Three things I knew very little about.

I usually kept my mouth shut when they got into these areas of discourse, but I always worried about not saying anything at all and them feeling like I didn't fit in or had nothing to contribute. Remember what I mentioned about the drinking, fitting in—particularly as the singular female—was always key. So every once in awhile I would try to throw in a somewhat intelligent comment or question just to remind them I was there and, for all ~~intensive~~ *intents and* purposes, fitting in. But one particular time (and I have yet to live this down, I should have kept my darn mouth shut) I proved the exact opposite.

It was just a few months into my short legal career—because any longer immersed with these men of Mobile, Alabama and I would have known better—and I was still green at the time. The guys were talking about some old high school buddy of theirs who had made a lot of money on a patent for a product he had invented. They mentioned it several times during their back-and-forth and I had only heard of this product in one context. It was a tree stand. *A tree stand?* They said it a couple of times and—for whatever reason—I felt the burning need to interject at that moment. Curious, I asked:

"A Christmas tree stand?"

I swear every fork at the table dropped. Chewing immediately stopped. Men craned their heads to get a good look at me. I looked to my closest buddy at the time, a fellow associate sitting across the table, and tried to fix whatever faux pas I had just committed.

"You know," I pleaded for his assistance, "the little red base with the screws in it that holds up the …" No sooner than I said it did the light finally come on. *Oh, a tree stand. Those things up in the tree that you sit in while you wait for a deer.* "Oh God." The words just came out of me, uncontrollably, like a fart. I could feel the heat from my own blood in my face. Thankfully the men just let out a few chuckles and kept talking about their buddy.

I didn't say anything else that day, but the tree-stand story always managed to come up at every subsequent firm gathering or, ironically, firm Christmas party. Any time we had some clerks working with us for the summer and a joke was made about saying something awkward, my name and the infamous tree-stand moment would come up. And I played right into it. I mean, it was funny. If I can't laugh at myself, that's a lot of wasted material. Just goes to show you, though, how big of an idiot I was. I'm lucky they hired me.

But, after a few years, the luster wore off and my efforts to blend wore thin. I am such a people-pleaser. I would worry myself into a sweat-frenzy with the petrifying thought that I was going to disappoint a partner, fail to ask a critical question in a critical deposition and screw a whole case up. I spent hours at night reading documents, depositions and records to try and make sure that didn't happen.

Then sometimes it still happened—because it's just going to happen sometimes—and it was always a shitty day in the life of Annie when it did. I found the practice to be consuming, hostile and incredibly stressful. Some people thrive off this. Some people love it. I just didn't. Like I said: it was me not the firm. They were very good to me. And I was very good to them until I freaked them, their spouses and the entire Mobile legal community all out by telling them I was going to sail, I was going to write, I was going to quit.

I guess it's no secret now. I was a lawyer until I quit. I guess you could say I still *am* one. I have the license and the big fancy degree to hang on the wall, which now sits in my dad's barn up in Cullman, Alabama collecting dust. He probably curses and bangs it every time he has to reach the tackle behind it. But I certainly don't practice anymore—again, whatever that means.

With all that practice, it's funny to think no one ever really perfects it. Don't get me wrong, the law is not a terrible profession by any means. It can be an interesting profession and a noble one. In certain practice areas you can find on a daily basis that you're actually helping someone. In other areas, you may find that realization is far more rare—coming only in glinting, intermittent flashes at best—among the far more common angry client, angry partner and angry opposition. It can be a very hostile profession. It just depends on how you choose to use that dusty degree.

As a litigator, you basically spend your days arguing—over time, information, liability, money, value, on and on. You get paid, every day, to argue pretty much—in person, through email, over the phone, in writing. When I look back on it it seems in a way I was also paid then to write—motions, briefs, objections, responses, requests, more motions which always elicit more objections and more responses, replies and sur-replies. I believe there are even sur-sur-replies. Lawyers like to argue that much.

I did a lot of writing during my short legal career, and was certainly paid far more handsomely for it than I am now, but I didn't enjoy the pay as much. The fat bank account, the growing 401k, the IRA, the stocks, etc. were never *enjoyed* as much as they were looked at. Numbers on paper that I glanced at on occasion just to make sure the pile was still there and to see how big it was. But, as the numbers increased, the enjoyment did not. They were still just numbers. On paper. That I looked at.

Obviously I need and want to make money, everyone does, but what dawned on me as I started to plot this whole life transition was that money itself—the physical thing of it, sitting in a pile in the corner of the room—is useless. I didn't want money to just hold it my hands and smell it, to stack it up in a big fluffy pile and make snow angels in it. It doesn't really smell that great and it makes a pitiful angel. What makes money a necessity is that it can be bartered to obtain the things you need and, after that, the things you want. That's what makes money important.

When I started to look at money that way, rather than a number on a bank printout, I started to think more about what I was trading my money in for: security, comfort, bills, solar-lit walkway lights. That's when I really started to see where my money was going. When you spend consecutive ten-hour days in an office, five days a week and sometimes Saturdays, under a fluorescent light, scouring stacks of documents in order to stuff your brain with information you actually care very little about, billing by the hour, making a lot of money, your mind starts to drift from what you *make*, to how you *spend*.

That forced me to think about the only commodity that's continually spent. Unlike money, it can never be made, saved nor stockpiled. It can and is always being spent. Every minute, every second. One after the other always, repeatedly spent. If you were to see it as a number on a paper, it would be constantly ticking down. Imagine if you looked at *that* number every day? Would it change you? I felt like I could see that number like a rolling ticker above my head. I was young, vital, capable, curious and yet I continued every day to report to a job I did not want to do.

I had not always felt that way. I believed, like many others, that there would always be more time. I could do the things I wanted to do and live the life I wanted to live when I was done working. But suddenly my life seemed so finite, so fleeting. It was the divorce, I know, that changed me. There is liberation in finally facing the truth that there's something fundamental about your life, yourself, that you don't like and finding the courage to change it—even in the face of an unknown outcome. But just because it is the right thing to do does not mean it will be an easy process of emotions to endure.

How does a divorce feel? It hurts. Even if you wanted it it still does, maybe in ways you didn't expect—emotionally, financially, socially. There was previously a way of life you may not have been entirely happy with but there were things about it you liked, things that made it comfortable. Once those things are gone, it hurts. Even if you survive the initial fall, you're still going to bleed out for a bit. It's a form of catharsis but it can be a therapeutic one. Because you know what a divorce does to you? It shows you who you are. You, the singular, with no one else around to help you or hurt you. There is no one to blame. There are no coattails to ride. There is no one but you. You are what you are and you do what you like. It may surprise you what you like.

For instance, I didn't know I was going to like sailing. I knew nothing about it at the time of my divorce. It was the sailing, though, that actually made me give up something more valuable, more meaningful to me than my marriage—my career. You may think that's a horrid statement: *What can be more meaningful than marriage?* Having experienced it though, I feel at least from my vantage point, I can say that in earnest. I believe marriage is right for some people but not for others. Like you, I look at some seventy-year-old couples who have been married for fifty years and think they look so happy together. Their love is so genuine and complicated that I admire it. I don't believe it takes marriage to achieve that, however.

On the contrary, I feel marriage, for other people, becomes a toxic, eroding bond that they cling to because they don't feel like they have any other option. They made a promise a long time ago they feel they must stand behind, even though they can barely stand one another. They're like two snarling dogs chained together. Sometimes marriage is tragic and it's horrible to watch it twist and rub what once was love into hot, searing sibling-like hate. While I know I am relatively young, and my life and emotions are still evolving, having experienced it and speaking as a self-made divorceé, I simply believe marriage is right for some but not for others. Some people should just be adventure companions for some period of time.

While making that decision—the this-is-not-right-for-me revelation—may be easy, the getting out part is not always. A divorce can be devastating, even when you think you wanted it. Even when you still do want it. It certainly was for me. I lost a lot. I lost my truck, the rental property, tons of furniture and household stuff. You may be wondering, *Did I get to keep the house at least?* The big, sprawling solar-lit walkway house? Yes. That fucking albatross. With both the house and the apartment to keep up, I had to try and sell it. That's when I learned what the term "under water" meant. The marital estate went into foreclosure. Thankfully it sold in a short sale and I was able to pay the deficiency—roughly the price of my truck so that's where that went—to get out from under it.

Like I said, blood was shed. I had asked for it though. It was all my doing, but the divorce blew me flat like an atomic bomb. Most of my personal belongings, all of my available cash and my credit shot out of me during the blast. My life felt a bit like that stupid 'Annie' picture from New Mexico I had clung so hard to—irreparably damaged and unfixable. Nothing about it was going to prop me up or make me comfortable anymore. I was stupid to think it was going to be easy, but over time, the dust settled and I started to ease up. On my knees at first, still choking and hacking on the stirred debris and then finally on a new set of financial legs. After a while, I began to breathe a little easier.

It's just money, right? I told myself. That's not the real stuff life is made of. And you really only need credit if you want to borrow more of it to buy more things. *That wasn't the life you wanted, remember Annie?* Obviously not, because I had essentially shattered and cracked my former life over my knee. There was no longer a big house, a nice car, a full bank account. There was just me, a run-down apartment and a particleboard pool table. I had chosen this new life and there was nothing to do but move forward in it. It was time, once again, to throw away the crutch and walk away anew.

Enduring a life metamorphosis like that—losing things you thought you couldn't live without and somehow mysteriously not only surviving but thriving in an unexpected new way—makes you assess everything in your life differently. I found I had developed a new set of values. What once was seen as important—necessary even—now seemed wasteful, harmful even. After I survived the shock wave from the divorce and began to gradually stand again, I knew I was starting to feel the same about my career as I had about my marriage. At least my breed of it—the stress-ridden ten-hour hard-fought days of a trial attorney, buried in a fluorescent-lit office under boxes and stacks of medical records, depositions, pleadings. When I would come into the office every morning at 6:00 a.m., I was starting to stare spitefully at all of those banker's boxes stacked around my desk just as I had those solar-lit walkway lights from the cab of my truck that fateful night. *Who needs all this stuff?*

I asked myself again—*Why is this important to you?*—although I already knew the answer. It wasn't anymore. But what really sickened me was how much *time* I had spent poring over all of that stuff. That was time I couldn't, wouldn't ever get back, used to earn money I didn't really need to buy crap I didn't want. You see what I mean? Deciding I wanted a divorce made me see everything differently. Some may call it selfish but if living the life you want makes you selfish, then I guess I am and I've come to terms with it. Over time, the realization seeped in before I could even detect it. Then one day it was just there and I knew. Like the marriage, the only reason I was still doing it—going to that office every day and working that damn hard—is because I thought I was supposed to.

The decision to turn my back on my firm, however, as opposed to my husband, was much harder. As much time and money as I had put into my marriage, I had put *way* more into my career. The thought of throwing it all away truly frightened me. I mean, this was supposed to be my lifelong profession, right? The thing I had worked so hard in high school for, in undergrad, in law school, hell, at the firm for. Yet I knew it was stifling me. Divorce is a catalyst for change. One year out from it and I knew I had another aspect of my life that was consuming my happiness. I knew I needed to make another—probably even more painful—life change, but I just couldn't get myself to do it. It was just too big a cliff to jump off.

Instead, I sat on my cot in my cell, picking at my prison mattress, and once again let fear stall me. Like the conversation I didn't want to have with my now-ex, I put it off. *When do you say it? How do you say it?* I was plagued by it. *You have to have it thought-through first*, I told myself. You need to know how you're going to present it, what you're going to say and how you're going to say it. You don't just mumble the words, "I think we should see other people," at the first moment the thought strikes you. No. Hell no! You hold back, pretend everything is the same until you get your head wrapped around it, make sure it is in fact what you want to do then figure out how you're going to do it. After that, it's a very simple matter of growing a pair and *actually* doing it. Until then, you remain a pansy. You go to work and pretend everything is copasetic.

Just as I initially had done with the divorce inclination, I tried to deny myself the idea. *You can't do this to them. They're relying on you.* I buried the dangerous thought of freedom and continued working as hard as ever. I gave appropriate, yet non-committal, responses when hints were dropped about partnership and I was handed new clients and new cases. I worked my way onto ten or so medical malpractice cases and I spent my days poring over medical records, studying deposition transcripts, interviewing and prepping witnesses, trying my best to be a good attorney, and trying even harder to convince myself I could like it. Love it even. I mean, isn't that what you're supposed to do so that you "never have to work a day in your life?" *I could do this*, I told myself. I *had* to do this.

And, so I did it. I kept doing it. I got more cases, more clients, more years under my belt. I earned the promise of partnership and a lucrative career as a trial attorney. In my world, that would be the achievement of all achievements, the mecca—to become a hard-nosed, seasoned trial attorney and be able to claim the notoriety and courtroom swag that comes with that title. Once you've achieved that, then you've really become something. You're wealthy, established, in the world of litigators—decorated. That was what I was supposed to be working toward and that end goal was supposed to make my daily toiling, the endless battles, all of the hard work I was doing worth it.

Then I went to trial. Then I knew I couldn't do it anymore.

It was a medical malpractice case that we tried in October, 2012—a shoulder dystocia. If you are not familiar with this unfortunate occurrence that can happen during childbirth, I highly recommend you Google it, look at some images and learn. The birthing process itself is fascinating and speaks volumes to the complex, yet highly capable and resilient anatomy of a woman—not to mention the durability of a newborn. It's truly fascinating stuff. And I did enjoy learning about the process. What I did *not* enjoy, however, were the hundreds, perhaps thousands of hours I spent reviewing the boxes upon boxes of medical records in that case, drafting motions, objections and trial pleadings, reading and summarizing deposition transcripts, sorting and organizing trial exhibits, worrying myself to death trying to memorize every fact in the case.

I suffered three months of absolutely brutal trial prep. Every day I was swallowed in a vacuum of records, depositions, witnesses, only to be spat back out ten hours later—drained and internally disheveled—but still hefting documents home with me every evening to finish yet another pleading by morning. While work had always been the biggest hindrance to my world-traveling/writing desires, these particular three months practically suffocated what little breathing adventurous spirit I had left in me.

I went nowhere but to the office, the hospital and home. I ate canned and cartoned food at night so I could spend more time working. I worked on the weekends, either at home or at the office. Friends, family and Phillip invited me out for dinners, excursions, weekend trips, but I continually had to decline. When I would try to explain to them—"I'm preparing for a trial. It's a *huge* deal."—I felt like they couldn't see the importance of it all. I had to offer the excuse so many times I started to lose sight of it myself.

What really bothered me was that if I was really on this track—headed in the exact direction everyone intended—then this would simply be the first of many trials. I would have to say this again and again, every time I was in trial prep. Was I really going to be *that* person? Miss I Can't Go Anywhere or Do Anything because I'm a trial attorney and that's such a huge deal?

The more I had to decline—the more adventures, experiences and getaways I had to turn down—the more I started to question everything about it, every single drive to the office and every late night at my desk where I would wave the cleaning lady off because I wasn't yet done doing my such-a-huge-deal work. I knew it would never let up. It was endless and consuming—a daily barrage of hostility and heated debate—and then it got worse. It was decided I would second-chair the trial and that I would give the opening statement. It was an incredible honor and one that I am still grateful for because it was just the shove I needed to make me jump off the track.

I wrote my opening statement, rehearsed it, changed it, rehearsed it some more, polished it and memorized it, then rehearsed it and rehearsed it again. I would say it in the shower, in the mirror while I got ready for work, in the car on the way to the office. I would go for a walk every evening after work and make myself say it twice over all the way through (it was about thirty minutes long), before I would let myself go home. I lost weight. I lost hair. All that walking and talking and fretting, but my health was the least of my worries at the time.

I also lost friends. I lost opportunities and I lost so much time. There wasn't an option to devote it to anything else. So much was riding on this case. People's livelihoods were at stake. The hospital's good name was on the line, not to mention the hundreds of thousands of dollars that were invested. We were defending serious claims from an upstanding mother with a sadly crippled child. It was a horribly stressful culmination of years of work and litigation. I felt like this opening statement was the most important thing I was going to say. Ever.

It was decided I would give the opening statement, full-scale, to several partners and staff members at the office one day for critique, which turned out to be exponentially harder than the live performance at trial because I actually *cared* about these people's opinions. They were my colleagues, my bosses, my mentors. I worked with them daily, looked up to them. Despite my growing desire to leave the firm, I still had a deep-seeded need for their approval. I worried for days before that in-house presentation, sweated at the thought of standing up before them.

I had to take long, slow breaths to soothe the involuntary clenching of my stomach before I stood up to give it. I was physically repulsed by the stress. My body tried to fight it like cancer. When I finished they attacked me—ripping up my analogies and tearing huge holes out of my opening. Rightfully so. A lot of money was at stake. I was new to this and they had a better eye for what would work and what wouldn't, but I felt shredded afterward—chewed and gnawed and now with the sickening realization that I did not want this. If this is what it took out of me, then I didn't want to be an attorney. I didn't want to go to trial. I never wanted to do this again. That day changed me.

By the time we got to trial, I was numb. I didn't think anything could revive me. I went to the office in a zombie-like state, trying to shut off my emotions—my internal scream for release—for another ten hours as I battled my way through another hostile day. It's a good thing it was hard, consuming work that occupied every facet of my mental capabilities, because if I would have had just five minutes to sit and ponder my hell, I would have bolted. They would have seen just a flash of blonde and pearls as I sprinted in high heels out the door.

I even avoided the Friday lunches at Oliver's because it wasn't lighthearted laughter and old southern jokes for me anymore. It was my life and I was pissing it away in a poorly ventilated office with a phone that never stopped ringing. I couldn't avoid it anymore, couldn't try to bend and shape and beat myself into the right position. It was clear. I was never going to fit in. This was not the place for me. It felt like prison.

I thought if they caught me in a moment—like the one I feared near my packed-out truck, standing in a puddle of shame—with no case to distract me, no quick answer or witty quip, that they would see it on my face: my desperation. I wanted to break through the blocks of my cell and escape. Just as I had with my divorce, I eventually knew it needed to be done and I found myself, again, just waiting for the right time. I wasn't emotionally, procedurally or financially ready to seriously quit and I didn't think there was going to be some textbook moment when it would be right. But I knew at the very least that I couldn't do it right before trial. I was going to disappoint them when I left, sure. But I wasn't going to sabotage them.

I stayed on. I studied and I worked and I rehearsed and the day of trial I sat at the defense table, my stomach convulsing again, my chest radiating with heat, my sweaty hands leaving moist outlines on the table in the cold courtroom. Then I stood before an audience of strangers and performed with what little sliver of feeling I had left for that case and told our story. Then we battled for days, evenings too—filling the war room and courtroom with our legal bravado and expensive demonstrative aids, billing hundreds of hours and spending thousands more. Then the verdict came back.

CHAPTER TWELVE

Go to Danglin'

"We, the jury, find in favor of the defendant ... "

We won. The trial. The one that almost killed me. We won it. The jury came back with a verdict in favor of the defendant—our client, the hospital—as well as the doctor. And rightfully so. As sick as I was of that case, I believed from day one that the nurses and medical staff we were representing did everything they possibly could for that poor woman and the injury that resulted was simply an unfortunate but unavoidable consequence of a risky childbirth. But—while this may make me seem a terrible person, I will admit it—the best part about that verdict, for me, was the fact that it was over. That gut-wrenching, stomach-convulsing terror ride was over.

I knew the minute the verdict came back that I would never do that again. I would rather climb a mast mid-sea, ten times over. The thought made me chuckle as I sat on the foredeck—rubbing the welps and gashes the mast and all of its accoutrements had left on the insides of my thighs during my daring mid-sea mast climb—but it was so true. I would plop my happy ass down in a bosun's chair and climb a mast every single day for the rest of my life before I would ever sit again at a defense table to try a case. The stress and worry, lost weight and hair—not to mention the thousands of hours of my life that had been devoted to it—were just not worth it. For me, it would never be worth it. I never wanted to live another zombie-like day again.

And, at the rate things were going for us—not a week into our big Keys trip and we'd already suffered some gear failure, picked our way through impenetrable fog and undertook a swaying, rocking, mid-Gulf halyard retrieval—I couldn't fathom the thought of ever feeling numb again. There was so much to experience—hard things, great things, painful things, scary things. I couldn't imagine *not* feeling every second of it because I was out here really doing it: living on a boat and cruising to new places. I didn't know who was answering that blaring phone in my old office, but it sure wasn't me. Not anymore. Reminds me of that Joe Walsh song: "Leave a message, maybe I'll call."

And it felt great to be so self-sufficient. The boat and our bodies were all we had to take care of. Once you figure out how they work and the fluids don't scare you as much, you just modify and repair as needed and keep on trucking. Case-in-point: as we were detaching lines from my bosun's chair and hooking everything back up after the climb, Phillip started looking at our busted lazy jack. The one on the starboard side that had snapped during our first night on passage.

He then hatched the brilliant idea to raise the stack pack "sail catching" lines back up with the staysail halyard, which pulled it back up pretty much exactly where it had been previously attached to the eyelet on the spreader. The captain's real smart like that sometimes. But that's one thing I have really learned to love about sailing. It's all about improvising: learning your systems and—when something doesn't work quite right or fails—knowing how to accomplish essentially the same result using another system or a different method. I call it "creative systemizing" and attribute it initially to the time my dad slapped a sticky hunk of chaw to my face with a maxi pad to soothe the wasp sting I got while doing my business on the side of the road.

But it seems cruisers have been creative systemizing long before my run-in with the alien wasps. Phillip read a story to me some time during this trip by Cap'n Frank Papy from *Sailing: Impressions, Ideas, Deeds* that has always stuck with me. Apparently Papy was sailing a beat-up, broke-down, falling-apart boat from Jamaica to Ft. Lauderdale that was leaking from every orifice (think floating floorboards) with the bilge pumps unable to keep up and just when he was about to throw up his hands and throw in the towel, he thought about the engine. It's constantly sucking raw water in to cool itself, then pumping it out. It's essentially a water-sucking machine when you really think about it. And when Cap'n Papy did, he promptly closed the engine seacock, detached the raw water hose and ran it straight into his flooded bilge—well, cabin floor by then—to both cool his engine and pump out the bilge. *Blows my mind.* And while I know our lazy jack repair is decidedly "small-time" in comparison to Papy's heroic Hail Mary, it still reminds me that sailing is all about improvising, and it's an incredibly rewarding and exciting challenge.

With our lazy jack back in action, and our sights set on Clearwater, we settled back in the cockpit for a nice morning sail. And, I'll tell you, they must call it Clearwater for a reason, because that was the most crystal green water we had seen on the trip! It was jewel-toned, a brilliant aqua-green, absolutely stunning.

That was, until we handled our business. It was our first time pumping out via the macerator and, funny thing was, we couldn't really find our "business" at first. During our first harrowing adventure in the Gulf, we were too fraught with rough seas, a flailing dinghy and a seasick mate to worry about pump-out, so this being only our second time out in the Gulf, it was our first opportunity to use the macerator and make sure it was indeed working.

The macerator on the boat is pretty much what you would imagine when you see the word. I picture it like a meat grinder with all of these teeth-like gears that spin together to grind stuff into pulp, except the "stuff" in this scenario is a bit more explicit than meat. When you "pump out" at sea, the pump pulls your "stuff" from the holding tank on the boat through the macerator to grind it all up then passes it through a sea cock (fancy name for hole in the hull) to flush it out to sea.

I can't tell you how many times I checked to make sure the sea cock for the macerator was open. Don't ask me what I thought would happen if it was closed and we engaged the macerator and started pumping our business toward it. I pictured it swelling up like a water balloon on a spigot and then. *I told you not to ask me.* Hence the double- and triple-checking.

But after all final checks were made, it was time to test that puppy so we initiated the launch sequence and it kept going and going but I couldn't see anything topside. I was looking around on either side of the boat right at the beam. Again, don't ask me why. I guess I thought it would come shooting out so hard it would launch straight out both sides like a rocket jetpack. That would be some serious shit! *No, seriously.* Phillip hollered up for me to check near the cockpit. *Ahh, the water travels aft when sailing. Brilliant!* And there I found it. Our business. Headed out to sea. Not really a picturesque, jewel-toned vision but important to see nonetheless. It was good to know all systems were a-go if you know what I mean.

It turned out to be a fun day of firsts as we caught our first fish of the trip right around noon. Scared Phillip and I both half-to-death, though, when the hand line popped suddenly over the rail. We both jerked up from our books, looking around wildly, thinking: *What the hell just happened?* Trust me, when something snaps loudly on the boat, it's hard not to think the worst. *What crucial piece of equipment just failed?* is the first thought that paralyzes your brain.

And—more often than not—that's usually a pretty good instinct. Stuff just fails. No matter how tedious and meticulous you are about your maintenance. It's just going to happen. And when it does, it often is accompanied by a very loud pop or bang. It had happened to us during our last Gulf Crossing when the bolts on the dinghy davit bracket began to shear and pop off. *Ping!* they went as they clattered to the cockpit floor. Pops, pings and bangs are generally regarded as bad things on a boat. So, needless to say, Phillip and I were both relieved when we found this ominous bang was just the trolling line. *Whew! Just a fish on! Reel her in!*

Who knows how long she'd been on there. One final swish of her muscular body—probably trying to free herself and she broke the stretchy band we use as our "fish-on indicator" clean off. It took a team effort to get her hauled into the cockpit, but we finally got her slick body hoisted up in there. Then Phillip hollered for the "fish kill." During our Keys preparation, we thought we were real smart in bottling up some isopropyl alcohol to use to douse a flopping fish's gills to sedate her. This is what the cruising and fishing guides recommended in lieu of a bloody beatdown in the cockpit. However, I decided the perfect alcohol-dispensing device would be a little travel hairspray spritzer—Suave Ultra Hold No. 4 to be exact.

I popped down below to get our little fish kill sprayer while Phillip held the flopping beast steady on the cockpit floor. I handed him the bottle when I came up, Phillip took aim at the fish's gills and pulled the trigger. It was the most anticlimactic spray I've ever seen. Like a mouse sneeze. And it only seemed to anger Flopping Frita because she really started bucking and kicking then. I had my hands on her tail and torso and Phillip was trying to catch and hold her head. She was wild! After a few more failed spritz attempts Phillip finally unscrewed the lid and started dousing her, but still, that stupid little bottle only holds like two ounces. It was just enough to baptise a baby and she was still kicking strong.

"More!" Phillip shouted. While we hate to waste alcohol, I guess if it means dinner for a week and saves us from a fish clobbering, it doesn't really count as a waste. I went down and grabbed a bottle of rum for Phillip to dump on her and he started really saving her soul. Frita's flop finally started to slow and she eventually just laid still on the cockpit floor. We eyed her suspiciously—certain she was saving her biggest romp for the minute we pulled out a knife. But, she was done. She never flopped again. We tried our best to make the process quick and painless for her and set about cleaning and filleting her. It was unanimously decided the hairspray bottle was a total failure but we had a great time reliving Phillip's epic *ka-chew!*

Then the real fun began though. The blood bath. Looking back on it, perhaps cleaning a fish it in the cockpit floor wasn't the best of decisions but this was our first fish to clean and cut on board. We were just kind of going with it. I started hacking in and cutting off huge hunk-fillets. Even with Frita half-mutilated, it was still hard to take your eyes off her, or leave your toes exposed next to her white fangs. I truly thought she might snap to life and bite a small appendage off. She was so powerful!

After a great deal of sawing and cutting, I'd say I carved around eight or nine pounds of meat off her—enough to feed us for a week. That was worth the dumped rum drink in our book. Phillip looked Frita up in the fish guide book and found we had caught ourselves a king mackerel! How's *that* for royalty? It was a bloody mess though. No British accent needed. And a bloody good bit of work. From the time of the catch-and-drop in the boat, then the gut-and-clean to the dreaded wash-and-scrub of the cockpit, the whole fish debacle turned into about a three-hour chore. But I mean—what else are we doing, right?

After the fish fiasco, we made our way into Clearwater Pass around mid-afternoon and started to ease our way into the channel. As most of you may be, we (well Phillip, actually as he's the primary helmsman) are avid users of Active Captain and he had seen on there that there was some shoaling in the Clearwater channel after you come under the bridge.

Knowing that he made a wide turn to try to avoid it and unfortunately (we think) his cautionary wide turn turned out to be a little *too* wide and he found the shoaling on the other side—with our keel! The boat lurched to a stop and we knew immediately we'd run aground. *I hate that feeling!* There's no mistaking it.

Phillip was quick to act. He threw it in reverse, threw the boom out over the portside and told me to climb out and "go to dangling." Okay, that's not what Phillip said exactly. He doesn't talk like that. I do. But that's how my brain processed his message and I knew exactly what he needed me to do. You might call me an expert dangler. I've dangled from many a thing, plant and animal for many a varied purpose. First there were the monkey bars at Highland Elementary where I would kick and flail double-handed from one bar to the next all the way (and I was the only girl in the third grade at Highland to accomplish that feat thank you very much). Then it was the branches of Mr. Christian's crab apple tree (different from his super-tall tree) so we could get apples to fall out to throw at each other. I'm sure Mr. Christian loved having us as neighbors.

Then there was the occasional animal. Yes, animal. Horses, mostly, but there were also several cows, dogs and one mule. Animals require some particularly high-end dangling skills. The likes of which I knew Phillip needed from me now. I knew exactly what he needed me to do because I had done it before. I remember the feeling of the slick leather in my hands that day—one on the horn and one on the cantle of the saddle trying to keep my body up on it. Yes up. Because, you see, I was most certainly down.

"And this one goes here, right?" I was asking my dad how to fasten the saddle for the first time on my old paint pony, Patches.

"Yep," my dad said, showing me how to hook the cinch to the flaps under the stirrups. Then he showed me how to pull the long leather strap back and forth—kind of ratchet-like, to get it nice and snug around the horse's soft belly—weave the leftover length from the flap down to the cinch and back up again before making one final swoop around and back through itself with the tail end to make that really cool knot. I was excited about the knot. I practiced it three or four times, at least.

Dad got to working on some things at the other end of the barn while I un-did and re-did the cinch a few times on my own for practice. When I was through I thought I was ready to go. I scooched the old milk crate that I used to hop up next to Patches, swung a leg around and settled in nice in the saddle. I wiggled my little seven-year old bottom around a few times. Everything felt secure so I clucked Patches around and headed out. I was just going to ride around on the farm a bit so I didn't tell Dad I was leaving. I usually had pretty free range as long as I stayed inside the fences, which was fine with me. That left one hundred and thirty-nine whole acres to romp and ride around in. That was plenty!

And boy was I riding that day! Patches and I trotted along the perimeter up near Mr. Rury's place, around all three of the little lakeponds on the property and even out to the blackberry patch on the north side before I turned Patches back toward the barn. But you know horses. If you don't, then let me teach you a quick bit. Horses love to go home. While riding is fun, when they sense they are headed back to their stable, they can't help it. They start trotting, then they gallop, then they lope,

then—if you let them—they all-out run. It's like run-home-syndrome or something. If the horse is stubborn, then it's hard to break. Patches wasn't too bad about it, but she had a twinge of it as most horses do. To tell you the truth, that was probably my fault. The lope home was often my favorite part of the ride, so I often just let her do it.

This time, though, something went wrong. As Patches began to trot faster and faster I could feel my saddle sort of bumping around on her back, moving way more than it normally did or should. When she broke out into a full gallop I knew. I was sliding. Inch by inch my saddle was making its way down to her belly. I let go of the reins to tug on her hair in hopes of righting myself, which was a mistake. Not only did the hair-tug not work, it made Patches whip her head up, throwing the reins up high on her neck and out of my reach. Now I had no way stop it. The saddle kept slipping.

In my little-kid brain I felt I only had two options: jump off and hope Patches didn't step on me as I tumbled underneath her or just hang on. Being a pretty good hanger-onner in my mind, I chose the latter. And there I was—gripped like a scared cat to the ceiling—to the saddle which was now upside down underneath Patches's belly. I curled up in hopes that she wouldn't knock me with one of her hooves and just rode it out. I knew if I fell then she was sure to trample me—unintentionally of course. If Dad was worried when he saw Patches trot toward the barn with me clinging to her undercarriage, he sure didn't show it. He laughed so hard it spooked Patches and she finally stopped just before the gate to the barn.

"Lord Babes," my dad said between chuckles as he eased his way toward Patches and grabbed a hold of the reigns. "What are you doing down there?"

Relieved to see Patches's legs finally standing still and me with a hope of getting out from under her without suffering a hoof imprint, I finally let loose the saddle. I let my bottom thud down on the dirt and I scrambled out from underneath her, a little shaken but no worse for the wear.

"The saddle," I started in, kind of fumbling and embarrassed and trying to pat the dirt off my jeans. "It just slipped down. I don't know what happened."

Dad started moving a few saddle pieces around—lifting some leather and flaps here and there and inspecting things—then he came up with the unhooked end of a long leather piece. Upside down, I was kind of confused by it at first but dad just held it up until I recognized it.

Ohh, the breast strap. The minute I realized what it was, I realized I hadn't clipped it. *Dammit!* Yes, that's literally what I said internally at age seven. I was already thought-cursing by then. It's when they start popping out as actually-said words that you get in trouble. You remember the brother and the bar of soap on *A Christmas Story*.

It was the damn strap. That's why the saddle had slipped. I forgot to clip the breast strap to the cinch. That's the piece that goes around the horse's chest. Between his front legs and attaches to the cinch under his belly to make sure the saddle doesn't, you know, slide around or anything crazy like that. I didn't say anything. Dad could tell I knew what I'd done. I just pouted and shoved my little-booted toe in the dirt. But he knew how to bring me back around.

"So now you know," Dad said with a smile. His face was still laughing at me. "You clip this one last so that you don't … go to dangling."

Well, it was time to dangle this time, Dad. Who knew those dangling skills would come in handy? What is it they say? "Everything happens for a reason." I guess my upside-down Patches incident was meant to train me for our equally exciting run-aground event in Clearwater because I was ready to dangle now! Phillip pushed the boom way out to port and sent me out on my dangling mission. I made my way monkey-bar-like out to the end of the boom, hand over hand, hunched my knees up and went to danling! Like my life depended on it.

CHAPTER THIRTEEN

April Showers

"That's good. That's it," Phillip shouted from the cockpit. "Bounce some more." *You got it. Bouncing away out here.* I bobbed and bounced some more and could then see the boat slowly moving forward. Phillip summoned me back to the cockpit and I got the boom squared away while he made our way off the shoal. *Thank goodness.* Another disaster averted. It was a good lesson in how to respond quickly to get the boat moving again. Go to danglin'!

Needless to say, after that small scare, I was all nerves and eager to get our boat docked up securely and settled in for the night. The last time we pulled into Clearwater when we were first bringing the the boat back from Punta Gorda, we had twenty-knot winds on our stern and two corn-fed Larry-the-Cable-type guys holding our bow off the dock. We were not in any kind of mood to repeat that scene this time. So I was thrilled to see when we pulled up to the fuel dock that they had courtesy lines—already pre-set at just the right length and ready to toss to you for tying up—which was awesome. *Thank you Clearwater!*

Even the quick little motor over to our transient slip was completed without a hitch. Thank goodness. *No docking debacles today!* Once we were filled up and docked up, we gave that boat a good scrub-down, which she was in sure need of. As were we! We showered up, dressed up and set our sights on cocktails and dinner, in that order.

We decided to save the mackerel we caught earlier that day as our next passage meal and head to town to provision, explore a little and get real crazy with dinner. Phillip found this little Middle Eastern place that had rave reviews on Trip Advisor: Mana Mana. It seemed like a little hole-in-the-wall type place—which is usually our favorite—and when were we going to get good Middle Eastern food again on our way south to the Florida Keys? Who knows, which is why this venue was right up our adventurous alley.

Phillip and I began walking to town and hailed a taxi on the way, which was a good thing because the restaurant turned out to be about five or six miles away. This crew was pretty beat by then. After a day on passage, Philip and I had certainly worked up an appetite though. We probably looked like those cartoon characters, hooked by the nose and wafting in on wavy scent lines. We were famished but ready to feast!

Mana Mana turned out to be even quainter than we imagined. There was a tiny deli-style walk-up counter in the corner with a concession-stand menu board behind it, one guy running the joint and just a handful of wobbly diner tables scattered about. Phillip and I were a little skeptical at first, but when we started to smell the food and see what the shopkeep was dishing up, we knew we were in for a real treat.

The guy running the place was great too—a true small-business owner. He made all of the food himself, was eager to serve us up some of his own authentic Israeli Middle Eastern specialties and even bring us a few extra treats and sides that we didn't even order, just because he was proud of them. And the food was incredible—savory falafel with perfectly seasoned chick-pea balls smothered in tahini sauce, succulent shawarma beef, grape leaves, fresh pita. Aren't you hungry now? Phillip and I ate ourselves absolutely sick. Seriously, we wiped both plates clean and didn't leave a single crumb in the pita basket.

We were both satiated. Probably a little too full but it was totally worth it. It turned out, rather than a cab, we had managed to score a personal driver for the evening! We found while we were checking out that our cabbie had decided to eat at Mana Mana as well. While we were buried in our flavorful dishes, he had ambled in, ordered and sat around the corner and ate, too, while waiting to drive us back home. *Smart man.* He knew we would need to get back to the marina, so we were a guaranteed hit. He gave us his card on the way back to the boat, though, and—I swear, I can't make this stuff up. His professional "cabby" name was Johnny N.

We decided the "N" was for Nitro. *Yeah buddy!* We had Johnny N take us to the CVS by the marina so we could stock up on supplies—water, milk, coffee, OJ, paper towels and some milk to marinate the mackerel in. Just a few basics. We savored the last burning embers of the sunset on the way back to the boat and then crashed hard. After a mid-sea mast climb, our battle with Flopping Frita, an inadvertent run aground

and a big, filling Middle Eastern feast, the captain and I were beyond exhausted.

The plan was to jump out the next morning back into the Gulf and make our way down to Charlotte Harbor. Some cruising buddies of ours had told us that area—Cabbage Key, Pine Island, Cayo Costa—had some really beautiful tucked-away anchorages, so we wanted to check it out on our way down to the Keys. From there, we would cruise down to Ft. Myers then make the twenty-four-or-so-hour jump to Key West. That was the plan anyway—almost a meaningless term on a sailboat.

We woke the next morning, still full, but eager to get up and going and start making way on the approximate one hundred-mile, twenty-four hour run to Charlotte Harbor. We waved at the rising sun, made our way back out into the Gulf and had one of the best sails yet of our trip that morning. It was thrilling to have our mainsail all hooked and ready to be hoisted with a simple tug on the line—no flailing halyard, no mangy mutt with shackle-panties in his mouth, no halyard whipped tight around the backstay and, most importantly, no mid-sea mast climb. While I can definitely say it was an adventure, it was not an experience I was chomping at the bit to repeat. *Hoist the sails! Let's just cruise.*

The water around Clearwater really is the most brilliant green. Like turquoise but not so blue. It's heaven. It's the most beautiful sight to see under the hull of your boat. We had a great east wind, right on our port bow, around ten knots. "Now we're cooking with Crisco," the captain said. It was a great sailing day, which may have been the problem. Sailing karma is a real bitch.

We threw out the trolling line again, hoping for some good fish luck, and we got a few bites but no snags. They kept chomping off our expensive lures. One even yanked so hard he busted the stretchy hose we use as our fish-on indicator. Again. So they were definitely out there and biting and we were definitely "fishing"—just not "catching." But we really didn't mind. Spirits aboard the *Plaintiff's Rest* were soaring.

Case in point: our sails got back-winded at one point—when we were messing around trimming them and tacking—and it turned us around. It was no problem for this cheery crew though. We just whipped back around, this time an *intentional* jibe, and got her back on track. The only hang-up, literally, was the trolling line. We'd had her out when the accidental jibe occurred and she got caught on the rudder. But that was quickly deemed "no problem" either. The captain jumped right in for a nice swim in the Gulf and got her untangled.

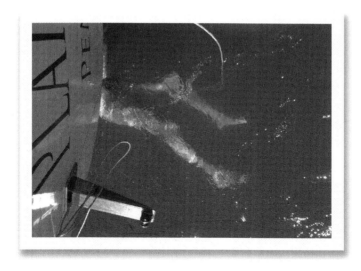

It was like nothing could get us down. I couldn't help but sing it. It was our anthem for the trip: "Ain't nothin' gonna break-a-my stride. Nobody gonna hold me down!" I know you want to sing it with me. Well, come on then. "Whoa, no! I gots to keep on movin'!" Apparently the only thing that could dampen this crew's mood was rain. Yeah, rain. You would think that sailors—their entire means of transportation and living being one-hundred-percent dependent on the weather—could handle a little rain. Not this kind apparently. The skies were clear, the sun was out, the conditions were ideal. And yet, it still rained.

The winds started to kick up mid-morning, so we decided to reef the Genny in a bit. As we were winding her in, we heard a loud pop from above. Remember what I said about pops, pings and bangs on a boat. Once we heard the pop, we stopped pulling immediately.

Then it rained ball bearings. All over the boat.

CHAPTER FOURTEEN

When It Rains ...

It seems on our boat, April showers do *not* bring May flowers. Phillip and I made our way gently up onto the foredeck to try and figure out what in the heck on the boat had just totally busted. We each started picking up these little bronze-looking balls that were strewn haphazardly along on the way. It was clear they were bearings. *But to what exactly?*

While having a furling headstay can be a real plus—the sail is always up there, curled up and ready to fly—it is also another system on the boat that can fail. We inspected the drum at the base of the forestay that spins and makes the Genny furl (fancy sailing term for roll up). I always remember it in that if you have a furler, you can curl her (up). Little Annie nautical slang for you there. You're welcome.

The furling drum looked fine but we could tell the bearings in the drum were the same type that had rained on the boat, so we figured it had to be the swivel shackle at the top. We knew we were going to have to let the Genny down to have a look at it. Not a *real* problem. Yet. *Perhaps we can fix it?* The thought rang out collectively among the crew. True to our "Whoa no!" mantra, we were being optimistic.

Phillip started to un-cleat the Genny halyard at the mast and lower the Genny while I positioned myself on the foredeck, ready to grab and flake her as best I could when Phillip eased her down. But there was no *easing* about it. As soon as Phillip un-cleated the halyard and let just a little slack in it, our big, whopping 135 Genny all came toppling and tumbling down onto the foredeck. *Wha-boom!* Thankfully she fell so quick that she landed all in a heap, and—more importantly—all on the boat. All on me, as well. I was buried in the Genny, but that was fine. I would rather be hidden in her heaping folds *on the deck* than trying to heave all 135% of her—heavy, wet and sucked into the grip of the Gulf—over the lifelines.

I may have mentioned this before, but it bears repeating: Genny is huge! I honestly don't know whether I could heave her in from the water, even on a calm day. The fact that she had landed all on the deck was just pure dumb luck. We were confused, though, by her immediate fall. Phillip did not lower her by easing the halyard down. No. He let out a little slack and Genny then came zipping down on her own, leaving a halyard at the top of the mast (again!) and a very baffled Phillip below, an un-lowered halyard still in his hand. Puzzled, we wrapped her up with the Genny sheets and secured her on the foredeck. She looked so sad there too. Our big, ethereal headsail all tied up in a ball on the deck. Instead of the bright-eyed, fresh-faced Genny you saw in the early parts of *Forrest Gump*, ours looked more like the strung-out, cocaine-snorting leaper she turned into. Our Genny was totally busted. So I said it, with the full Forrest Gump accent and all. I couldn't help myself. I had to. It was just too fitting.

"Jenn-AAYY!"

Unfortunately, the bad news just kept coming. We discovered why the Genny had come tumbling down all at once when Phillip let just the tiniest bit of slack in the line. The halyard shackle up top had come apart. There are two parts to the shackle that raises our Genny: 1) the part that clips to the head of the sail and spins when the Genny furls and unfurls, and 2) the part that clips to the halyard and remains still when the Genny furls. It's like a Lazy Susan. One part remains stable but allows the other part to spin. Hence the need for ball bearings in between.

The real bummer about what happened to our halyard swivel was that—when Phillip let just a little slack in the line—the shackle came apart. Meaning the part that attaches to the head of the sail came down, while the part that clips to the halyard stayed ... Yep, you guessed it. At the top of the mast. Not *one day* later in this trip and we had another halyard stuck up at the top of the mast. *What the bloody hell?*

We inspected the part of the shackle that had come down—the part that attaches to the head of the sail—and she did look to be in semi-working order, assuming the ball bearings were put back in. There was no obvious crack or visible defect. But we had no idea what the other piece that was still at the top of the mast looked like. It was clear there was going to be yet another mast ascension in this mate's future to retrieve yet another halyard. So the troubleshooting process began, which on our boat generally starts by whipping out what we call the "manuals bag"—an old canvas bag our previous owner kept on the boat that is filled to the brim with the owner's manual to every single part and system on the boat. I'm telling you: manuals are key. Keep them (all of them!) and read them first when a system fails. It's amazing what you'll learn.

After a quick review of the manual for our Harken furling system, Phillip and I were definitely of the opinion we had perhaps pulled the halyard up too tight when we raised the Genny after having the UV cover re-sewn during our Keys preparations.

"The halyard should be within the top four inches of the foil," the manual said. "Snug but not too tight," it said. *Snug but not too tight? How the hell can you make that determination from fifty-feet below?* I was kind of peeved at the manual. As if a four inch difference at the top of the mast is something that can be determined with any kind of precision from the deck? (Insert frown here.) But we figured we had likely pulled her up too tight when we raised her, causing pressure on the joint between the non-spinning part that attaches to the halyard and the spinning part that attaches to the sail—like putting too much weight on one side of a

Lazy Susan. This resulted in the pop-and-shower when we were furling the Genny.

We certainly didn't mean to, but it seemed we had caused the failure. That's usually the case, however, on the boat. Many—if not most—failures can be attributed to operator error. Once we started to think it back through, we felt kind of lucky that the two strained pieces of the shackle had somehow miraculously held together until the very moment we had *decided* to drop the sail, when we were bobbing gently, standing on the deck on a clear sunny day, hands outstretched, *ready* for her to fall.

Can you imagine if the shackle had come apart in heavy winds, when the Genny was under full load? The whole thing would have crashed into the water. Along with the Genny sheets. And what if we had been motoring? And one of the sheets had caught in the prop? *What if* ... When we actually started to think about it, we started to consider ourselves damn lucky that it had happened the way that it did. Perhaps Genny was looking out for us after all. Maybe she *does* know what love is.

Once we had pretty much diagnosed the problem—we no longer had a furling Genny—we started working toward a solution. What does that entail? Phone a friend! Phillip got some of our cruising buddies on the horn to let them know what happened and get their thoughts. We were somewhat close to Punta Gorda—where our previous owner used to keep the boat—so Phillip also decided to call the previous owner to see if he could recommend a good marina in the area. Jack referred us to Embree Marine, where apparently they had done some work on our very boat before. We called a few times but unfortunately no answer. Didn't help us that it was a Saturday.

The captain and I began to realize we likely weren't going to be able to actually talk to anyone about repairs until Monday. And—to add just a little more dung to our already-heaping pile—Phillip did some research on our Harken furling system (checked their website and some sailing blogs) and found that the fine folks at Harken don't make the halyard swivel for our furling system anymore. Apparently ours was the Model 1 series, and they were now on like Model 7. *To infinity and beyond!* There was the real possibility we were going to have to have a whole new furling system put on the forestay.

What is it they say? "When it rains, it ... "

But do recall our motto for the day. "We gots to keep on moving!" I kept piping back up with it now and again to keep morale up and because it was true. We had to keep on moving. And so we did. Phillip and I knew we were going to have to pull out of the Gulf and into Tampa Bay for repairs as Embree Marine was located in St. Petersburg. It was getting to be late in the afternoon, though, so we decided we would anchor for the night and make our way across the rather vast Tampa Bay the following morning. Phillip started checking the maps and cruising guides and we found Egmont Key. The cruising book described it as a "quaint island with tall palm trees and clear and glistening waters, where couples stroll along the white beaches without a care." *Without a care. Sounds heavenly. We could be that couple!*

"Who needs a furling Genny?" Phillip said smugly. "I mean, really? Sailors have been hoisting their Gennies somehow without them for hundreds of years." I had to smile at his gumption. Perhaps my "Whoa No!" mantra was wearing off on him. But he was right. Either we were going to get her repaired or we would just hoist her the old-fashioned way. We still had a forestay and a headsail. We decided to consider ourselves lucky. *Let's pull on into this glistening-waters anchorage here, make us some dinner, and keep on enjoying this trip shall we?* And so we did. I mean we *had* made it to our very first "key." And it was gorgeous there. Sugar white sands surrounded us. A classic lighthouse blinked out and crystal-green waters lapped at our hull. Egmont Key was kind of nauseatingly perfect.

It was nice to hear the anchor chain rattle out and know we were about to spend a quiet, still night on the hook. No two-hour shifts, no worrying about running into anything. We snubbed her up and jumped in for our first swim of the trip! While Phillip had, technically, jumped in earlier out in the Gulf to un-snag our fishing line, we decided that was kind of a necessary dip—a work-dive if you will. This was our first, elective pleasure-plunge! The water was so clear you could easily see down the ten-or-so feet to the bottom. Phillip swam down to check our anchor and even picked up two nearly perfect palm-sized sand dollars from the bottom. "That'll be two dollars, ma'am," he kept saying as a joke while he was making cocktails and handing them to me in the cockpit and I would pretend to hand him the sand dollars as payment.

We enjoyed a nice solar shower, cheersed the sunset from the cockpit, cooked up the fabulous mackerel we had caught on the way to Clearwater and called it a night. We decided not to worry about Genny any longer. We would deal with whatever she had in store for us tomorrow. For now we were on anchor, nice and secure. Nothing could bother us. But it seems that would never be the case. It seemed the spirits of the Gulf, Mother Nature, Neptune, whom-the-hell-ever constantly wanted to screw with us. That night, on anchor, we pitchpoled. I kid you not.

CHAPTER FIFTEEN

The Stress Dial

There is a very distinct, specific type of nightmare boaters have, often when they are trying to sleep on their boat and the wind is howling and their most prized possession seems to be holding precariously to only a single tiny hook in the ground. Nights like these spawn "boat nightmares." I had my very first one that night at Egmont Key.

I don't care what that stupid travel guide said—with its shimmering images of a couple, hand-in-hand, playfully frolicking on the white, sandy shore—it was wrong. That guide totally screwed us. Egmont Key may be a great place to drop anchor for the day and play but it is a terrible place to drop anchor and spend the night, particularly if you've got an east northeast wind, which we did. A strong steady one kicked in after midnight and howled all morning across Tampa Bay to Egmont Key. Tampa Bay is huge. It's massive! And, when you've got a good seventeen knots of wind screaming across it, it feels even bigger.

Our night at Egmont Key was the worst we have ever spent on anchor. The. Worst. We bounced and popped and whipped around on that anchor like a balloon hanging out the window of a semi flying down the interstate. I gripped the covers in my hands and cringed every time the boat started to groan and creak and I wouldn't breathe again until her gut-wrenching wail was over. I seriously thought the bow roller—or better yet, the whole bow pulpit—was going to break off. Phillip and I tossed and turned all night, mumbling and groaning every time the boat did, in empathy.

We debated pulling the anchor and motoring into the bay in the middle of the night but—with the wind right on our nose—that was going to be a massive chore on the winch, not to mention the crew and the engine. And we were holding—popping and jumping and groaning, mind you—but we were holding, so we decided to ride it out. I peeked out the v-berth hatch to see if the snubber—a sacrificial rope we attach to the chain and cleat to the deck to take the weight off the almighty God-sent machine that actually raises our anchor chain, the winlass—was still on and in place. I was relieved to see it there, even with its chafe guard (a patent-pending towel and duct-tape contraption) still in place to prevent the rope from shearing on the bow roller.

But even though everything was in place, that didn't lessen the popping and groaning. It sounded like it was so painful for the boat. I just wanted to pluck her out of that mess and coddle her. Phillip kept telling me, though: "It's what she's built for. That anchor's designed to hold in a hurricane." *This is worse than a hurricane!* I thought. I know that's nowhere near true but that's what you thought-scream when you're down in the berth, trying to wince away the boat's cries. I decided then and there I don't want to be anywhere near the boat if she ever has to ride out a hurricane on anchor(s). I don't want to see, much less hear, her scream and flail like that ever again. It's absolutely gut wrenching.

We were finally able to fall asleep in spurts in the wee hours of the morning. While my conscious mind really did think the whole pulpit on the bow would snap off and we would sink, my subconscious mind apparently thought that when that happened the boat would rear back like a raging stallion and pitchpole—because *that's* the nightmare I had. In my dream, the pulpit snapped off—leaving a gaping hole in the bow. In response, the boat kicked back up on her stern (yes, this was possible in my dream), went flying backward only to have her mast stick mightily in the shore like a flying sword.

It was incredibly vivid in my dream. Just as it had been when I envisioned my truck drifting off the interstate at seventy miles per hour and starting to flip upside down into the rocky shoulder. But this time I could *feel* it all—the boat moving underneath me, the rumble as the pulpit ripped off, then the entire cavity of the berth rolling back and lifting up. I woke with a jerk, and a choice expletive, I'm sure, only to find myself safe in the v-berth, with the boat still gripping mightily on the anchor. But I was shaken. It was real in my dream.

While I can easily say our first night at *a key* was nowhere near the peaceful, dreamy stuff Sandals Beach Resort commercials are made of, we at least survived it. Despite my horrific and vivid night-magination, I was thrilled to wake just before sunrise the next morning and find the pulpit on the bow had in fact not snapped off and the boat had not flipped over during the night, but we had spent an incredibly rough night at anchor. As soon as one stray shard of morning light struck the deck, we pulled the anchor and high-tailed it, motoring our way across Tampa Bay at daybreak.

But, do recall, it is one big-ass bay. We still had a ways to go before we would make it to St. Pete. We did enjoy coming under the SkyWay Bridge around mid-morning. Phillip and I having both been to St. Pete by land, the bridge was sort of iconic for us—a true monument to how far south we had actually come by boat. And I know the thing is like eight thousand miles above the water—give or take—I swear it still feels like you might hit when you go under.

I hate watching our mast go under bridges. Well I guess I can't say that's true, because I always *do* watch. It's like a train wreck. You can't take your eyes off it because you want to be sure it's not going to hit. I wonder why though? I mean, what are you going to do at the moment of impact if it *does* hit? Nothing I suppose, but I watch anyway in case I can help it with my mind. I stare at the mast, squeeze all my muscles and think short thoughts. I like to believe, because I did, that we cleared the SkyWay Bridge just fine.

While we did have to motor that morning because the wind was still east northeast, dead on our nose, and the bay was pretty chopped up, we enjoyed traversing new waters and were excited to see St. Pete come into view on the horizon. Phillip called ahead to see if we could find a transient slip or a mooring ball and luckily they had room for us in the mooring field in the Vinoy Basin. That meant it was time for another adventure. Phillip and I had never snagged a mooring ball before and with our long-standing list of docking debacles, I was sure I would find a way (somehow!) to royally goober us up. I seriously imagined myself hooking the ball and it somehow pulling me over the lifelines. Then

I'm bobbing around on the ball, all of this slimy ball gunk on me, while Phillip is left mate-less on the boat. Don't ask me where the "ball gunk" comes from. It's just there in my vivid imagination.

My mental image aside, I knew grabbing a mooring ball is not always easy—particularly in heavy winds or current—or with novice-slash-clumsy crew. *Who me?* But I was ready. Now that we were down a boat hook, I had our fishing gaff in hand and a dock line all tied and secure on the portside bow cleat. I was ready! I was going to nab that ball! And surprisingly, I did! Many kudos to Phillip and his savvy helmsman skills. He put the ball—which did end up having gunk on it thank you—right in my path. I snagged her right up on the first try and secured that boat in no time—faster than a hog tie. *Done!*

When we finally got a chance to look around and take in our surroundings, Phillip and I both agreed, this was an awesome place to stop for repairs. Like I've said, the boat just kind of takes you to new and neat places all on its own volition sometimes. The Vinoy Basin was beautiful and nestled right in the heart of downtown St. Petersburg. It had its own dinghy dock too—within rowing distance—and we were within walking distance of all the facilities and the downtown strip. Fourteen bucks a night for a waterfront, city view and all the amenities. *Hot damn!* The basin also offered a hell of a lot more wind protection than we had next to Egmont, so we knew we would be sleeping better on the ball.

Phillip and I felt like royalty in St. Pete. And we must have been because the dockmaster—real nice guy although I can't quite remember his name, I'm sure it was Bill, or Billy, or Mack or Buddy—came to pick us up at the dinghy dock in the famous "Dock Mule": a little ATV side-by-side he cruises around on. He toted us around a bit and gave us a quick tour before dumping us off at the showers. It was Sunday afternoon and Phillip and I knew we weren't going to make any headway with our headsail dilemma that evening, so we collectively decided to just forget about her for the night and go carouse about in town. The basin is literally just a hop and a skip away from the main downtown drag where we found a ton of upscale bars and restaurants, a resort hotel and even a super swanky rooftop lounge where we could look out and see our very own boat glistening in the basin. I swear she was wagging her tail. She liked it in St. Pete.

From what I remember about the evening it was definitely fun, but it was a short-lived celebration. The captain woke bright and early Monday morning and put to work his crew. It was time for this mate to get back up the mast to get the busted half of our swivel halyard down. While it was not our fault this time, it was kind of shocking to know we had yet again—not *one day* later—another halyard up the mast that needed to be retrieved. But, this time at least, we were not pitching and bobbing along in two- to three-foot seas, which feel like seven- to eight-foot monsters at the top of the mast. We were sitting nice and calm in a mooring field. Compared to what I had done last time, this was cake. I even decided to take my phone with me to get some footage and all-important selfies from the top of the mast. I found myself to be ridiculously excited about this proposition: a picture of me smiling up, with all fifty feet of mast and the beautiful deck of the boat below me. *Boats rule!*

"I see you smiling," Phillip said again as he was hooking me up in the bosun's chair. He said that a lot to me on the Keys trip. I didn't say a word in response, though, because it was true. I was busted. I was just so damn happy. Sure I was about to be hoisted fifty feet up in the air by just a couple of ropes. Sure one might consider that a bit scary, even death-defying. I considered it life ratifying. *What an awesome thing to do. What a sight to see!* I was smiling the whole way up, feeling so lucky.

It was a Monday and I wasn't sitting at a desk. I wasn't staring at a computer screen. I wasn't worried about the next number that might pop up on my phone. I wasn't worried about a deadline or a deposition. I wasn't really worried about anything. Sure our headsail was busted but we would either fix it or re-rig it. It wasn't really something we worried about. We just got to fixing it, that's all. To be honest, I was so proud of myself that I had done this. That I had changed my life from ten-hour days in an office, to months on a sailboat headed to the Florida Keys. *How fucking awesome!* I was so grateful I had found the courage to make that change. I hadn't been near this brave when I did it, but I did it.

The steady creak of the halyard as Phillip was raising me up the mast reminded me of the fan blades creaking around in his office that day and my mind took me back. The dark blue paint on the walls accented the matting on his framed degrees and the old floorboards groaned underneath my chair as I sat in his cave of an office. That was a Monday, too, when I blurted it out. Words that would once again change my life. But I did it. I said it and I stood behind it, even though it was hard, disruptive and ridiculed. I could see him once again, his eyes squinting with the effort and his hand locked tightly on the dial.

I was one year shy of partnership. Five years of the grueling worker bee life as an associate and I was standing on the brink of what was supposed to be my bountiful reward. I don't know if they actually say it in law school but it's whispered. Young lawyers see partnership as the shining promise of certain wealth, status and social standing. It is the coveted rank, the achievement worthy of the years you spend working at your desk until dinner, reviewing and summarizing records on the weekends, running to your partner's office every time he calls, pen and legal pad in hand. Partnership is the carrot at the end of a long, trying stick and I was there, at the end. I had put in the years, I had spent the necessary hours, I had my hand outstretched for it. They were about to hand me the keys to the kingdom but I say "No thanks" and walk away from it all? What makes a person do that?

A lot of things but, for me, it started with that little seed that had taken root so many years ago—when I saw the cinder block prison I had built for myself and knew I wanted to tear it all down. Once again, I knew my goals were different. Their kind of paradise could never afford me this crystal blue horizon, this unfettered sense of freedom. Theirs involved board meetings, trial prep, depositions, fundraisers, more networking, more drinking. Their paradise was a professional feat that granted them more stature which meant more money and more security. And they needed that. Their worlds revolved around their professional reputation which enabled them to bring in cases so they could continue working and making more money. They needed that too. A lot of it. They had nice homes and kids to send to college, well-dressed wives and luxury vehicles. Money afforded them the things in life they wanted. It simply didn't for me.

I was definitely the oddball—always struggling to join their easy banter about local politicians, community matters, football, fishing and tree-stands. And it only got worse after the divorce. Then I was single, running around and living in a rented loft apartment downtown. I didn't have a husband or a family. I didn't even own a *home*. *Tssk*. *Tssk*. Looking back on it, I bet my divorce worried them more than I could understand at the time. It was a faint scribbling on the wall. I was now an obvious rogue. Without an oppressive mortgage to pay or private school tuition checks to write, I didn't have near the need for a six-figure salary that they did. Fewer obligations afforded me more choices. An associate with such a status was likely feared—maybe even envied.

I'm sure my sovereignty spelled instability and they tried to reinforce my place at the firm the only way they knew how—by offering me bigger cases and more money while on my coveted partnership track. And it was a good offer. It was what every young lawyer should want and should be grateful for. It was the promise of a secure future, a safe place, the best a firm can provide. Unfortunately it translated in my world to an obligation to take on more of what I already carried and loathed—more worry, more responsibility, more stress—and give them in return the only thing in the world they could not offer me: more time. Sadly, the numbers on my paystub just didn't hold the same value for me as it did for them. I needed more time. That was the number I saw ticking above my head. I was young and healthy and I needed to break free. Again it was clear, I simply did not fit in their world.

When Phillip and I started to talk seriously about cruising, I knew I wanted to go. I wanted to live aboard our boat and travel the world. *What an incredible thing to do.* But with the way my life was structured at the time—me poised for partnership, about to ingrain myself even further into the infrastructure—I knew there was no way I would be able to make that dream a reality. And that realization crushed me. I went to work every day with lead weights on my chest, oppressed by my own confinement. I felt like I was about to add twenty years to my sentence, in my sad little cell. That, or I was going to break out.

I had done it before—changed something huge in my life and weathered the incumbent storm—so I knew I could do it again. This time, though, was far more frightening. These were my partners. At the firm. This was my job, my *livelihood*. Again, I was not eager to broach the subject. I waited—because just like last time—this was going to be hard to say, it was going to hurt people and I was scared. I was going to disappoint people I cared about, again. But—much like the night in my truck—I didn't select the moment, it found me. When it did the clarity of my needs struck the fertile ground of my soul like a thunderous bolt and the words erupted from me involuntarily—like electricity escaping through my eyes. What did it you ask? It was the stress dial.

A few weeks after the horrendous, haunting, life-changing trial, one of my partners called me into his office to talk about a few projects and discovery matters we had pending. I walked in and sat down across from him like I always did—legal pad and pen in hand—as he began flipping through a stack of papers on his desk, trying to find a set of discovery requests he wanted me to start working on. As he was thumbing through, he came across a letter from a plaintiff's attorney in another case I was working with him on. It was another medical malpractice case, this one was a drawn-out, pulmonary embolus matter—even more involved than the shoulder dystocia we had just tried.

He scrolled through it with one finger held up in the air—instructing my silence until he finished—then he told me the attorney was asking if we would agree to a trial date in that case the following February. We weren't halfway through November, we'd just spent the last three months (three gripping, grueling months!) preparing for the shoulder dystocia trial and now we were supposed to turn around and do it all again? I quickly did the mental math. *November, December, January ...* If we were going to try that case in February, we would have to start now. *Now?*

If I didn't do or say something, now—in that very moment—I knew I was going to embark once again on a trail of tears to and from the office every day and half the weekends over the course of the next three months. Not to mention working through Thanksgiving, Christmas, New Years, and potentially every other holiday in my foreseeable future, preparing for yet another massive med-mal trial. I watched the fan blades as they slowly creaked around, their haunting chorus harmonizing with the shrieking voice inside my head. I found myself curled up again on my prison cot, my arms wrapped tight around my knees, my eyes piercing out from behind them. This was my moment.

I'm sure my face exhibited some form of shock-turned-horror, because my partner set the letter down slowly and eyed me like prey in his scope. Sensing my hesitation (or at least what he perceived as mere hesitation—which was, in actuality, gut-wrenching repulsion) at the thought of preparing for another trial, my partner pushed back from his desk, laced his fingers over his stomach and eased back in his chair as he began to explain to me what he said he had explained just recently to his second-year-in-college son: the little matter of the stress dial. Yes, the stress dial.

"Just like I told him, the more successful you want to be, the more you've got to turn that stress dial," he said as he turned an imaginary knob in front of him with his index finger and thumb. "The more money you want to make, the more you've got to turn the knob," and he turned it again a couple clicks to the right, squinting a bit in mock effort.

All I could think was how much *less* I wanted. Less money. Less stress. Less turning of that *fucking knob!* I felt like my knob had all but blown off in the last trial. I had no knob left, much less one that I wanted to crank to the right with a precocious squint. The stress dial did it for me. I found the courage or, rather, the courage found me.

"If you want to become a partner, and ... "

"I don't," I said boldly, surprising myself even, at the bluntness of my own statement, and my interruption of him which is something I rarely did.

Silence swelled between us. The fan blades limped around a few times. He blinked. Opened his mouth. Shut it. I blinked.

"You don't ... "

"I don't," I said immediately, interrupting him again. "I don't want to try cases. I don't want to go to trial again. I don't want to ... be a partner."

That's how the conversation started. His hand-turning, stress dial speech about more money and more work did it for me. Now, I would *like* to say that I was composed and resolved and held steadfast during that exchange but, well, I didn't. I didn't all-out cry, but I teared up, I mumbled, I sniffled, I apologized—several times (although I wish now that I had *not* done that)—but I did get through it. And I did hold fast. I did not want to try cases. I did not want to do med-mal. I did not want to become a partner and I did not want to make more money. That was the real shocker for him. Partnership meant professional security, social standing, certain wealth. Isn't that what everybody wants? What everyone is *supposed* to want? More money?

That's what I was lead to believe. But once I had it, I did not. If making partner meant working more, taking on more obligations and trying more cases, I didn't want that either. If making less money meant turning that stress dial back about ten or twenty notches then that was the first damn thing I wanted. Less stress. More time. Time to take off from work, to travel, to go to places I had never been before. I did get that out at least.

And the conversation was very awkward, as were the ones that followed while the managing members of the firm tried to get their heads wrapped around me and my insanity and tried to figure out what the hell they were going to do with me. I was a little worried, sometimes embarrassed, when I was faced with these difficult questions, because it seemed I only had lofty, ethereal answers to them. I had no solid, socially-acceptable reason for my seemingly mid-life crisis.

"What do you want to do then, Annie?" they would ask.

"I want to sail around the world and spread sunshine and rainbows!" is what I was sure my answers sounded like.

I knew precisely how silly it sounded but I *did* want to sail and see the world! I still do! And if sunshine and rainbows could be stored on board and spread about during the process, I'd be happy to do that too. Surely it would beat how I currently spent my days: in hot heated debates. I wanted this and now it was time to stand behind it. And there was liberation again, at least, in having just said it. It was now out. I felt like a lead suit of armor had been taken off me. I was frightened and exposed but I was no longer hiding behind anything. At the very least, I had told them the truth. What they were offering, I simply did not want.

My position, however, was unorthodox and interrogated. Once the news broke, I had several attorneys come to my office to see if it was really true. I felt a bit like an exotic animal at the zoo. They all seemed to cock their head to the side and eye me curiously when I told them, again and again, that it was the truth. This was what I wanted. I knew I had to stand behind it. I had faced the same hidden shame and embarrassment in the first few months after my divorce, feeling I needed to apologize for something I had chosen and saw through, something that was right for me. Yet I had overcome *that* and looked back in wholehearted agreement that it was the best thing I had ever done for myself.

I told myself, in time, I would feel the same way about this severance. While some of my partners were hurt by it, and I have to live with that, there were a few who I think envied it. They seemed to give me a slick, half-smile when they passed me in the hall—the equivalent of a secret fist bump. But, I knew it wasn't going to be easy. This was still the shredding of my career. I had only taken the first step. The same is true for an opening statement at trial. It's merely the laying out of your initial position and how you *think* things are going to proceed at trial but you never know what's actually going to happen. A rogue witness may come out of nowhere and sink your whole case, your expert may get disassembled on the stand, your client may crumble on cross-examination.

I, too, faced similar unknowns. I didn't know if they would decide to fire me within the month out of spite, ask me to pay back contributions they had made to my 401k, sue me for breach of some unknown employment contract. They are lawyers you know. Smart ones at that. I had no clue but I trusted them and I trusted my decision. For now I just had to weather the storm but I had done it. Broken that ground. The hardest part was behind me. I had given my opening statement.

CHAPTER SIXTEEN

Up Salt Creek Without a Shackle

It was a Monday I remember. And I walked back to my office wild-eyed and trembling. I didn't really know what I was going to do with the rest of the day—the rest of the week. I had stacks of work to do, sure. I always did. But soon it might not be *my* work to do. What if they took it all away? What if I never had any more work to do there? It was a kind of freeing feeling but a frightening one as well.

I remember how scared I had felt in that moment, as his fan blades squeaked around. I was scared to say it, but more scared of what would happen if I didn't. So, I did it. I just blurted it out. And then I was frightened to the core once I had. What were they going to do with me? What had I done? *Did you really just throw your legal career away Annie?* But it just takes time sometimes for the dust to settle so you can see your path and determine whether you made the right decision. I knew one thing for certain, even as I sat there in my office—just kind of breathing and taking it all in—my Mondays were never going to be the same again.

As I reflected on it now—a little over a year from the stress dial day and once again at the top of our mast—I knew I had made the right decision and I had to chuckle at the irony. It was a Monday too, although a very different-looking one from my previous life. A regular day like this in my old office and I would have been scouring documents, fielding hostile phone calls, prepping witnesses who probably never wanted to see my face again and spending half of the day, I'm sure, with a thick wedge of worry furrowed into my brow. That's what my previous Mondays looked like. Every one of them just about the same. But now where was I? Swinging lightly in the breeze way up high, taking selfies at the top of the mast. It was hard getting here but I had done it. *Mondays rule!*

Thankfully this time we were able to use the *main* halyard to raise me up the mast which is far more reliable than the spinnaker halyard we had to use in the mid-sea mast climb and the whole process, ascension to descension, was—I hate to say it but it's just true—fun. Just pure fun. Phillip and I were both in a great mood.

We were excited to get on the phone and start scoping out options to repair the Genny. It was an invigorating challenge. And the first step of that was retrieving the busted half of the halyard that had remained at the top of the mast so we cheerily set to it. I'm sure we looked like the seven dwarfs—all whistles and smiles out there while rigging me up. Some people would probably want to shoot us. Thankfully it was just the two of us, though, alone with our happy contagion so we were safe. It was a beautiful day too. We were moored in an incredible basin in St. Pete and the view from the top of the mast was absolutely stunning.

Once I made it to the top, I shimmied the broken half of the halyard down to Phillip so he could inspect it on the deck. From what I could see when I was up there it didn't seem to have any defect—no visible cracks

or sheared parts. Although I will say I had never before taken a good look at our swivel halyard so I knew I wouldn't be the best judge. Down it went to the captain.

Phillip said it seemed the sir-clip had just popped off, which caused the shackle to come apart, allowing the swivel part to fall down the forestay and the halyard piece to remain at the top of the mast. But, even if it was put-back-together-able (that's an Annie term), we were still missing some bearings, so repairs were certainly in order. I also pulled off what looked like some marred black plastic at the top of the foil on the forestay. I didn't know what it was but I bagged and tagged it like a forensic field expert so Phillip could make heads or tails of it later.

I also put the inner forestay back in on the way down. If you recall we had taken that out when I climbed the mast mid-sea. Why? Because it was banging, remember? And apparently we don't like banging, at least not *near* as much we like having an—I don't know—easy to rig storm sail in dangerous storm conditions. Because rather than simply re-route her on the deck to a stanchion post or something to stop the banging, we took her down entirely. *Don't hate us because we're brilliant.* Thankfully we soon wised to the folly of that decision and decided—since we're on our most epic journey in the sailboat ever—it might be a good idea to put our storm-sail stay back up the next time we climb the mast. We didn't think that "next time" would be not two days later, but that's the beauty of sailing—all the pleasant unexpectedness!

It was interesting, though, what really brought that to our attention. Remember the creative systemizing I've been preaching? Well when our Genny had her crack-induced fall-out, one of the first things Phillip said was, "Well you know what? We can just hoist the staysail. Use that as our headsail and keep on cruising." Except that we couldn't. Because we had taken that stay down. But, I'll tell you, with cruising, if you're not out there screwing up and learning from your mistakes, then you're not doing it right. So, we chalked it up as a lesson learned, popped the storm-sail stay back in while I was up there and—aside from this very public write-up about it—no one was the wiser.

The great news was, we made it back up and down the mast a second time safely and we now had both busted parts of the Genny down, as well as the Genny halyard. *Done and done. Hopefully no more mast climbs this trip.* The good news, though, just kept coming. Once we got down and situated, Phillip got on the horn with the folks at Embree Marine—who our previous owner had recommended in St. Pete—and they referred us to a local rigger: Steve Smith of SMMR, Inc. We gave him a call and—while he had a few boats already lined up to work on that day—he asked us if we could motor over that morning so he could have a quick look at our Genny shackle and give us a diagnosis. We told him we were tied up to a mooring ball in the North Vinoy Basin and, turned out, he was just a short hop out into the bay and around the bend, up Salt Creek.

"You bet Steve. We'll be right there," Phillip said with a goofy grin, pointing at me to ready the boat to go.

Another great discovery about the mooring ball? It's the easiest thing to leave. You just un-cleat and go. It's fabulous! It wasn't ten minutes after we hung up with Steve that we had the engine cranked and warming. Phillip could tell Steve was real sharp over the phone. He knew immediately what had happened to our Genny shackle and the likely problem we were going to have fixing it. The ball bearings weren't really the issue. Steve had plenty of them lying around the shop that he could use to replace the ones that had fallen out of our shackle.

The real problem would arise if our shackle turned out to be too damaged to be re-assembled. If it was in fact broken beyond repair, we would need a new one. And—while we do have an incredible, sturdy, wonderfully-built old boat—she is still an *old* boat and the Harken furling system that had been put on her was decidedly outdated. Meaning, a *new* shackle likely wouldn't fit on the old foils that were put on our forestay for the old Harken system. Old parts often don't talk to new parts. We needed our old guy to hang in there.

Hopes were high as we motored over to Salt Creek so Steve could have a look at our shackle. Now I will say I was fully expecting to encounter many a salty sailor-type when we met Steve and his crew. You know, some old rough-handed, leathered, weathered riggers. I certainly wasn't expecting Walter White but that's who we got! I swear Steve Smith was a spitting image of everyone's favorite close-shaven meth chef from the *Breaking Bad* series. Have you seen that? It's based in New Mexico so I'm kind of partial. Steve Smith was every bit as smart and resourceful as Walter White too. After talking to many folks about him afterward, we learned he's the best rigger around those parts. So we were very lucky to have the privilege to pull right in unscheduled and have his surgeon-like rigger hands on our boat.

Steve took one look at our busted shackle and knew just what to do. He was going to have to unpin the forestay from the pulpit to get the shackle off so he could see about repairing it. I have to admit that kind of worried me: *Un-do the forestay? You mean like really detach it from the boat? What if it doesn't go back on? You know we're headed to the Keys, right? On this awesome, epic life-changing trip? Right?* I didn't like the idea but I didn't voice my concerns aloud. Surely Steve knew better than I. He had us loosen the backstay to ease the tension on the forestay so he could get it off.

It was strange to see the forestay disconnected from the boat. While I know Steve is an incredibly knowledgeable rigger, it still gave me a stomach ache to see him unpin her and let her go free and dangling. It's like watching a wing being stripped off an airplane. *Put it back!* She is just such a crucial piece of rigging. The life of our Genny was certainly in Steve's able hands. Once he got the shackle off and had a good look

at it, Steve agreed with Phillip that it was possible the sir-clip could be put back on, the ball bearings replaced and it might be all right. He said he wouldn't know, though, until he got in there and started re-assembling her and—like I said—Steve already had several boats lined up that day for rigging repairs. But, Steve started eyeing our swivel halyard curiously—turning it over and around in his hand—and said, "You know, I think I may have one of these in the shop."

Shut up! Really?! I was floored. An old part that nobody makes anymore? The life-saving swivel piece that could save our Genny? And this guy—the one guy we came to in the entire Tampa area—and he's got one "just lying around the shop?" *Get out!* Phillip and I prickled with energy as we watched Steve walk back to his shop. Minutes passed slowly.

I kept licking my lips. Not a word was exchanged. Then he emerged! I'm sure Steve wasn't as overly dramatic about it as I remember, but (to me) he looked like the bad boy from the final scene of *The Breakfast Club*. Walking all purposeful and slow-like, his hand thrust defiantly into the air. Except he had a swivel shackle in it! *Hallelujah!*

Likely sensing my budding excitement, Steve was quick to warn us that the shackle he had found was the Model 2. Ours was the Model 1, so there was a chance it wouldn't fit. I didn't care though. All I could think was: *So, you're* telling *me there's a chance.* Despite his already full line-up for the day, Steve rolled up his sleeves and set to work on us immediately to see if the replacement shackle would word. Steve slid the "new" used shackle around the foils on our stay and it was a perfect fit. I've never seen anything fit snugger (on something that wasn't a Kardashian).

"Now, we're real proud of our old used crap around here," Steve told us as he was re-securing the shackle. "I'll have my wife look it up and see what price we can give you for her." Phillip and I hadn't really even processed the thought of payment. Steve was fixing our boat! Making it go again! *Can you even* put *a price on that?* Sadly, you totally can and we were hoping this little inadvertent trip up Salt Creek wasn't going to force us to pack up our little Key-West-bound wagon and head back home. I kind of squinted a little and turned my head to the side, hoping it would help. *Lay it on us Steve.*

CHAPTER SEVENTEEN

Have Genny, Will Travel

The night before—when we were out galavanting and painting the pretty town of St. Pete red—Phillip and I had been discussing the potential outcomes of this Genny halyard fiasco, one of which would require replacement of the entire furling system on the forestay. If we couldn't find a replacement swivel halyard that worked with our old foils and furling system, that was totally possible. It was also totally possible *that* little investment might run us in the thousands. Yes, multiple. You can see why we drank the night away. Now, standing in Steve's shipyard, we knew the damage would likely be less, but we still didn't know how steep it would be. I think Phillip squinted and winced a little too while we were waiting to hear back from Steve's wife. But we got incredibly lucky. You know what Steve charged us for his "old used crap?"

A hundred dollars.

Yes. Just a hundred. That was it. For a part no one makes anymore, that we couldn't order or buy online. A part that instantly fixed our furling genoa for the entire trip. I'm not one to toss around hundred dollar bills but—to us, in that moment—it was chump change. *Done deal,*

Steve. No more restaurants in St. Pete. We'll eat beans. And the hundred was just for the part. Steve wouldn't let us pay him anything for the labor, although we tried. "Just send folks my way," was all he said. And boy have we tried! Hence the mention here. Thanks again Steve at SMMR, Inc. up Salt Creek. Without you, we would have been up shit creek, without a headsail.

Phillip and I motored out of Salt Creek on our second "life-high" of the trip and had a great time recounting our spontaneous, fortuitous stop at Steve Smith's shop, his Sanford-and-Son approach and appearance and his keen resourcefulness. I'm sure the man can conduct nuclear fission with a little battery acid, duct tape and bailing wire. I'd only met one other man in my life that I would say that about and I had a great time impersonating him for Phillip as we made our way back to the Vinoy Basin.

"You never know when the law might be looking," I said to Phillip, all country twang-like, shifting my eyes suspiciously and tipping my pretend greased-up ball cap.

It was this old buddy of my dad's—Johnny Milwood. He actually worked as a roadie for Hank Williams, Jr. back in the day and could pick and rip with the best of them. Johnny lived in an old run-down trailer on the outskirts of his sister's property—totally off the grid because he liked it that way. I think he ran an extension cord like one hundred yards—hell maybe two—from the nearest barn to power his little fort where he spent most of his time watching one of his seemingly ten thousand movies (for the third time, he could quote them all), monitoring his homemade apple wine and cleaning his guns. Man, that guy had some guns. Why?

"Cause you never know when the law might be looking," he'd say, as he eyed the perimeter of his rickety porch suspiciously. Then he'd drop his greasy head back down and get back to polishing a muzzle.

His little shack, though, looked about like that Sanford & Son guy's place—half-deconstructed trucks, ATV's, TV's and satellite dishes littered the yard—kind of like Steve Smith's self-proclaimed "boat graveyard shop." Johnny had an incredible knack for fixing things you thought would never run again. Dad and I often took him starters, mowers, weed-eaters—all sorts of piddly farm type items we figured were for sure 'goners'—and not a couple of days later, Johnny would have them running again, with some jerry-rigged type solution: two wires you would have to hold together to make it start, a plug you had to push on while you gave it gas, a pull string to crank a car. You could never predict what he would come up with. But—nine times out of ten—the thing was fixed. We would hand him a twenty and a six pack of Budweiser and Johnny would hand us our good-as-new device and a mug of his wine to go with it.

Johnny got a real kick out of my screwdriver-start car when I drove it up to Cullman during college. I think that kind of won me into his good graces. Dad joked that it rivaled the pull-cord-start Johnny had made for him. At the time, Dad used a little green Ford sedan to run hay around the farm. While he really did only put the hay in the trunk and haul it around trunk-open, the stuff just gets everywhere. It covered the seats, the floorboards, the dash. But that green machine ran for years and years. Until one day I couldn't get it to crank. I had come up for the weekend from college in Tuscaloosa and had hopped in the "hay ride" to follow Dad up to the barn as usual but I couldn't get it to go. The steering column was all open and mangled. I couldn't even find the ignition. Dad was already snickering and laughing by the time he got my door open, excited to tell me about Johnny's latest "fix."

"Pull that stiff wire," he said, grinning. "That one there, with the loop on the end."

Then I saw it. Sure enough. There was a straight wire—with a loop on the end—sticking out from underneath the column. I looked at Dad kind of funny like, gripped it and pulled and—sure enough—the thing cranked right up. I would have never known how to crank it had he not showed me. "I'm not really sure what Johnny done," Dad said. "I just know it works and cain't nobody steal it." You should have seen the thing—hay sprouting out of every orifice like a stuffed scarecrow, the paint so dirty and dusted the car looked mustard yellow rather than green. *Trust me, Dad. I don't think anybody had their eye on it.*

Johnny was just a good guy though. Real salt of the earth. He helped us every time we needed it for just $20 and a six-pack. Never a complaint, or an "I'm busy." He was also smart—probably one of the most mechanically savvy individuals I have ever met, although Steve Smith would be a close second. You wouldn't think it by the looks of him: thin as a rail, long scraggly hair down to his shoulders, a couple snaggle teeth poking out. But he was. I'm not aware of a single thing Johnny couldn't fix.

I think I liked that most about him. He was so resourceful. "It can't be done," was never the answer. I liked that I was starting to become that way—bit by bit. Self-sufficient and—kind of like Johnny—a little bit off the map. Cruising will do that to you. I couldn't believe we had saved our transmission last year with some duct tape and a Dasani bottle. I was proud to see Johnny and Dad had rubbed off on me a little. I felt those skills were going to serve me far better in my new life than my ability to summarize medical records and bill for it. Turns out that opening statement wasn't the most important thing I was ever going to say—"I quit" was.

Because here I was, breathing in a Monday morning and I was greased up, sweaty, cruising on a sailboat down a salty creek, smiling for no reason (and every reason) and doing Johnny Milwood impersonations. I wasn't arguing. I wasn't worried and I wasn't stressed. For me, there was no dial. I certainly didn't miss the suits and heels and I didn't miss the money. The only thing I was missing was a jug of homemade wine to go with our Johnny-style fix on the Genny. But that would have to be about it. Phillip and I made it back to the Vinoy basin around mid-afternoon, fixed us up some good cold boat drinks and sat in the cockpit admiring our now-furled Genny. Sip. Smack. *Ahhh.*

The whole point, though, of fixing the Genny was so we could get back out there sailing again. The plan was to head out across Tampa bay early the next morning, pop back out in the Gulf around noon and just make the run straight to Ft. Myers. While we wanted to see Cayo Costa, Cabbage Key and that area in Charlotte Harbor, we were really eager—now that our Genny was back in action—to cover some ground in the Gulf and make our way south. While we had a great time in St. Pete, heading out on the town, checking out the rooftop bars and fine dining, Phillip and I were a hundred dollars short and both excited to be back out in the open water—just the two of us and the boat, looking out on a silky sunset and enjoying a serene night sail under the stars. We were making this trip by sailboat for a reason: we wanted to sail! With our canvas now fully functional, all we needed was some wind.

The minute I even thought it, I knew. I shouldn't have said anything. Not even thought-said it. It's always a jinx. It's like when someone is about to yank the pull cord on the outboard and you say: "Gee I hope it starts this time." *Doh!* As it seems she always does—even when I just think it, Mother Nature hears me.

She blessed us the next morning with 19.6 knots of spring breeze, right on the nose! *Hooray!* But we weren't going to let it get us down. We hoisted the main up to the first reef point and charged across the Bay. The wind laid down as we made our way out of the pass. *Never again Egmont Key!* And we ended up having a great sailing day—steady twelve- to fourteen-knot winds blew over our port stern all afternoon as we glided through crystal green waters. Our Genny unfurled beautifully and was holding true. *Thank you old used boat crap!*

At a steady six knots, our boat was really moving! The captain was thinking we would easily make it into Ft. Myers the next morning. This time it was he who did it. All that darn thinking. *She can hear you, you know.* Just when you think the weather's going to cooperate, Mother Nature likes to jack you around. The perfect afternoon and placid sunset were a deceptive omen.

The wind had been blowing a steady eight-to-nine knots most of the evening and it looked like it was going to hold true through the night. So after the sun dipped out of the sky, we decided to set up a movie on

the laptop in the cockpit and (now you know) I did it again—sealed our fate for another night of catastrophe aboard. I started it out the same way—with the whole "Movie Day" camel bit. "Uh-oh, guess what day it is," doing my funny little camel-imitation walk. And you remember what happened to us the last time we tried to have "movie night" on the ole' *Rest*. Perhaps we should have taken it as a sign: like when you wash your car and it rains. Because—it seems—every time we set up for movie night on our boat, shit tends to hit the fan. This is why the whole camel-day ritual is now banned.

It was around 9:00 p.m. and wasn't ten minutes after we'd nestled in at our little "theater," that the winds kicked up to fifteen miles per hour.

The boat heeled over and groaned but we were fine—a little overpowered for a quiet evening sail—but still fine. We paused the movie and decided to reef the sails a bit. *A good idea, no?* Chaos ensued. In a matter of five minutes, the wind went from fifteen to twenty to twenty-fucking-five!

We were trying to wrestle the sails down to the first reef but the Genny was whipping and popping in the winds and there was so much force on her, even luffing, she felt impossible to pull in. After struggling with the sails for several minutes we were turned every which way. The captain decided to crank the engine and drop the sails to get us back on course. It was the right call but still a bit of a dangerous proposition in and of itself. The wind had kicked up the sea state and we were beating into three- to four-foot waves. Since our swivel halyard explosion we had decided to bring the Jenny in by hand whenever possible, which meant we would be doing it now hand-over-hand, with at least twenty-five knots of wind billowing in her belly.

"I don't know if I can do it!" I shouted to Phillip through the wind. "It feels impossible!" I was trying to bring the Genny in by hand but just getting the line to pull back an inch took a monumental effort. We still had at least a good thirty feet left to go. Each time I would get some movement and use all of my force to heave back on her—gaining just a couple of feet—the minute I had to stop to move my hands up the line, she would come to a complete standstill again and it felt like I was tugging on a seated elephant. I really did not think I was going to be able to do it and the longer I struggled and heaved but failed in my sad, not-able-to-do-it state, the longer she was left out there—popping, snaring and snapping at us in the wind.

Genny acted like a rabid pit bull at the end of her chain. Each time she rared back, she would yank with all of her however-many-pounds of might (I don't even want to imagine) on the meager little blocks and pulleys and tackles holding her back—each one threatening, in my mind, to snap off the boat with the next ear-piercing pop of the canvas. It's like trying to hold a rearing elephant back with yarn and nails. Finally Phillip and I fell into a coordinated hand-over-hand pulling effort on the furling line—never allowing the momentum to stop—that allowed us to finally muscle her in. But I will never forget the intense and immediate fear of that moment when I truly did not think we were going to be able to contain her. A Genny out of control is like a tornado at the bow of the boat. She can destroy everything.

Once Genny was secure, I then headed up onto the deck to wrestle the mainsail down into the stack pack—sure this time to don my safety harness and clip in everywhere I went. And it was a good call. There were several times a wave hit and the only thing I had to grab onto for balance was my safety line. It was a bit of a *Deadliest Catch* moment but, after a battle, we got the sails down and secure.

That was just the beginning though. The wind definitely brought some rough seas and we were beating into waves, bare poles, fighting our way through the Gulf. Now should we have kept some canvas up for stability? You bet. But we believed—at that time in our novice cruising career—trying to deal with sails in those conditions and tack back and forth tirelessly into a fearsome headwind was not worth it.

Whether it was the right decision or not, we chose to secure the sails and bash through it. The boat actually felt like it was leaping sometimes.

It would lunge over the top of a wave, then come almost to a dead stop at the blunt face of the next one. It's hard to imagine a thirty-five-foot, sixteen-thousand-pound vessel can be so agile—can *move* or *be moved* so easily—but out in the open Gulf, I assure you it can. It's incredibly humbling to be reminded of how absolutely tiny and fragile you are out there in a vast body of indifferent water, no matter how big your yacht.

The Gulf was not our friend that night. The sounds of the boat groaning and pounding into waves was deafening below. There was no way either of us was going to be able to sleep in those conditions. Phillip and I both hunkered down and clipped in in the cockpit—our eyes glued to the instruments, pleading with the wind to ease off. But she wouldn't. She kept coming at us in swift torrents, holding a steady twenty-five to twenty-eight knots for hours on end. Around four in the morning, Phillip was on his eighth hour straight at the helm and all we could do was hold our course, hold onto the boat and hold out until daylight.

As I sat curled and soaked under the dodger, watching the bow of the boat crash into black-wall waves, words seemed to rise up from deep within me. Her smoke-charred voice puffed up through the cracks of the cockpit floor and swirled around me, muffling the sound of the waves:

"I thought I was going to die."

CHAPTER EIGHTEEN

Waste Not

She shocked me when she said it. In her day, my grandma—better known as Big Mom—was a pistol. She outlived two husbands and kept all one hundred thirty-nine acres of her cattle farm up in Cullman productive and profitable for fifty years. I always remember her with that ratty old sweat band pushed up into her white, wet curls—headed outside to hang clothes on a line, pick grapes from the vine, pull weeds from the "flahrs" (flowers) or "go count the cows."

That woman could work circles around me, even in her seventies. That wasn't true in her eighties though. It was one of the hardest things I've ever had to watch—Big Mom's sad, steady decline. It took years and it took every scrap of her dignity before it eventually took her. Smoking will do that. But, hell, anything can do that. It can happen to the healthiest person alive but it's one of the worst things I can ever possibly imagine: a slow death to disease.

It did let me see a side of Big Mom, though, I might never have. In her final year I got to spend the kind of time with Big Mom I never could have before, because she was always working, cleaning, washing, scolding. She was always worrying too much after us to sit down and tell us stories, but I wish she would have known how valuable they were—almost as much as her worrying, scolding and her heaping helpings of cabbage, turnip and mustard greens.

When Big Mom was finally unable to do all that cooking and canning, she was finally content to sit around and tell us stories. I asked her about a picture one day I had looked at all through my childhood. It hung on the paneled wall of her bedroom—right by her bed—and I realized I didn't have any context for it. It was an obviously posed family photo, very Olan-Mills-like, of Big Mom, her husband—my grandfather Herbert who died when my dad was fifteen—my dad, around the age of four it seemed, and his sister, De, seemingly around the age of ten. When I asked Big Mom about it that was the first thing she said.

"That's why we took it," in her craggle voice. "'Cause we thought I was going to die."

I was taken aback. Out of all the things she could have told me about that photograph, that's the one? And I couldn't decide what intrigued me more—the fact that Big Mom thought she was going to die at like the age of twenty-nine or the fact that, because she *did*, they needed to sit down and take a family photo. I guess it made sense. Capture what exists before it doesn't anymore. But, man, what a morbid photo shoot. Can you imagine? "Now you sit right there, Miss Devena, in the middle. You get the special chair because—you know—you're about to die and all."

I was intrigued by the story. Apparently at twenty-nine, Big Mom had been in a real bad way. It was weird to hear these things about her—as if she had lived a completely different life before I came into cognition—but she had. I couldn't even picture Big Mom svelte and young, wearing those 1950's housewife dresses with pearls and primped brown hair. I could only imagine sweat bands, her white, wet forehead curls and her big glasses with the chain. But Big Mom told me she'd had some kind of issue with her liver that they couldn't diagnose and it had caused severe gastrointestinal problems. It also caused her skin to yellow (which was why the photo was black and white).

Big Mom told me she went to several different medical facilities to try to find a cure and they eventually punched a valve through her abdomen—much like a colostomy bag—that allowed bile to drain from her poorly functioning-liver. The prognosis at the time was that she was going to die—pretty soon too. The valve-bag solution was merely meant to provide some comfort during her "last days." This was why they booked the happy family photo shoot. I had to ask—out of sheer curiousity—if my dad and Aunt De had known at the time that this was the reason they all went to take the picture. Big Mom kind of chuckled at my appalled face when she told me they did.

"Death was a lot more matter of fact back then," she said. "It was either going to happen then or it was going to happen later. We didn't really see fit to worry about it. We just wanted to get the picture for the family record and move along. You know, get on living."

I was amazed at this. What a great way to approach it? It's going to happen—to everyone at some point, either now or later—so why worry about it. So simple it's baffling. And I guess fate saw fit to reward Big Mom for her matter-of-fact heroism because a few weeks later she got an appointment at some new facility "up north" and they put her on some protein kind of enzyme medicine that turned everything around for her. To be honest I don't recall the particulars, I'm not sure Big Mom even did when she relayed the story to me in her final year—probably because they really didn't matter. What mattered was: Big Mom thought she was going to die and it didn't phase her. She was ready and **she had no regrets. Maybe that's why she** didn't. She had some more living to do.

"You get a second chance, Annie, you take it," she told me.

I was so struck by that. It was kind of funny but I seem to couch everything in my life—even the sad, tragic, trying times—in humor. I guess that's just how I process them. The fact that I had asked about *that* photo—the only one they'd taken because they thought she was "gohn *die.*" Dad laughed when I told him about it later, telling me how it was, in fact, true and how he remembered that day and the fact that Big Mom had wore a dark black dress and powdered her face extra heavy in hopes of making her sallowed skin look more white in the picture.

He actually remembered it. At the age of four! But it wasn't a sad memory for him he explained. "Death is just part of it." I think my dad still would have chuckled if Big Mom had passed all those years ago as predicted and I then asked about the photo. They were just ready. It was just matter-of-fact. Death didn't worry them. How you lived your life was more important.

The thought kind of soothed me as we pounded into the black churning waters of the Gulf, the boat crying out with each crash. Not that I thought we would really die out there but if in fact we did—instantaneously in a boat-shattering catastrophe—I would have been okay with that. I would pick *that* any day over the slow, debilitating decay I watched Big Mom endure, losing first her ability to breathe after ten steps, then her ability to walk without assistance then, tragically, her ability to recall me, my dad and so many people who loved her. Big Mom passed away on November 13, 2013.

The Annie she had known when she was last lucid no longer existed. In my former lawyer life, I was the jaundiced, sallow woman posing for my last morbid photo. But that image had been shredded. Now I was a wanderlust writer whose future was anything but certain. After I broke the news—gave my opening statement—it took the guys at the firm months to believe I was really going to do it—step away from the practice to sail the world—and while they were a bit shocked by it, they were very good to me during the transition.

First they moved me to a different practice area—bankruptcy and creditor's rights (collections suits, basically)—which was better. It was definitely not as sexy as medical malpractice defense or trial work but it was far less stressful, time-consuming and unpredictable. While it showed me there were areas of law I could practice in that didn't require me to lose weight, hair or friends, it also told me I could do all of that when I was old. I would always have the degree. If I couldn't hack it as a venturesome writer/world-traveler, I could always come back and get by as a well-traveled collections attorney in my saggy years.

Sadly, everything the firm did to try and keep me only reaffirmed my belief that this was not the time in my life to hold an office job. For me, the practice of law became merely a backup plan. And I'm thankful I got the degree and got a glimpse of what life as a lawyer is like, because it is a pretty lucrative plan B and perhaps was the reason I felt I could be so brave in venturing out. I know I have a better fall-out plan than many others but I earned it.

Once it became clear my mind was made up—I was leaving—the firm phased me out slowly over the course of 2013. By November, I was working the first of my last two months for the firm remotely. December would be it—the last of my "lawyer dollars." After that I would be—for all intents & purposes—unemployed. I had some plans for income but writing was never expected to provide me an immediate return on investment. For the foreseeable future, all I had were plans and time. Not a bad deal. Certainly not a permanent situation but—for the present moment—a fortuitous one. Because what did Phillip and I plan to do with my new-found work-freedom? Stuff it in a boat and take it to the Keys!

Early November, 2013, Phillip and I found ourselves picking dates and passages for the Keys trip. We had planned to take a short ten-day offshore shakedown voyage over Thanksgiving to help us identify any last issues and make repairs before we would officially shove off in April the following year, bound for the Keys. But—as it always does—life happens. Big Mom passed and we headed up to Cullman, Alabama for the funeral instead. As it stood, I was headed up to pay Big Mom her due respects and I was thirty-one, divorced and—since it was just a month out, I could pretty much say it—unemployed.

You might think I would have been a little embarrassed about it, worried that poor Big Mom might be ashamed of me. Rolling in her coffin I assume. But the truth was, I knew she'd be proud. I knew she'd see the gumption in what I had done—the courage in it. "You get a second chance, Annie. You take it." Isn't that what she'd told me? *Well I damn sure did Big Mom!* Much like her, I didn't die at twenty-nine, as a streak of blood and glass on the interstate. I no longer lived in a house filled with frustration, resentment and hate. I no longer drank myself into oblivion and I no longer sat—paunch and pasty—at an office doing something I didn't like. I was now living my life for me and somehow, deep down, I knew Big Mom knew that.

And I felt a big part of why I embarked on this whole unchartered soul quest was because of Big Mom. One of the most important lessons she taught me was the old "waste not, want not" adage. Like her second chance, Big Mom showed my brother and I if you don't waste what you've been—"by the Grace of God," she would say in her charred, craggle voice—given, then you won't want for more. Sometimes life is going to hand you a rough deal and you just have to suck it up and make the most of it. At least you've still got cards to play. You're still in the game. Her teachings went hand-in-hand with mom's, who schooled us in the "less is more" way of life. While mom's version of a simpler life wasn't some lofty, philosophical choice, it was simply a matter of economics and reality, she still taught us to appreciate what little we had by refusing to let us whine or want for things we didn't really need anyway.

As I saw it, time was the most important gift I'd been given. There is no way to get more of it, only less if you choose to waste your health or less out of it if you choose to spend your time wasting away in a supposed-to prison. When I realized I had, by some inexplicable stroke of luck, survived what could have been my last day on this earth, I felt like the ticker above my head started over. It was still dwindling but it was a new number, signifying a new time in my life—my own version of a second chance. With that simple premise, my simple beginnings kicked in and it was just a matter of going back to the way of life I had been raised on: appreciate what you've got and don't waste it.

Just because it sounds simple, though, doesn't make it easy. It actually makes it harder. Complicating things is so easy it's almost inadvertent. Maintaining simplicity, on the other hand, is so hard it's almost unachievable. Every choice must be purposeful, every move intentional. *No zombies allowed!* I knew the new life that awaited me on the other side of the prison wall wasn't going to be as comfortable or secure as my old one, but I was determined to find a way to make the most of it. At least I still had cards to play. I was still in the game. I had nothing to want for or whine about.

These were the lessons I learned from my "mothers." While sometimes the lessons were intentional, often times they were not. As a kid, you just pick up on and immolate the way of life of those around you. I learned a lot from the stubborn women of my youth and it seemed I had grown up to be just as stubborn—if not twice so. Case in point: the grapefruit crate.

At her funeral I told one of my favorite Big Mom "waste-not" lessons. There were plenty, I assure you. It was hard to decide. The woman re-used the cellophane wrapping they used to package produce at the grocery store. They still had the stickers on them. She also re-used the wrapping that came on meat. Ground beef, pork, anything. She washed it, if that helps. But she had a whole drawer of it, all wadded up and sticky. She would flail her hands toward it when you were helping her clean the kitchen and holding a hunk of meat or something she wanted you to wrap. We all secretly dug around in hopes of finding a wrap that had been on produce as opposed to poultry but—looking back—I'm not sure I should have worried about it. I never once got sick eating anything Big Mom served me. I think by the time I was grown, I was thoroughly inoculated.

The cellophane wrap was just the beginning though. There were also the hundreds of Cool Whip and Country Crock tubs Big Mom used as her tupperware, the "half-used" paper plates that sat wrinkly, stained and stacked by the microwave—waiting to be used two more times, at least, before they could be thrown out—not to mention the canning. Big Mom's basement was full to the brim, shelf upon shelf, of vegetables she had canned. As we were cleaning them out after she passed, we literally found a whole shelf that dated back to 1987.

Big Mom did not waste a thing. I imagine growing up in the thirties will do that to you. While my level of frugality would be dwarfed by hers, I do attribute it to her. Whatever the Great Depression did to Big Mom, Big Mom did to me. It all started with this huge crate of grapefruit.

I was probably seven or so at the time, just barely starting to form memories that would really stick. I was spending the summer—as my brother and I always did then—with Dad up in Cullman on Big Mom's farm. Big Mom took me with her one day—driving her boat-size Cadillac by squinting up through the cutout in the steering wheel—to the Spradlin's farm up on County Road 1251. The Spradlins grew their own fruit and vegetables and sold them year-round at a sort of farmer's-market-type roadside stand on the edge of their property. They always had what was in season and it had usually been picked that morning.

On this day the Spradlins had one of my absolute favorites—grapefruit. A ton of it. Okay probably not a literal ton, but it was a ton in seven-year-old measurements. I think they translate something like dog years. You could either get like six grapefruit for two dollars, twelve for five dollars or a whole crate—thirty-six of those damn things—for fifteen bucks. I can't explain why but I wanted those grapefruit more than anything in the world. They seemed magical. I would have gone all Jack-in-the-beanstalk style with it and traded Star Brite's rocking rainbow horse for them. *I wanted the grapefruit.*

I kept circling them like prey, imagining what it would be like to bite right into one—puncture the rind with my teeth and have juice squirt all down my neck. Mrs. Spradlin must have got a kick out of me and she must have been looking to unload some grapefruit because she gave Big Mom and I a whole crate as a gift. Big Mom had been buying fruit from Mrs. Spradlin for years and always brought her some freshly canned beans, okra and such when she stopped by her side-of-the-road stand, so Mrs. Spradlin threw a crate in the trunk of Big Mom's caddy—despite Big Mom's repeated protests—and said, "no charge."

My eyes probably bulged out the size of grapefruit. I was on a citrus high! I ate two right when we got back to Big Mom's, two the next morning and another two the next. Life was awesome. The next week I was still enjoying them in the morning, but my body wasn't enjoying them later. I had developed a serious case of the squirts. Again my body was baffling me. *Are those organs coming out? They must be organs ...*

Having no clue at the bright age of seven that the reason for my gastrointestinal dismay was the ruby reds, I kept at it. It wasn't long, though, before I put two and two together and I could no longer stand the sight of them, the smell of them, the bitter-rind taste of them. Big Mom and I were walking through the Piggly Wiggly that week and I spotted a box of Something Whatever Flakes and, again, I couldn't imagine anything in the world I wanted more. I was learning a lot about this whole "wanting" business. *Careful what you wish for.* Isn't that what they say? According to the homemade crate of grapefruit in Big Mom's basement, I still had everything in the world I had ever wanted, a whole quarter-crate of it still. And Big Mom was quick to remind me of this. Rightfully so. I'd been given a gift. That was not to be wasted.

"After you finish the grapefruit," she said. *After I finish the grapefruit?!* my kid brain shrieked at me. *Was she serious?* There were still so many. I didn't have many more organs left to sacrifice. Having everything I ever wanted was literally cleaning me out. But perhaps Big Mom didn't know me well enough yet because she had actually handed me a solution. The grapefruit had to be gone. I wouldn't dare try to throw them away or hide them. Big Mom eyed me like a nosy shopkeep every time I took two more out of the crate. I'm not sure where she thought I could hide softball-sized grapefruit on my little seven year old body but apparently she had some ideas. She didn't know it but she too had given me a gift—the key to my cell. Big Mom herself had said it: eat the grapefruit and I could have the flakes. It was decided then. I knew exactly what I was going to do.

When we got back to the house, I went straight for the crate, pulled out my little front-print kid tee and packed the last of the grapefruit in it. There were eight. *Just eight* I told myself as I trudged up the stairs from her basement. It might suck but surely eight wouldn't kill me. That's what I thought when I started but not when I was halfway through. After my fourth grapefruit—my belly extended and already gurgling—I was certain those evil pink spheres were going to kill me. I was going to die in a watery little grapefruit grave right there in Big Mom's kitchen. But that didn't stop me. *My God I was stubborn.* Big Mom didn't say anything either. *My God* she *was stubborn.* She eyed me sternly as she came and went while I shoveled spoonful after spoonful of the pink, putrid piss down and eyed her back.

My dad gave me a funny look when he saw me hunkered over my bowl of pity at the table. Seeing me at the table eating grapefruit wasn't a new sight. Pursuant to my agreement with Big Mom, I had been making my own squirty breakfast for weeks—cutting them in half, digging out each juicy triangle with my special grapefruit spoon, then squeezing each of the four halves into the bowl and slurping it down. As a kid, though, I never thought to rinse fruit. Hell I hardly rinse it now, particularly something with a rind. *You don't eat that part anyway.*

But, apparently, my dreaded grapefruit could have used a good scrubbing because the Spradlins marked each with a big, black Sharpie. After all the digging, scooping and squeezing, my juice concoction was a sad grayish-pink with little black bits floating around in it. That's what dad was eyeing—my bowl of watery gray slosh that looked anything like refreshing grapefruit juice. Keen on my "produce pact" with Big Mom, though, over the dreaded grapefruit crate and being a smart man not wanting to get between two stubborn southern girls, he just asked one question:

"Babes, how many of them grapefruit you got left to eat?"

"Two," I responded immediately, without stopping my squeeze-and-slurp routine. I had been at it for an hour, stuffing my pot-belly with citrus. I knew exactly how many were left every time I ate one. I was slurping up the black-speckled remains of Grapefruit No. 3 as we spoke. Dad just sort of nodded and went about his business. I'm sure he was a little worried about my Sharpie intake as much as the grapefruit. Hell, both were probably contributing to my "potty issues." But I imagine he thought two more wouldn't kill me, so he stayed out of it. Man how I gloated when I finished that crate. I slurped down the last of the Sharpie juice and took my empty bowl and sloshing stomach straight to Big Mom, sporting a huge black-speckled grin and expecting big praise. What I got was:

"Alright."

But she said it with a smile. I think she was kind of proud of me, for handling my business—taking what I had asked for and what I deserved and keeping my word by swallowing it down (literally) without complaint. After another noisy organ donation, she took me back to the Piggly that very afternoon and—I'll tell you—that first bowl of Something Whatever Flakes was the best stuff I'd ever eaten. If Big Mom hadn't been watching, I would have ate them all, the box too, for extra packing.

But I learned a good lesson. Waste not, want not—sure—but, more importantly: your wants may change. That's okay. Hell, it's expected.

When I reflected on the grapefruit story while I was preparing to tell it at Big Mom's funeral, I realized what I should have taken away from that whole saga was that no matter how hard I may have worked for something, how much of it I may have painstakingly stockpiled—like grapefruit in a crate—it may no longer be what I want and that's okay. I knew I might get a little flaky at times and want to change everything—my scenery, my surroundings, my goals and that's okay. Judging by my recent upheaval, it should probably be occasionally expected.

I simply vowed to listen to myself more closely. *Annie, are you gurgling?* If so, it might be my soul telling me it's time for a change. And I knew such desires would likely come at a time that seemed inconvenient and push me toward a path that seemed disruptive—as change often does—but I would just have to suck it up and make the best of it. It's like that played-out life/lemons cliche except you don't want to know what my little body made out of that grapefruit. I promised myself I would never again remain in a cell because it might seem hard to escape. I knew if it came to it and it was the only option, I would eat my way out! I don't think I formed a solid stool for six months after consuming the dreaded eight but it was worth it. Your life is always worth it: waste not.

The grapefruit saga seemed to be a big hit at the funeral. Me being me, I had to tell a funny one. The real kicker, though, was Mrs. Spradlin's reaction. To be honest I hadn't even thought about her being there when I decided to tell it, but she attended along with plenty other Cullman "elders"—folks who had been living and making a living in Vinemont County like Big Mom for the last fifty years. After the funeral as we were shuffling out, Mrs. Spradlin pulled me aside and—with a little thumbs up and a wink—told me: "Thanks for the plug!"

Big Mom would have loved that. The fact that her passing and my story telling could help someone, particularly someone she'd been supporting for decades. Big Mom was an incredible woman. Stubborn as a god-damned mule and ready at the drop of a hat to scold you for the slightest misstep, but also ready to teach you a valuable lesson the hard way, which took patience and persistence on her part but it's the only way they really stick.

Big Mom was also short with the praise but I think it was better that way. That way we weren't spoiled with it. I would say I was sad to see her pass, but I wasn't. By then it was a blessing. Rather, it was sad to watch her decay. To wither into this frail, sickly, skin-rag of a woman I once knew and looked up to, but she had lived a long, full life before I even met her.

"That can't be her," I said as we flipped through them. My dad and I had stumbled upon some old pictures of Big Mom after she passed, tucked away in a faded, floral shoebox in her basement—ironically just one shelf above where we had kept the crate of grapefruit that long-ago summer. There was one small faded album on the bottom that cracked open like it hadn't been touched in years.

"Oh, that's her," Dad said with a smile, as if he knew something about Big Mom that I didn't. As I looked harder though I could tell it was. She had the same features, the same dark curly hair and the same striking eyes as she'd had in her "gonna-die" death shoot. This time, though, Big Mom was posed out on some marina docks clad only in a bikini, a cowboy hat and high heels—pretty racy for her and for the times. Still, you could tell she could have cared less what anyone thought of her at the time. This was not a woman doing what she was supposed to. No. Big Mom—although I'm sure they called her Devena, or De, or something far more sexy than "Big Mom" back then—was kicked back, chest pushed out, one hand held up to her hat, the other on her hip, posing like a true Playboy model.

We all were kind of shocked to see her like that—the woman we could only imagine pulling weeds and canning. I looked at the side of the photo where there was a printed date: 1955. She would have been thirty. Just one year out from the dreary "they thought I was going to die" picture. I knew exactly what Big Mom was doing. She was rocking that second chance.

I felt a true kinship to Big Mom then. Her passing only reinforced my firm belief that what I was doing was right. Like her, I felt I, too, had been given a second chance at twenty-nine, and I damn sure wasn't going to waste it. How you spend your time is a choice and I knew I was not doing anything I was supposed to but everything I wanted to. And the next time I got my hands on a cowboy hat and a pair of heels I knew exactly what I was going to do.

CHAPTER NINETEEN

Want Not

"**N**ineteen. I'll take nineteen!"

Phillip was shouting at the wind instrument. We were both glaring at it, pleading it to change, to decrease, to tell us something different. But it wouldn't. Occasionally—once every hour maybe—the wind would drop below twenty knots and we would cheer and beg for a downward trend to begin. While nineteen knots of wind on the boat is still not fun—it's way better than twenty-something. No matter how hard we pleaded, though, the winds would not let up. They held steady at twenty-two, twenty-five, sometimes twenty-seven knots—all through the night.

Each time the bow would rise up to climb a wave I would hang my head down and cringe because I knew the next sound was going to be a loud crash of the hull against the water. Sometimes the boat falls into a wave just right and the crash is more of a gush—not near as gut-wrenching—but other times, the bow will slam into a wall of water with such perfect timing that the boat stops entirely from the collision, or at least it feels that way. Any forward momentum you had comes to an immediate halt. Your body flings forward in reaction and often an ominous ringing of metal follows.

I don't know if it's the shrouds that hold up the mast vibrating from the blow, or the mast itself snapping forward and back like a tuning fork, or perhaps the pulpit crying from the impact, but I hate that sound. It's the sound of something breaking and a reminder that it all can break and fall apart out there. Something can crack, you can take on water and it may be enough to sink the boat. The water really is that strong and while our boat is too, that shrill metal ringing reminds you that it is possible.

"What was that?" Phillip asked, snapping his head to me after we'd heeled hard to port and heard a disturbing crack thunder up from the cabin below. We had the hatch boards in place and the cabin buttoned up to keep the water out, which was spraying and crashing over the dodger, but the sound was loud enough to push through it all. It wasn't a sound I had heard before. While we try to stow away everything below before any passage—because you never know when you may find yourself tipping and heeling in some unexpected swells or even just a big wake—it's common that something wiggles its way out or a cabinet door flings open and things spill out.

This is why most of our dish and pantry items on the boat are plastic, not glass. But you can generally recognize that sound. "Oh, that was the cup cabinet. The Tervises tumbled out again." It's just a sound you've heard before and you know exactly what happened and there's no worry. It's just plastic. But this sound? The thunderous rip that had emanated from our saloon was unlike anything we had heard before. It wasn't cups merely tumbling about. It sounded destructive.

I pushed the companionway hatch back and shined my flashlight down below as I had been doing every ten-or-so minutes to make sure the floorboards weren't floating. There were plenty of cups, pillows, coozies, Tupperware and all sorts of piddly cabinet crap that had busted its way out.Everything was now bouncing around with every kick and buck of our boat, but that didn't matter. It was the thunderous crack we were worried about. Then I saw it.

The weight of the table when we had heeled so far over had ripped the floorboard underneath it up, letting the removable bilge access cover next to it slide underneath—like tectonic plates. The table was wedged up now, almost leaning on the port side settee but there was no way we could fix it in this sea state if the screws had ripped out. With the wind keeping us heeled mostly to port, the wedge was actually a more secure position for her anyway. I relayed the status to Phillip and he decided to leave it. "I don't want you down there trying to wrestle that thing alone. Close her up." So I did.

We carried on like this for hours—metal ringing, hull bashing, more tumbling and crashing of stowed items below—with Phillip manning the helm and me keeping a lookout for other ships or obstructions and manning the flashlight-floorboard watch. After battling these conditions all evening, we decided a little after midnight to pull out of the Gulf as soon as we could and take cover in Charlotte Harbor. It was clear the wind was not going to let up. We had wanted to make it from Tampa Bay all the way to Ft. Myers in roughly twenty-four hours to beat the "numerous thunderstorms" that were set to come in later the following afternoon but—with the horrendous night we were having—it just wasn't looking feasible.

We had both been up for about twenty hours straight at that point. We were beat but the the Wind Gods didn't care. "Please stop, I'm tired," is not a request they will listen to. We just kept beating into black waves. At one point, both Phillip and I caught a whiff of something terribly foul. It smelled like the holding tank. I can't really describe it exactly because it smells like shit, yes, but there's more to it than that. It has the rubber scent of the joker valve in it (the flush mechanism in the toilet, essentially), the stench of the putrid water that sloshes around in the tank and just a hint of, I don't know, corn perhaps? It's just a distinct smell. I'll bet every boat owner can tell you instantly if they get a whiff of their own holding tank.

"Oh God." The words just leaked out of me, because we both knew what it was. I wondered if we had been heeling and tipping so much that the contents of the tank had sloshed hard enough against the screw cap to ooze out. The tank, mind you, is under the bed in the v-berth—the big, absorbent, foam bed in the v-berth. I closed my eyes to try and shut out the thought of what I might find down there. I looked at Phillip to see if he wanted me and my flashlight to go investigate.

"Don't," he said. "There's nothing we can do about it. I'd rather it stay down there." I put my flashlight back in my pocket and remained curled under the dodger watching our perimeter. We didn't smell it again and the thought didn't stay with us for long. While that's disgusting, sure, it was the least of our worries. The integrity of our hull constantly colliding with waves and the ability of our engine to keep us chugging toward Charlotte Harbor easily took precedence over a little shit in the bed. It just didn't matter that much. One more bang of the bow on a wave and the incumbent ringing metal afterward and I forgot all about it. I watched, furiously, as the wind instrument continued to rise. *Twenty-seven. Twenty-eight.*

Hours passed like this and our boat continued to charge toward the inlet, crashing and beating her way to shore. But just when you think things are going to get a little easier, in sailing it seems that's just about the time they get a little harder. Always pushing you to your limits. Here it was, 4:30 a.m. and we were coming into a new harbor at night, in four- to five-foot waves and twenty-five plus miles-per-hour winds. Always an adventure and right when we're both beyond exhausted. The entire night I think I might have fallen asleep for two minutes, twice, out of sheer exhaustion, but then a loud crack on a wave and my head would bang against the companionway and I was up again. Phillip never shut his eyes. Not once. All night long he held that wheel.

He finally took a break around 4:30 a.m. as we approached the channel markers for the inlet to do the one thing that mandated he leave the helm. As I took the wheel for the first time since we had seen yesterday's sun, I was shocked to see how hard it was, how hard it had been for him all of those hours upon hours of wind. Phillip pointed out two lit markers on the horizon—red on starboard and green on port—and told me to stay between them while he went down below. *Easy enough*, I thought. Wrong.

The bow of the boat was tipping and swaying wildly—like it was drawing one of those infinity symbols over and over again. Keeping *the bow* in between those markers might have been easy. Keeping that erratic, ever-shifting infinity symbol between them was not. *How had Phillip done this for so long?* When Phillip emerged again in the cockpit, I tried not to let my relief show but I was thanking every kind of god that he was back. I wanted more than anything for him to take the wheel back, immediately, but I knew how tired he was. What tiny little relief I could afford him was needed and well deserved. I held fast as Phillip sat next to me massaging his arms and rolling his neck for just a few minutes.

"Okay, let's get in here," he said finally as he took my place behind the wheel. I can't say I know how he did it, but somehow Phillip steered that infinity symbol between every marker and brought us safely into Charlotte Harbor in the black of night, leaving the tumultuous waters of the Gulf behind us. We pulled into the pass just as the sun was coming up.

I don't think I've ever been so thankful to see warm rays of sun on Phillip's face. The Captain really stepped up that night bringing us in safe in those conditions. I was so grateful for him. We were both grateful for the boat. She was the real champ. Beating and bashing into those waves all night long so we could stay safe and somewhat dry in the cockpit. She was certainly a hearty broad. Time and again, she has proven to us that we chose the right boat. I can only hope she feels the same about us.

I can't really convey the relief Phillip and I both felt that morning. To this day, that was still our very worst night on passage. Now that the sun was out, the horizon was visible and we were intact—me, Phillip, the boat and every little block, tackle and belt on her. We had all somehow made it through that harrowing night with just a few screws ripped out on the floorboard underneath the table and—much to our delight—no shit in the bed. It must have just been a perfectly aimed whiff that came out the overflow valve on the port side and made its way back to us in the cockpit. *Way to hold it, holding tank!*

We could now see land on the horizon. I've never been so thrilled to see dirt and bushes. We pulled into the harbor and found the first place with a decent swing radius off the ICW to drop anchor and get some rest. *Ahh, rest!* It was around 8:30 a.m. by then and we had both been going twenty-six plus hours. I don't even remember crawling into the v-berth and shutting my eyes. In fact, I'm not even sure how I got *in*to bed. That's not the first time that's happened, though, and I'm sure it won't be the last.

It was a short reprieve though. We hadn't been asleep an hour, at most, before the Captain sprang back into action. He was up, walking around on the deck, making sounds that sounded all too much like he was readying the boat to go. I was cursing him from the v-berth below. I can't remember the last time I felt so exhausted—as if it was going to be physically painful to make my body move. But I finally roused (with only minor pain) and asked him what the plan was.

"We're going," Philip said all cheery and bright. Like it was just another sunny day for a sail. Not like we had just almost died the night before. I kind of wanted to curse him but he was just a little too cute in his euphoria. "It's beautiful out here. Not a cloud in the sky. We can make it to Ft. Myers today."

That man. He's got a sailor's heart, no doubt. But his enthusiasm was infectious. I started nodding my head slowly, then with a little more vigor, like a slow standing clap-ovation. *Yeah. Yeah. Yes. Why, I do believe you're right. I believe we can.* Our plan had been to make it to Ft. Myers that day and—after surviving the most horrendous night we have ever had in the Gulf—we were now here, safe in the ICW, just a short five- or six-hour motor away from our goal. I actually think our heroic feat invigorated us. *By gollie, let's do it! Let's get to Ft. Myers today!* I hopped up topside and started readying the boat right alongside him.

And if there is anything out there like "sea karma" or "Gulf good will" (which I believe there is), we had certainly earned ours because it was a gorgeous day to cruise down the ICW. Phillip was right. The sun was shining, the weather was exquisite and the sights were superb along the ICW—Cayo Costa, Cabbage Key, all of the state parks along the way. We had definitely earned some favors from the Sea Gods. I tied on some swimwear and let my hair down. It was a glorious day on the boat!

The solar shower warmed on the deck all day and we enjoyed a luxurious cockpit shower in the afternoon. It's amazing how much you can take for granted the feeling of just being *clean*. I've showered a thousand times in my life, I'm sure. I hope at least. But ninety-nine percent of them felt like a chore when I was dragging myself out of bed at 5:00 a.m. for another long day at the office. Stop the alarm, roll out of bed, jump in the shower, throw on a suit, go to the office. Then do it all again tomorrow. Lather, rinse, repeat. There was nothing rejuvenating or invigorating about the shower because it was just part of my everyday routine.

But when you pull yourself out of that routine and find yourself bashing into rough salty waves all night, in a wet, uncomfortable cockpit, a shower is suddenly a revelation. Your own dry, clean skin is the best thing you could possibly imagine. A long, rough passage makes you appreciate so many little luxuries that—in all the hustle and bustle of a stressful day-to-day life on land—seem perfunctory. And I love that about cruising. The long, wet, uncomfortable stretches make those moments—when you're dry, warm and curled up with a book and a hot cup of coffee—feel like one of the best hours of your life.

The irony is I spent so many hours warm, dry, with a hot cup of coffee in hand, reading, yet wishing the entire time that I was somewhere else. I took the experience for granted because I had it every day. But when the experience is rare and juxtaposed with one like we'd had the night before in the unforgiving waters of the Gulf, it is suddenly realized and appreciated for all its previously unseen worth. What was once just a mindless daily activity, now brings pure pleasure.

We spent a beautiful sunny day motoring the ICW through Pine Island Sound, over to San Carlos Bay, by Sanibel Island, and under the Sanibel Causeway Bridge to Ft. Myers Beach. The crew were really excited to see Ft. Myers Beach in the distance. *We made it!* The same day we originally had expected to nonetheless, which was shocking considering the night we'd had. It was strange how the howling winds and treacherous waters of the Gulf now seemed a million miles away. Nothing could phase us here in Ft. Myers!

We made our way under the bridge and snagged a mooring ball in the Matanzas Harbor which was, again, another pleasant surprise—only fifteen dollars a day, with a dingy dock, restrooms, shower, laundry, pump-out, you name it. That place rocked. I was so glad we had paid our dues the night before—fighting and leaping our way across the Gulf—because I think we racked up just enough good will to save us from one last catastrophe: a storm of biblical proportions.

Once we were secure on the ball, we set about our typical just-dropped-the-hook routine. We straighten up the cockpit from passage and stow away the anchor gear. I often snap a few shots of our new locale and Phillip sets to making us up some boat drinks. We didn't quite get to the cocktails this time but I was glad I had taken a few pictures because the comparison afterward was eerie. Not ten minutes after we got secure on the ball in Ft. Myers, a shelf cloud appeared on the horizon—ominous and lurking. Recall those "numerous thunderstorms" we were trying to beat when we left Tampa? Yeah, I forgot about those too after our twenty-six hour bash across the Gulf. But here they were.

The sky grew a sinister, boding gray as the shelf cloud rolled toward us. Then the rain came in sheets. Torrential, hard-hitting sheets, burying the boats around us. I really felt like I was going to start seeing animals, paired in twos, running along the shore to safety. The last register I saw on the wind instrument before I took cover below was forty-two.

Phillip and I hunkered down in the cabin as the rains pounded our boat. We each looked out the port lights but could not see a single boat next to us. They were completely hidden in thundering sheets of white rain. We couldn't even tell which way we were pointing as the boat groaned and tugged on her mooring ball. The storm was intense and immediate. Frightening but thrilling at the same time. And while the thought didn't strike me until the storm had passed, I can only wonder now what we would have done if that storm had hit fifteen minutes earlier.

Fifteen minutes prior, we had been out there—motor-sailing with full canvas out—making our way into Ft. Myers. What if we hadn't been able to reef or drop the sails in time? I don't think I want to know what forty-two-mile-per-hour winds can do to your mainsail. What if we had been in the tight channel when that wall of wind hit? And the rain! There would have been zero visibility. I didn't think about these things until after the storm passed but they gave me this sickening, goose-bump feeling that made me shiver. If there really is such a thing as boat karma, I can only imagine we had earned just enough the night before to have brought us to that ball at that very moment, minutes before the storm hit.

But—as fast as it came—it went. The sun came back out and we found ourselves high and dry, safe and secure. Now it was time for a drink or three. The bridge and boats around us came back into view. Phillip and I were astounded at the pictures. I had taken some from the cabin below during the storm. The rain was so thick, we couldn't see boats that were twenty yards from us. An entire bridge on the horizon—less than a mile away—was non-existent.

It had been one hell of a storm. But, as it seems is often the case, wicked weather brings breathtaking sunsets. It was almost surreal to watch our view transform from ominous, brewing clouds and sheets of pelting rain to now—a serene sunset, the sky stained with shocking pinks and burning yellows.

It was so beautiful it silenced us. We both sat in awe, enjoying the slow movement of our chests rising and falling in gratitude, as the realization started to sink in. We had made it all the way down to Ft. Myers—by boat! Our next stop was Key West. We would be making the jump across the Gulf in just a couple of days. *This was it!* We were on it—the trip we had been planning for months, preparing and provisioning for for weeks, dreaming about for years. And here we were. Truly living it. But Phillip and I both knew we were enjoying every stop, every step and every breathtaking sunset along the way. It was the destination that had motivated us, initially, to set our sights on the sea, but it was now the journey that was capturing us, calling us onward, always, for more—to anywhere and nowhere in particular by boat.

I couldn't imagine a thing in the world that I was wanting for in that moment. I had everything I needed—a healthy body, this beautiful boat, the freedom to go places in it with a companion who challenged and inspired me. And as soon as the thought struck me, I started smiling to myself at the memory. It's one my brother, John, and I always conjure when we're feeling pretty damn content, when we're feeling there's nothing more in the world we could possibly *want*.

"I want a bun," he said—in this whiny little brat voice—as he pushed the plated burger away from him like it was rotten. "And cheese." John and I each took another huge bite out of instinct. We were mighty content with our cheese-less burgers and we wanted to make sure Mom knew it. *No problems here.*

"And burgers don't come on bread," he continued.

What a little shit? In our house they did. Anything sandwich-like did. It was always one of those white perfectly square loaves that looks like it came out of a machine and costs ninety-eight cents. Or at least it did back then. I don't think it was Wonder Bread but it was yellow with a bunny on the package. I do remember that.

It was Bunny bread and so many other things. Two Bunny slices was a burger bun. One folded over was a hot dog bun. Smash one flat and it was a tortilla. Pick out the little blue mold spots and it was sourdough. It was everything. Actual dome-shaped, sesame buns for our burgers was a luxury John and I just weren't used to. And it's a good damn thing too. If having special sesame buns made you shove aside that awesome Bunny burger because you don't feel it's good enough, then I'll take the bread.

I think John and I were literally frightened for him. Jack Eichenberger. I will never forget that name. He just sounds like a brat, right? Maybe that's just my memory tainting it but he definitely was. Jack was a neighbor that lived down the street from us back in Clovis, New Mexico. We didn't play with him too much because—well, like I said—he was just bratty. And one time he told mom on us for jumping off the roof onto the trampoline and got John and I in a heap of trouble. Thank goodness he was never around when we did it with the bowling ball.

Although we still played with him begrudgingly when the occasion arose, we never let Jack jump with us on the trampoline after that and this was his first and last time to ever stay over for dinner. Mom had cooked up some burgers for us kids—me, my brother, John, our cousin Jay, and now Jack who had lingered. Now Jay stayed over all the time. Like John and I, he was wise to mom's ways. The minute Jack shoved his plate away, Jay, John and I all perked up. We knew Jack was about to set her off. The three of us made motions behind her putting our breadburgers to our mouths and taking big, exaggerated bites, waving our hands encouraging Jack to do the same. *Dude, just eat the burger. Trust us.*

"Oh, okay," Mom started in and we could already hear the tone. She was loading her weapon. "Well you want dinner, right Jack? You're hungry?" Her voice sounded sweet. But that was the problem. Mom's voice was never sweet. It was sharp, strong, clear—not sweet. She had now pulled back the hammer and was preparing to fire.

"Yes," Jack said. "I want dinner. It's just ... I don't eat burgers on bread," he said it again. Jack had no idea the hell he was about to unleash. John, Jay and I kept eating—our burgers almost swallowed whole by now—watching the scene play out with big white eyes.

"Well tonight you do. And if you complain you'll eat two."

Jack blinked.

"And we don't have any cheese."

Her sweetness was gone now. That was Mom speaking right there. But she wasn't being harsh. It was just the truth. Fancy little sliced cheese was not something we had often either. We didn't have sliced cheese. Or buns. It was like Jack couldn't comprehend it. He stared at her in disbelief, his face conveying his thoughts so clearly: *Had she not just heard me? Burgers don't come on bread and I want cheese.* But our faces conveyed ours even clearer: *Did you not hear her? Eat the damn burger!* John, Jay and I again took another collective bite. We'd tried to help as best we could. If Jack couldn't take the hint, he was on his own.

Jack didn't say a word. I think he was stunned. I don't think an adult had ever talked to him like that, which explained a lot. No wonder he was such a little snot. He watched in horror as Mom pushed the plate back toward him, sat back in the chair next to him and lit a cigarette—her eyes never leaving his. That's when Jack knew. She was going to sit there and watch him until he ate the whole thing.

"Well go on," Mom said after her first puff. "You said you were hungry." Jack's lower lip started to quiver and we knew he was about to lose it. Big, bulbous tears started to form on his lower lids, threatening to spill over. Those weren't tears of embarrassment. I think he truly was afraid of her, as he should have been. You didn't push food back with a snarly little face at our house. That's not how kids behaved.

"I ... I don't ... " Jack started and Mom cut him off.

"Tonight you do," Mom said, interrupting him with her resolve. "One more word and it's two."

I hate to say it but John, Jay and I were now having fun watching. This was a great show. And it was just a burger—a perfectly good one too. They're great on bread. All he had to do was eat it. We didn't feel sorry for him anymore. Mom was treating him right. She had been clear. After a long minute, Jack finally picked up his bread-burger and took a little bird bite—chewing with a look of disgust—like it was the worst thing he'd ever put in his mouth.

Mom just sat there, taking long draws, watching him. Jack sniveled and sniffed and ate slowly at first but once he realized she was really going to sit there and watch him—until every burger bite was gone—he wised up and started eating faster. Soon the burger was gone and Jack just kind of sat there, looking at Mom wondering what she would do to him next. But there was nothing more she needed. It was a simple expectation—eat your food without complaint—and once he'd done it, Mom was satisfied.

"Take your plate to the sink now," was all she said as she snubbed out her cigarette in an ashtray and left the table. Jack pouted his way across the kitchen, put his plate gingerly in the sink and wiped a tear away from his face with the back of his hand. The boys and I followed in behind him and dropped our plates in, avoiding eye contact with Jack. He didn't stay long after that and he darn sure never stayed over for dinner again.

I didn't feel sorry for him though. If anything I was proud of Mom. Jack deserved it. You don't act like that when you're a guest at someone else's house. John and I knew better. We also knew to eat what Mom made us because that's all you were going to get for dinner. Be it bread-burgers, bread-hot dogs, just bread and margarine—you ate it. It was either that or do without. Mom made sure we were grateful for what little we did have.

We didn't need our burgers to have a bun or cheese or come in a McBox with a McToy. And don't even get me started on super-sizing. Bottom line is those burgers were perfect just the way they were—Bunny Bread and all. I know Mom didn't choose a simple lifestyle for us as part of some trendy, philosophical plan—it was just a product of the way things were—but I'm still grateful for the experience and the lessons John and I took away from it. Thanks to Mom, the less we had the more we seemed to appreciate it. We didn't feel like our lives were lacking anything. When it comes to superfluous McStuff: want not.

I want cheese. I chuckled to myself in the cockpit. That was just funny. And I loved how Mom just sat there and watched him without remorse. She was trying to teach him but he would never admit that burger was perfectly fine without the cheese. He can't help himself. The Jack Eichenbergers of the world will always want. It starts with a bun and cheese but it soon progresses to a new bike like the neighbor's, an expensive Trapper Keeper to start junior high, a new car when he gets his license, a big fancy job that pays six figures and finally, a McMansion with $260.00 solar-lights for the walkway. They will always want, want, want until it's all stacked around them like cinderblocks and they forget what truly brought them happiness in the first place.

I can't really explain how life starts to warp you. It just does. Over time you just morph. I know because I did it. I wanted and acquired and shopped and bought until I found myself brainwashed by it all: "This is my cell and this is my cot." This is my Cox cable package and this is my million dollar life-insurance policy—you know, for when I die and can't spend money anymore.

I smiled at the bread-burger memory as I sat in the cockpit sipping my first crisp, cool glass of wine in two days. I wasn't wanting for anything right now. Not a damn thing. I was just grateful. Nothing like a tough-as-nails mom and surviving a wicked storm on your boat to make you feel grateful—for every breath, every moment, every sip of wine, every ray of sun on your skin. I was so proud of myself for being there, for bringing myself there, for fighting my way to that moment. It seemed I was going to make all of those rainbows-and-sunshine goals I had been talking about really happen.

I was also thankful for my youth and my healthy body that had allowed me to embark on such adventures. Little did I know that would change tomorrow. It's sometimes easy to forget that in one snap moment—with just the slightest stroke of unfortunate luck—everything can change. As much as we try to control it—to structure, plan and prepare for it—life truly is that unpredictable. But isn't that what makes moments like this so rich? When you realize it's all just as good as you could possibly have imagined it to be? You want for nothing more when you're reminded it could all be gone tomorrow.

CHAPTER TWENTY

"Annie, Are You Okay?"

"**H**uh?" he would say as he inhaled quickly and flinched himself awake, acting as though I had woken him with a question. I'm lucky he didn't flinch his wine right out of his glass while he was at it. Phillip is eerily good at flinching without spilling. I have to admit, though, I sure had fun watching him nod off again and again. It's amazing how quickly you can fall asleep when you're really that exhausted. You wake up, but you're out again in mere seconds.

The last sunset-pink slivers were just streaking down under the bridge at Ft. Myers and I believe it was somewhere during our second round of sundowners when the captain started to nod off. I said the sunset was beautiful. I didn't say it was invigorating. If anything, it was only furthering our exhausted state. Minus the quick one-hour nap in Charlotte Harbor, we were still rounding out a near thirty-hour stint and the adrenaline had clearly worn off.

Phillip's head started to dip and bob and he shook himself awake a time or two as the sun set. It was around 6:00 p.m. and we were both fading fast. Phillip kicked back on the settee to "close his eyes for just a minute" while I threw some dinner together—one of our go-to's on the boat: chicken tiki masala with naan. The funny thing was, though, I was banging around, clanging pots, opening cabinets, shutting doors, doing a great number of things—any one of which would usually have the Captain sitting upright, looking around—but none of it phased him that night. He was out. Gone. Done for. Knee-deep in REMs.

I roused him for supper and watched with a wicked grin as his head bobbed and wobbled above his plate and he shoved clumsy mouthfuls in, barely taking the time to chew before swallowing. His entire plate was gone in under six minutes and he was back in a deep sleep within the seventh. I have to admit it was pretty entertaining. I have never seen him that tired. We both fell asleep around 6:45 p.m. and slept till about 8:00 a.m. the next morning.

We had big plans that morning to dinghy to shore, go explore Ft. Myers Beach, get some lunch, check out the facilities. You know, get the lay of our new land. But, unfortunately, when we decided to leave the "house" that morning the "car" wouldn't start. That's pretty much what your dinghy is when you're living on a boat: your car. Your means to shore. While we probably could have rowed to the dinghy dock, it was about two hundred yards away, against the current. And we were planning to stay there in the mooring field for a couple of days before making the jump to Key West. *Sure would be nice to have a car.*

So Phillip set to it. He cranked and pulled and yanked and cursed that thing—for half an hour at least. When he looked in the oil window, Phillip could see the oil in the outboard was murky, which meant it had probably taken on water—likely during our horrendous night in the Gulf. It was mounted on the stern rail but there had been some some pretty tall waves crashing about. To this day we are still not sure exactly how that happened. But *c'est la vie*. Water had gotten in the oil, so we had to change it. And boy was it murky. The oil almost looked like chocolate milk. Phillip ended up changing it three times before it began to look anything like actual oil again.

Then he tried to crank her again. She would sputter and fire and run for a bit and then die. So he would crank her again. She would sputter and fire and run for a bit and then die. So he would crank her again, and so on. *What was I doing, you ask?* Laughing and taking video of course. I know, I'm terrible. But it was funny. And there was nothing really else I could do to help him. Either I could pull the cord or he could and she was going to decide to either run or not.

The great thing was all of our boat neighbors started to get in on the action. They had been watching Phillip jack around with that engine for about two hours now, listening to her crank and die, crank and die, crank and die. Several of them would throw their arms up and cheer when she cranked and heckle her when she died. "Booo!" It was better than football. And—when the outboard would crank and Phillip would get going a bit—other boaters would circle the wagons and check on him to make sure he didn't get stranded.

Boater: "You got her running there, partner?"

Phillip: "I believe so, but don't go too far. Thanks."

We even had some folks swing by and drop off what they called their "magic juice," some special lube they always spray on the carburetor of their outboard when she gives them fits. Because everyone's outboard gives them fits. It should just say in the manual: SOMETIMES SHE WILL CRANK, SOMETIMES SHE WILL NOT, AND THERE'S NO REASON WHY. That would at least squander the hope that she's going to run like she's *supposed* to.

But the Captain was persistent. He stuck with it and finally got her purring. Then he started zipping around all over the mooring field, lavishing in the cheers and hollers building around him—the roar of the crowd! It was hilarious. But it was also done. The car had finally started, so it was time to go ashore. We packed that puppy up while she was running and made our way to dry land. We stuck a little thank-you note to the "magic juice" can and dropped it off on our neighbor's boat. Such fun the exchanges you have with fellow cruisers. Then we were on our way to Ft. Myers Beach. It was high time for a margarita. All of that laughing and cheering and pic-snapping was tiring!

Ft. Myers was fun. We poked around the little bars and shops and strolled along the beach. I even spotted a bar called Top 'O the Mast. *Hey, I've been there. Twice!* We spent a couple of days lounging on the boat, playing ashore, washing pretty much everything aboard and getting rested up for another passage. Key West was calling and we were ready to go. While we love being on anchor (or on the ball, or at a marina, or however we find ourselves stopped and secure for the time being), what we really love is sailing. Getting that boat going. She loves it too. It's what she was built for. We woke to a beautiful sunrise on our last morning in Ft. Myers Beach, brewed our coffee, filled our mugs and tossed our line off the ball. *We are going to do some sailing today, kids!*

"I see you smiling," Phillip said. It was starting to become an inside joke on the trip, which—I guess if it's just Phillip and me—there really is no 'outside' but it was fun to share a known-but-unspoken sentiment. I just smiled bigger and kept sipping my coffee as we made our way out the pass.

We expected about a thirty-hour passage to Key West. We left Ft. Myers Beach around 8:00 a.m. with plans to arrive in Key West around mid- to late-morning the following day. While there is a mooring field near Key West, the Captain had booked us at the A&B Marina in Key West Bight. It is an awesome location in Key West. Excellent facilities, right in the center of all the downtown action and no wet dinghy ride from the mooring field. He figured, since it was our first time there by boat, and this was the expected highlight of the trip, then might as well splurge a little, huh? "Go big or go home!" he said. *Isn't he great?* It was a gorgeous morning for a sail too. Blue waters, a bright sky and a nice seven-knot wind quartering our starboard bow. Of all the things that could have happened that day, I never would have guessed this would be one.

You ever have one of those days that starts out perfectly normal? You begin your typical routine; you go about your business—completely unaware that *this* day is probably going to stick out in your mind for the rest of your meager existence. Everything seems so routine, so mundane and then BAM! It happens. Whatever it is—a car accident, a fire, an unexpected encounter, you win the lottery (let's all hope!)—it's something that makes *that* day stand out among the hundreds of bland, uniform days that preceded it.

I guess being on this big trip to the Keys—which was a daily adventure—sort of changes that equation, in that every single one of our days on this trip held something new. Something that will probably stick out in my mind for decades to come, but still I thought we were just going to get underway that morning and make passage to Key West. I thought we might see a shark, perhaps run into some weather, catch a fish, or some other predictable Gulf adventure I was mentally prepared for. But I was not prepared for this. As often as I say it—"Sailing's such an adventure! It's so challenging but fulfilling. Expect the unexpected!"—I guess I forget to do it, because I never expected this.

Remember Hal? Running around with the shackle panties in his mouth? Yeah, him. *You turd!* Remember how I said that was Part One of what apparently needed to be a two-part lesson to teach us not to unclip our main halyard from the mainsail? Well this was Part Two. Now, we never (ever!) unclip the halyard from the mainsail. It stays clipped all the time. Did you get that? All. The. Time. Now we just pull some slack out and cinch it back away from the mast so it doesn't bang, but Hal remains securely clipped to the sail—say it with me: "All the time."

Back then, though, we used to unclip it every time we dropped the sail and secure it to the deck. After the Hal incident, we thought we had wised up. "You know, we should never try to clip that thing while underway," I remembered telling Phillip, as we were de-briefing after the mid-sea mast climb on our way to Clearwater, "We should always clip it to the sail *before* we leave."

"You're right," Phillip said. "Good call."

Ah, gold stars all around. We're so smart!

No we're not. An even better idea would be to never unclip it in the first place. That way it will *never* go whipping around and you never have to go leaping, lunging and mast-climbing to retrieve it. That is how we do it now, but that is not how we did it back then. This is precisely how "back then" became just that.

Once we made it out of the pass, we wanted to hoist the sails and do some sailing. We'd already forgot our new clip-before-you-go mandate and I had even chuckled when I went topside and saw our main halyard clipped to the deck while we were what? Underway. *Tssk, tssk crew.* But it was fine. The conditions were pretty calm—just a little two- to three-foot chop, bright sunny skies. We'd clipped it plenty of times underway before and this would be the last. We'd get it right next time. This is what I told myself as I unclipped the halyard from the deck and headed to the mast to clip it to the mainsail.

Unfortunately, and this is yet another reason to not unclip your main halyard and secure it to the deck—all lessons are free today, you can thank me later—all of the slack in the halyard from the mast down to the deck whipped around and got caught on the starboard spreader. This had happened before, though—particularly when the wind is on your stern and is blowing the halyard fore-ward toward the bow—so I wasn't particularly worried. I knew what to do. I let out more slack and embarked in an ancient rope-whipping dance (do recall my country roots), that thankfully freed the halyard.

You would think the hard part is over but I have to move quickly to get the slack pulled out so the line remains free and untangled and we can raise the main. I'm holding the shackle end of the halyard in my left hand and pulling down the slack at the mast with my right. Now I'd like to think I had a pretty good hand-hold on the halyard in my left hand but my focus was on my right, quickly pulling and tugging down the slack so it wouldn't get caught again on the spreader. I certainly didn't want it to get caught on the spreader! I also certainly didn't want it to get yanked out of my left hand and go flying but that's exactly what it did. The minute it happened a sickening chill ran through my body.

How fucking stupid! I had yanked it out of my very own hand. With everything we had been through on this trip with that stinking halyard I was not—mind you *not!*—going to let Hal get away. *Not this time, you turd!* Since we were underway, I knew if that bastard got away, it would mean another mid-sea mast-climb for this little mate. And while that experience was invigorating and inspiring—*when it was over* and my feet were planted back firmly on the deck—when you're up there, swinging wildly back and forth clung to a fifty-foot mast, your one and only thought is: *Get me the hell down!* Followed immediately by, *I'm never doing this again!*

I was not going to let that happen again. I was going to *get* that halyard! Nothing was going to stop me! *Get over here you mangy mutt!* Hal was swinging around just out of reach. I didn't think the Captain knew what had happened yet and I thought if I could retrieve it and snap it on the sail before he knew, that would be even better. I jumped up on top of the boom. Yes, the boom. I told you: I was going to get that damn halyard if it killed me. Sadly, it nearly did.

Up there, I was eye-level with it. I had a fighting chance! I just needed it to swing my direction. In those random, bouncy two- to three-foot waves, it could happen. I believed it would happen. It came so close several times and I almost had it.

"ANNIE!" Phillip shouted from the cockpit. *Shit!* He'd done seen me by then. "Be careful!" he bellowed. It was not a request. It was a demand. And I was. I felt like I was. My feet were planted firmly on the sail. I had a good handhold on the lazy jack line for balance and the halyard was *right there*. I had touched it twice. I was going to get that effin halyard!

And I knew not to tug too hard on the lazy jack line. After we had ripped the one on the starboard side clean off the spreader during our very first night in the Gulf on our way to Port St. Joe, I knew it didn't take much to pop one off. So I was just using it for balance. I was. I swear. Until the halyard came swinging toward me. Finally! *There it is!* I could reach it.

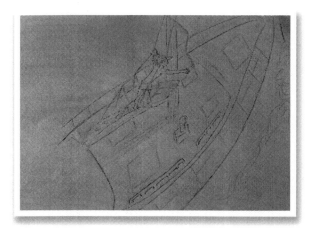

I stretched a hand out toward it, leaned out with all of my might … then SNAP!

With the halyard in sight—my fingers finally feeling the threads on it—I am sure my light little for-balance-only hold on the lazy jack line became a full-on death grip and full-weight-dependent tug. Just as I clinched my hand around the main halyard shackle, I heard a loud snap. I can't remember what I saw or how my body reacted, but I felt a sickening thud.

The next thing I remember, I'm raising myself from a crumpled position on the starboard deck (between the cabin and the lifelines) with the main halyard in my right hand. Phillip stepped out from the behind the bimini with a horrified look on his face, his voice commanding: "Annie, are you okay?"

"I, I …" I couldn't really form a complete sentence. It was like I didn't know how, much less *what* to say if I even could. I just held onto the halyard and laid there.

"ANNIE, ARE YOU OKAY?" Phillip persisted, his voice now a stern shout.

"I don't know," I finally told him. Because I didn't.

CHAPTER TWENTY-ONE

Life is Not

The first thing I remember seeing after the fall was the big, white meat of my arm. Between the time I hit, opened my eyes and blinked several times at it, my left forearm had grown twice its size. I knew it had hit ... something and I knew it hurt, but to see it swell—so *suddenly*—truly frightened me. I honestly thought it was broken. I didn't know what else could cause such immediate swelling. It was so fat at the base.

In all of the wild antics of my youth—gymnastics, barrel racing, cheerleading, jello wrestling and other numerous, countless stupid decisions in college—I had yet to break a bone. *Knock on wood.* I was thinking this might be the end of that lucky streak. I clenched my fist a time or two and rolled my wrist. While my entire forearm was numb and throbbing, everything seemed to be working fine, so I decided the bones were at least visibly intact.

"I'm okay ... I think," I said to Phillip finally, then repeated it to myself for reassurance. "I'm okay." Just as John had said to me when I was lying on the ground beneath that tall tree in New Mexico trying to breathe life back into my lungs: "You're okay, you got that?" It wasn't a request. And just as we had lifted my little Care Bears shirt and inspected my red swathed torso, I now gave my belly and appendages a good once-over and didn't see any blood anywhere so it appeared there would be no need—this time—for a toilet-paper mummy wrap. That was a good sign.

I heard Phillip set the auto-pilot so he could come on deck to check on me and I held the halyard out to him first thing. If I had risked life and limb for that bastard, yet again, I was damn sure going to get it in safe hands. At least I had brought it down with me when I fell. *One point for Annie.* But I couldn't recall the moment I grabbed it exactly. It was like some void. I don't remember blacking out or anything like that. It just felt like time had been spliced—like a movie reel—the incident was just cut out and the film put back together. One second I was leaning out, reaching for the halyard, then—Snap!—and I was on the deck, holding it in my hand. The snap then got me thinking about the fall. *Why had I fallen? What had snapped?*

"The lazy jack snapped," Phillip said, as if hearing my thoughts, as he stepped up on deck. I didn't even look up—assuming I even *could* turn around to see it. I felt a little like my six-year-old self after the tree fall. My arm was all scraped up and I was struggling a bit to breathe and turn my head to the left. But I knew exactly what Phillip meant. The rough winds we had encountered on our way into Port St. Joe had caused the mainsail to put too much force on the starboard lazy jack line, ripping the rivet right off the spreader.

What we gathered from that incident was that the lazy jack lines are not intended to hold extensive weight. We have since learned—from our trusty rigger back in Pensacola—that this design is intentional so that the rivet for the lazy jack line will fail before excessive strain is placed on the spreader. Makes sense. The spreader is a far more crucial component of the boat's overall integrity than a lazy little sail-catching line.

But clearly this riveting (no pun intended) fact somehow escaped me as I was doing my circus act up on the boom, reaching with all my might, one strained out-stretched hand to the halyard, the other bearing all of my weight on the not-to-be-tugged-too-hard-upon portside lazy jack line. "Well now they match," I said from my crumpled position on the deck. We now had two busted lazy jack lines and we hadn't even made it to the Keys yet. Worse, though, we now had a potentially busted mate.

Phillip began lifting and inspecting my limbs gingerly, asking what I could move without pain, what joints were capable of bending the way they used to and so on. "Let's get you back in the cockpit," he said as he eased me up. I was thrilled and amazed to find I hadn't broken anything. There weren't bones jutting out through jagged skin or anything gruesome like that, which would have been totally possible considering my fall. It's not a great height from atop the boom to the lower deck, maybe five or so feet, but there are a lot of obstacles on the way down.

I knew my left arm had taken the brunt of it. It was already ridiculously swollen and starting to develop huge purple swaths and welts from my armpit down to my wrist. But, again, I could bend and straighten it and make a fist, so I was optimistic. As I started to stand, though, I discovered a new pain—my knee. It seemed it too had hit something and it, too, was already swollen. Phillip gave me that same look my brother had as I raised my ragged body—worry and disbelief with a little bit of how-could-you? He laid a sturdy hand on my shoulder and told me to sit tight for a minute while he secured the halyard. *That was the whole point, right?*

He then helped me to my feet so I could hobble back to the cockpit. Like my arm, my knee was numb and throbbing but it appeared to be working. Phillip seemed to be comforted, slightly, by the fact that I was somewhat satisfactorily mobile but I hated to see such a look of worry and anger on his face. While I had managed to get that bleeping halyard down, it was at a serious cost. It was clear the captain was not impressed with my ... heroism.

We set me down in the cockpit for a good once-over. The arm had developed some gnarly purple streaks where (I can only assume) it sheared down the lifelines on the way to the deck. It was fat and painful, but—like I said—working. The knee had developed this strange ping-pong ball-shaped lump on the left side of my kneecap.

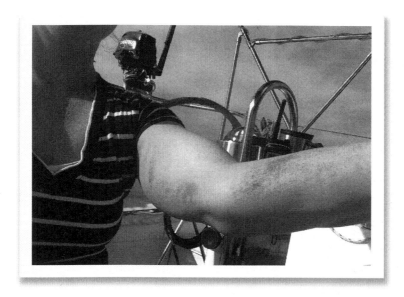

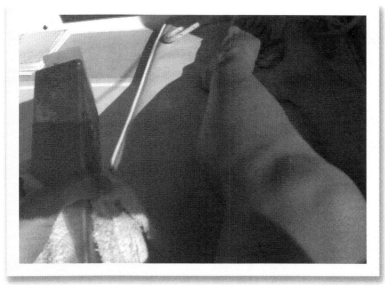

I wasn't even sure what to make of that. *Why the perfect round lump? Why swelling in such an isolated spot?* I had injured my knee before—this very knee (the left) actually, years and years ago. I tore my ACL while tumbling in high school and had it surgically repaired back in 2000. When that happened, the whole knee swelled instantly, like a cantaloupe. But just the year before, I had sprained the MCL in my right knee during my first attempt at skiing. And, again, it had set off the cantaloupe sequence. Those injuries both caused global swelling of the whole knee—not just a perfectly segregated ping-pong ball lump. I was a little worried about the lump. But all we knew to do at the time was ice everything and see what developed.

As I sat there, looking back on it, I couldn't promise I wouldn't jump back up on that boom to try and retrieve a swinging halyard. It is such a monstrous chore to retrieve it once it inches its way out of your reach—but I guess the best I can say is I hope never to let go of the halyard again. We already knew this lesson, we'd learned it several times, but it just *happens*—sometimes as a result of rocking waves or other hazards, other times just as a result of a senseless human error. It is entirely possible to just accidentally let go of something. I mean, you have hands to hold things, but they're human hands, so they err. I am hopeful, at least, that we have now sufficiently modified our halyard-shackling procedure to eliminate the frequency of the latter.

As a direct result of this incident—and from good advice after we told a trusted sailing friend, Bottom-Job Brandon, *about* this incident—we now leave the main halyard clipped to the mainsail at all times. Repeat it with me: all times. We just pull it off the mast a bit and clip it to one of the starboard lazy jack lines so it doesn't bang. That's it. It's actually an infinitely easier and safer halyard routine. But what did it take for us to learn that? Apparently a Frankenstein butterfly contraption, a dog-chasing shackle panties party, a mid-sea mast climb and—now—a busted-up mate.

In sailing, you learn something new every day. Sometimes it's something you've been doing for years but one day you just find a little better way of doing it and it makes life just a little easier. It's all about getting out there and doing it—making mistakes and learning—but continuing to do it. A fine example is our stack-pack lazy-jack fix. If you recall, when the lazy-jack line on the starboard side busted, the Captain came up with an ingenuous way to raise it back up using a somewhat-of-a spare line (the staysail halyard), so that we still had a functioning stack pack for the remainder of our trip to the Keys. He's kind of smart like that sometimes. And, since we'd done it the last time, he knew exactly how to "fix" the one I had now busted on the portside: he raised it back up to its near exact previous position with the spinnaker halyard.

"We're running out of spare lines on the mast though," Phillip said to me with a smile when he finished re-rigging the portside lazy jack and came back to check on me in the cockpit, which I had to chuckle at. With all of our rigged-up modifications and me now laid up on a pile of ice, the *Plaintiff's Rest* crew was a bit of a comedy of errors. But we were still going and isn't that the whole point?

For the time being I was numb but not broken and feeling pretty damn lucky for it. We decided to hold the ice on for the first hour or so to attack the swelling, then we would remove it and have me move about a bit later in the day to assess the real damage. I laid back on the ice, the captain handled the sails and we set out for a beautiful day of sailing toward Key West.

All you could see was beautiful blue water to the edge of every horizon and all I could feel was gratitude. I knew how incredibly lucky I was. I could have pulled up off that deck with an arm twisted backward and a white bony shard or three sticking out of it. If that had happened, I would have likely been spending the next week in the hospital back in Ft. Myers. Better yet, what if I had broken my back, snapped my neck, sheared some nerves and found myself never sailing anywhere again,

much less Key West. It was possible. It's always possible. Realizing that and living accordingly is the takeaway. Every moment matters.

I learned it from Big Mom's jaded, jaundice photo shoot: death is inevitable. Life, however, is not. It was just dumb luck I fell the way that I did and survived it as well as I had. And what a hell of a brute body to take that full-frontal impact like that and stand up and walk away from it. I was feeling like the luckiest damn sailor alive. I diligently put the ice back on and kept everything elevated and stable as we sailed toward an endless blue horizon, hoping I would be able to walk tomorrow.

CHAPTER TWENTY-TWO

My Tunnel, My Time

"Can you put weight on it?"

It had been over four hours since my crash that morning to the deck and we figured it was time to run me through a few paces to see what my battered body was capable of. Despite the stinging of the ice, it did feel incredible to be back out in the Gulf. Otto was holding great, we were making good time and the sea state was perfect. Other than my sad condition, it was really one of the most exquisite sails we've ever had in the Gulf. Like that sunset after the storm in Ft. Myers. Cruising seems to throw at you all at once, both ends of the extreme.

What's done is done though. I had fallen. I couldn't change that. *Might as well assess the damage*, I told myself. I was sure there was going to be some (potentially severe) soft-tissue injury to my knee. The ping pong lump was just freaky and fluid-filled. I couldn't imagine that was a good sign. And what an annoyance on a boat! When it's always up and down the companionway, kneel down here, squat there. I couldn't imagine losing the full function of such a crucial joint during our big-damn-deal trip to the Keys. I know, I know. I said I knew how lucky I was to be alive and not broken. That doesn't mean I didn't worry and pout a little about it. I was nervous and anxious about my limbs, though, and my ability to fulfill my duties as First Mate for the remainder of the trip, so I rose for an inspection.

Whether it was the beautiful sea state and our accompanying sailing high, or just my damn impressive durability, after a couple of hours on ice Phillip and I were both ecstatic to see I was pretty functional. The knee would shoot a hot twinge of pain and a emit a slight pop when I knelt down on it—not great but not life threatening it seemed. The arm was hideous—all fat and squishy with meaty slashes of purple and rust red—but it really didn't hurt that much. It was just ugly and I was fine with that. I couldn't make a tight fist without pain but the elbow straightened and bent just fine, the wrist swiveled.

I would have said she was running at about ninety percent. In all, after the first assessment, we started to think I might be okay after some rest and healing time. We kept with the ice-and-elevate routine throughout the afternoon and I'm sure that was a big impetus to my recovery. The Captain was adamant about it, fetching me food and water and my book and handling all the sails himself.

We were still on a perfect heading easing into the night. Our bellies were full and our hearts were content. We were really out there. Sailing across the Gulf. When the sun rose again, we would finally be there—the Florida Keys! Two more assessments throughout the afternoon showed the ping-pong ball lump on my knee had gone down considerably and the kneeling pain lessened. The left arm was still ugly but functional. The crew thought it was likely I was going to make a full recovery in time and deemed it an absolute freaking miracle. Other than the ice-and-ease-it routine, things were pretty close to being back to normal as we began our night shifts that evening which for me begins with a little Lionel Richie.

"Gonna be a sweet sound! Come. In. Down. On the night shift!"

I started singing it well before sunset. I often do. Phillip won't admit it, but he kind of likes it. I've caught him singing it once or twice. Even when we're tired and sleepy, we still get a little excited about our night shifts on the boat. There's just something magical about them. Phillip and I do two hours on, two hours off. And, when you wake, you're often a little groggy, slightly annoyed about the 2:00 a.m. wake-up, but once you get your bearings and get settled in at the helm, it's transportive. You feel so exquisitely alone—in this great big mysterious body of water under a smattering of stars. Sometimes a dolphin will come up and breathe the night air right along with you. You're often tired and a little worried about the boat but you feel so alive. Everything is crisp.

Some nights are tiring though. You don't really want to get up *again* after just an hour and a half of sleep, at four in the morning to hold the wheel in heavy winds. You don't really *want* to, but you do, because you know you're on an adventure. You're traveling somewhere completely new. In just a few hours you'll watch the sun rise over the bow of the boat and the work of the night will make it all the more beautiful, all the more rewarding. The sky will be pinker, the air fresher and your coffee richer, because you stuck it out. You served your shifts and sailed your boat under a blanket of stars into a new day.

But, even with all that glorious ethereal talk, sometimes my shifts start to feel a little long. They drag on at an excruciating pace. I know I'm tired, it's late and I'm in charge of the whole boat. In order to stay focused and occupy myself, I check the instruments again, scan the horizon, note the sails or engine temp if we're motoring. But that occupies only five minutes then I'm right back where I was—tired, sleepy and excruciatingly aware of how many *more* minutes I have left on my shift. Sometimes it's like that.

Sitting alone that night during my shift, on our way to Key West, I started sweating and a sense of nausea came over me. I had this kind of lingering malaise. Stupidly I started to think maybe some kind of sickening toxin that is usually safely encapsulated somewhere in my body had been cracked open and released during my fall. I know that sounds kind of ridiculous but with everything my body had been through recently, I didn't know what to make of it at times. I wondered whether I was actually physically ill or whether it was all in my mind—as if my thoughts were literally sickening me. It gnawed at me the entire first hour. Then it finally hit me.

I was scared.

I was worried, anxious and kind of sick with thoughts of my future. I was sitting here in the cockpit of this amazing boat but she and everything on it were just about literally all I had. I didn't have a house. I didn't have a job. I didn't have a husband. I didn't have much money. Now I was banged up, broke and just going. I started to question myself: *What are you going to do when you get there?*

Get where? I answered my own inquiry, which spawned a litany of others: *Well, where are you going? How are you going to get by?* I massaged my swollen arm a bit, flexed my knee and winced a little at the pain. *Are you even okay? Can you do this?*

As soon as the questions started tumbling at me, I remembered asking myself those things before. It was right after I'd finished driving from Big Mom's farm up in Cullman down to Tuscaloosa to start college at the University of Alabama, when I had just shed my New Mexico skin and was trying to start anew. I had my dad's Dodge Ram stuffed to the gills. The back window of the cab looked the same way it had when I made the move from my McMansion to my downtown Mobile apartment—shoes and hangers and a T.V. all plastered against the window pane—and the entire bed bubbling over with my desk chair, Wal-Mart room-in-a-bag and crates and boxes tied down with bailing twine.

I didn't really feel alone until I got there. When I pulled into the parking lot, there were girls everywhere—all dolled up in heels and high-fashion dresses. I didn't know what was with the big pearl earrings but every single girl had a pair on. Guess I didn't get that memo. And who dresses up to move? That's when the questions started. *What the hell are you doing here? How are you going to get by? Can you really do this?*

My decision to go to college in Alabama had been two-fold. First, I love Alabama. Having spent my summers as a child romping and riding around on Big Mom's farm, I felt like I had partly grown up in the lush, green country and loved the fact that I did. Second, I'd had a pretty bad fallout with my mom around that time that is an entirely different story. It was a long time ago and we've since mended the fences—so to speak—but I wanted nothing to do with New Mexico or her at the time.

But, leaving the state I had grown up in meant I wasn't going to know anyone at college. And much less know them, I wasn't going to know what they were like. How they spoke. What they ate. How they dressed. Clearly I'd already breached the pearl earring pact. I also didn't have much money to live on. I got student loans for the tuition but there was still another couple grand to cover room and board, a meal plan and all the other crap you learn only when you finally fly the coop that you have to pay for just to live—toiletries, car insurance, gas, clothes. That doesn't even include fun things like buying a coke, going to the movies, whatever. *How was I going to get by?*

The thought haunted me as I sat in Dad's truck watching all of these high-heeled girls trotting around, eight family members in tow carrying their zebra-printed, monogrammed dorm decor for them. Dad had a long-haul cattle delivery to make that week so he couldn't come with me. Big Mom was a little sour on the whole college idea anyway, finding it "mighty expensive for a piece of paper," and she always had a full day anyway—picking in her garden, washing the clothes, hanging the clothes, cleaning the house, cooking, canning, you name it. Her time was not going to be best spent with a silly frolic to college-land. So I was going it alone. It hadn't really bothered me until I got there and saw what I was really dealing with.

"Well you can wait outside scared or you can just go in."

Her words came to me unbeckoned in the dusty cab of that Dodge Ram. It was my mom. Even though I was angry with her at the time—we weren't even speaking then and didn't for years—that doesn't affect someone's hold on you. I remembered her telling me that the first time she was dropping me off at gymnastics. They had a great free program at Play, Inc.—that was Clovis, New Mexico's version of "the Y"—every Wednesday night. It turned out my brute force was finally good for something. I loved gymnastics. I stuck with it for years, competed in ninth grade and tumbled all through high school as a cheerleader. It was one of the best things I did in my youth, but I almost didn't. Why? Because I was scared.

I remember seeing the spattered flyer for Play, Inc.'s gymnastics program taped on the concrete wall of the bathroom for the public pool. Mom had dropped John, Jay and I off one Saturday to swim for the afternoon and I was just wiggling back into my worn-out one-piece when I saw it. The flyer had a picture of a girl doing a back-handspring and I thought it was the coolest thing anyone had ever done. I stared at the flyer for a long time. At the bright age of six, I couldn't read all of the words but I could make out Wednesday, gymnastics, free and Play, Inc. and that was all I needed.

I looked around a time or two, then pulled the flyer off the wall. Having nowhere to stick it in my little-kid suit and knowing it wouldn't survive the pool, I folded it up into a tiny chiclet-sized tablet and stuck it under a clump of dirt behind the concrete wall of the bathroom for safe-keeping until Mom came back to pick us up. I squeezed it tight in my hand all the way home and it was beige, stained and worn at each fold-corner by the time I opened it back up in my room.

It took me days to work up the courage to ask Mom to take me. I was afraid she might just say no—right out of the gate—and it would all be over. She would probably have a good reason but it would instantly squelch my dream of *my* little body leaping backward in my own back handspring. If I wanted to do it, though, I was going to have to ask. I finally opened up my little beige chiclet flyer to her one day and was surprised to find she agreed, on a few conditions. I had to promise to clean my room every week and clean up after supper on Wednesdays too. *Done. Got it. Great.* I was ready to do a flip right then!

Even though I had taken the first plunge in asking and getting my ticket to ride, I still almost let fear stop me. I was fidgeting and bouncing and had just about peed putting on what I perceived to be my best gymnastics outfit the next Wednesday. It was that same garage-sale one-piece bathing suit I had worn at the pool that day with a pair of little stained cotton shorts pulled up over it. I still had the worn, beige flyer crumpled up in my hand and I squeezed on it all the way to Play, Inc. But when Mom pulled into the parking lot, I was surprised to see her put the car in park, then ease back in her seat, leaving her seatbelt buckled, and light a cigarette. *What was she doing? We're going to be late.*

Then it dawned on me. This was probably the reason she had agreed to take me in the first place. If I wanted it so damn bad, I was going to have to go it alone. My mouth cinched into a tight little pucker as I watched her take a puff, look at the doors to the building and then look at me. I wadded and massaged the ragged flyer in my palm and looked at the doors too, then back at her. She often made things hard for us, but I hadn't seen this coming. It was clear, though, that she was not coming with me and I almost stayed in the car. At the ripe age of six, I didn't want to walk into that big building alone, have to go up to that scary guy sitting at the front desk to ask where the gymnastics class was and then walk in *there* all alone too.

"Well?" she asked, a thin wrist cocked on the steering wheel and a Pall Mall perched between her lips. She rolled down her window, flicked some ashes out followed by a gray plume of smoke before she turned to look at me again—one eyebrow raised in inquiry. I was frowning and picking at the cracked leather on the seat of her old Cadillac and I was *so mad* at her. I remember often being so mad at her—probably because she pushed me so hard. "I'm not going to hold your hand," she said. "If you want to do it, go in and do it."

That was it. That was all I needed. *Fine then.* I heaved and pulled the handle to open the Caddy door with lots of drama and grunts and slammed it back harder than I ever have. Then I heaved and pulled those big Play Incorporated doors open and walked in with little balled-up six-year-old fists to that mean-looking guy at the counter. Sometimes you could curse her for being so damn mean, but looking back on it—at the end of the day—I think I was a little braver because I was mad at her. I was stubborn and I was grunting. I was going to prove to her I wasn't scared. In all, I think she mostly did right by us by not holding our hands. Mine were usually balled-up little fists anyway. I was all grit and guile and "I'll show you!"

And, once those words came back to me again, it was decided. *Well, that's it then.* I wasn't going to wait outside scared. I was going in. That Rita Hayworth poster was going to be a shredded mess after I punched through. I shoved the door to the Dodge Ram open—again with lots of drama and grunts—then slammed it shut, loud enough to spook some of the pearl princesses around me and they scampered away. *That's right. Back it up. Look who's scared now.*

I had to laugh a bit at my own fear as I started untying some of the bailing twine from the bed of the truck. I was going to college for Christ's sake! I was starting a whole new adventure. Those are supposed to be a little scary, a little unknown, a little overwhelming. What does the motivational poster say? "If your dreams don't scare you, you're not dreaming big enough." Well mine were huge! They were thirteen floors high, and filled with frilly little southern sorority girls, but I was going in. And—just like the gymnastics class—it all worked out. I found friends, I found a way to make a little money, I worked hard and I had a great time in college. It usually all works out if you stop being scared and just go in.

I smiled to myself as that memory came back to me in the cool, dark air of the cockpit. While I couldn't quite ball up both fists at the moment, I felt I still had the same I'll-show-you attitude that would get me through this whole rip, roaring transition. I slid my hands along the soft leather of the wheel and eased my own fears. *It's okay if you don't know yet how it's all going to work out. You know it's the right thing and you know it will if you just go in. Head high.* So I wasn't a lawyer anymore? So I wasn't going to be some big fancy partner, with a big fancy house? I didn't want those things remember. *Remember!*

I scolded myself into reckoning. The only thing that was really worrying me was the money. How was I going to find a way to get by financially? But I'd had that same fear that hot day in the parking lot at the University and somehow it had all worked out. I knew I would always be a hard worker. I was smart, creative and disciplined. I would find something that allowed me to pursue my writing passion. I knew—deep down—that I was right about doing this: leaving it all behind, saying "No thanks" and handing the keys to the kingdom back.

Just like I knew I wanted to do gymnastics and I wanted to go to college. This was just that moment when I was staring at the doorway and I let a little fear mess with me. But not for long. We were going to Keys! Assuming nothing else happened—*knock on teak*—we would be there tomorrow! And I was going to heal. I believed in my body. Then I was going to write and travel and make this work. I was going to make my life my own. This is my tunnel and this is my time. I was going in. Head high.

CHAPTER TWENTY-THREE

This Is Me Roaring

"Boat coffee's the best."

I had already said it was good, it was great, but now it had worked its way up to the best. You may already know this, but I'm going to let you in on a little cruising secret—the "boat version" of everything is better. Boat food is better. Boat mimosasa are better. Boat showers are better. Boat sleep is better. Boat you-know-what is better. Whatever you can dream up that brings you pleasure, the boat version of it is always better. And that morning, as Phillip and I were making our way south across the denim-blue waters of the Gulf, the boat coffee was the best I had ever tasted. Every creamy sip seemed to soak through to my soul. I was beyond content.

As crazy as it sounds, I might really believe in the Sea Gods—or boat karma or whatever you want to call it—because after my sickening clatter to the deck, fat purple arm and funky knee, our night passage from Ft. Myers Beach to the Keys was our calmest yet. No beating our way across the Gulf, no fighting for every inch of ground, no pulling out and making a risky night entrance into a difficult pass. Thankfully, there was none of that!

Aside from my little internal revival, it was a perfect night. The wind held all evening and we were on an easy broad reach, averaging six knots, until daybreak. The stars that night were mesmerizing. You could just sit and look out on the twinkling sky and *think* all night long—in complete contentment. If our bash into Charlotte Harbor wasn't example enough, some nights on the boat the only thing you can think about is the boat itself: *Was that a crack? Did something just break? Is she going to make it?*

But when you have a night that is quiet, serene, dusted with stars, it is such a rewarding, peaceful passage. Apparently we had racked up some Gulf good will or something, because we were rewarded in droves. Just when things seemed the most shaky—I was busted up, frightened and wondering if everything I was doing was right and true—those salty waters handed us a damn near perfect passage and the boat carried us like a thoroughbred.

My arm was squishy but fully functional. My knee swelling and pain were easing. I was confident in and grateful for my body's ability to heal itself and my soul's ability to right itself—even in the midst of upheaval. Even with everything torn apart and jagged at the edges, I just knew I would get through it. I knew on the other side things would be better. I was making my life better. You always have to break a few eggs to make a cake, right? At least I hadn't broken any bones. I broke some promises and had disappointed some people but I hadn't disappointed myself. I hadn't let my supposed-to life break me.

We sailed until around 7:00 a.m. when the wind finally died out and we had to crank up. But she cranked just fine and was running like Rocky Balboa that morning. We were so proud of that engine. That boat was cruising right along. And so were the dolphins! We had a pack of them racing each other up at the bow as we were making our way in. They glided and rolled around each other with such ease—so fast and slippery.

Soon Key West was in sight. We could see it on the horizon. We had done it—made it there by boat. Just the two of us—Phillip and I—on our courageous Niagara 35. Our one last worry coming in was the "stern-to" configuration. Yes, me and docking. I don't know what my ever-lovin' problem is but I just get all jittery and usually screw everything up. I can't explain it, I just get a little antsy. My heart starts racing. I jump around like a monkey on cocaine and squeal a lot. It's quite a sight. And, now I was half busted—hobbling and babying my battered limbs—but I was all Phillip had. And we were going to do this. Come in backwards.

The A&B Marina even had a whole section on their website devoted to the stern-to approach and docking—complete with a diagram and video. This was serious business. I was naturally unnerved by it. I seem to have a particular knack for botching a docking. During our initial passage—my very first—bringing our boat back from Punta Gorda, I failed to catch a stern pole as our boat charged toward the dock in twenty-five knot plus winds. The next time I jumped off the boat without a single line in hand, expecting to just catch our sixteen-thousand pound beauty all gingerly like in a catcher's mitt.

While I improved during our many dockings and de-dockings back in Pensacola, when we would take the boat out just about every feasible weekend leading up to this Keys trip, I still had my issues. And this was going to be my first stern-to attempt. There are no finger docks between the boats at A&B Marina—nothing to space them apart other than the pilings. The boats are literally about two feet apart. It was going to be tight.

While the stern-to docking definitely has its perks (easy boarding and loading of supplies via the cockpit, easy access to power, easy leaving), it was definitely not going to be easy *coming*. We were going to have to make a backwards entry. I hated just the thought of it. I was sure we were going to smash into something. Come all this way to bash her up? *No. Hell no!* I was going to rock this dockage. We looked at the diagram and decided the most important thing would be for me to catch a bow line on one of the poles as we were coming in. That way I could ease out the line and control our backwards entry. That was it. Catch a pole. Catch a bloody fucking pole.

I can do this! My country roots kicked in. *It's like lassoing, right?* I had done plenty of that. The image of that old hay bail my dad had stuck some bull's horns on so us kids could practice our lassoing on the farm flashed before me. He'd shown me how to slide the rope back through the loop at the end to make a big lasso, how to swing it wide and slow over my head gaging the right angle to sling it over the horns.

"Easy now, Babes," he'd say as I was swinging the lasso, about to make the pitch.

Being right-handed, my dad had taught me to pitch it at just the right angle to catch the horn on the right before it would loop over and—most times—then catch the horn on the left as well. As soon as it did, I would pull hard and watch it cinch tight around the horns. It always felt so good when it caught around the horns. I would pull extra tight and often cause the hay bail to jump a little and leap toward us.

"Easy now … " my dad would start in but realizing it was just a hay bail and some old Texas longhorns, he'd finally let me unleash all my might just for fun. "Aww hell, bring her in!" he'd shout and I would yank and jerk and pull and sweat and dredge that hay bail all the way across the dirt floor of the barn towards me. I'd look up at Dad when it was done—all glistening and heaving and proud—and he'd smile and shake his head.

"You did it, Babes," he'd say. "But you always do," as he'd laugh at me for getting such joy out of just pulling something across some dirt. I couldn't help it. It was such simple fun!

Invigorated by the memory, as I hobbled my way up to the bow, I knew what I had to do. I started feeding the dock line through the loop spliced at one end to make a big lasso. I cleated the bitter end off through the chalk and on the bow cleat. I was ready. I was going to catch that damn pole! I was nervous this time—maybe even more nervous than any other pole-catching time—but there was a steadiness to my hand, an easy swing on the lasso. The rope seemed to swoop gracefully over head each time it came around. As Phillip backed her in, the pole came near. It was about six or seven feet away from me as he eased by when I heard Phillip holler from the cockpit: "You got this!" Then I released.

I watched as my big dock-line-lasso-loop fell softly around the pole. *I did it!* The thought struck me before I even realized it myself. But I had! I had done it. The line was around the pole! Instantly, I pulled and yanked and cinched her tight. My dad's voice creeped in: "Easy Babes." But Phillip's took over.

"Hold fast!" he shouted from the stern. I looked back toward the cockpit and could see we were slipping in fast, coasting straight toward the dock. This was it. My chance to use all of that bottled-up might to save us!

I heaved and pulled with everything I could muster. My left forearm rang out with a pins-and-needles-type pain as I squeezed my hand around the line but I kept pulling. My knee pinched just enough for me to take my weight off it but I kept pulling. Hand over hand I heaved until I could feel the boat finally creeping toward the pole. I looked back—all glistening and heaving and proud—and could see that it was done. We had stopped short of the dock.

The boat was once again, after another passage, tied up, secure and still. And this time she was in the Keys. *We had made it!* We had sailed her all the way down there. *Plaintiff's Rest* was easily the smallest boat in the marina but she had—by far—the biggest heart. She wasn't shy at all. She seemed to puff out her chest and inch her mast up a little higher to fit in with the mega yachts. We were so proud of her. We were proud of each other. But I was a little extra proud of me.

I had really done it—left it all behind to hop on a boat and set sail. I was a little busted, but not broken. I was tired, exhausted, sweaty and salty and looking forward to that first rinse and an icy cocktail—such simple things but they bring such enjoyment when you're cruising. I was still divorced, broke, and unemployed. Yeah, there was also that but I was still the happiest I had ever been. I was living every day to the fullest.

My hair was bleached from the sun. I was tan, browned and fit. I hadn't pictured the elephantitis in the arm and the crick knee when I looked out through my picked-out hole from prison but, otherwise, I had pretty much fulfilled my vision. I was a far cry from that pasty, paunchy overworked attorney who sat in the driveway staring at the house she hated, the husband she couldn't stand and the life she didn't want. I had done it: ripped everything apart and built it all back anew and I was so humbled, grateful and inspired by my own journey. I had to admit, I was pretty damn interesting.

And I didn't have all the answers yet—no big, grand plan. I didn't know where we would go next, after our trip to the Keys, and I wasn't sure what I was going to do when we got there or how I was going to get by but I wasn't going to let the financial uncertainty scare me. *It's just money.* It had only annoyed and irritated me when I had a pile of it anyway.

No more stress dial. No more prison cell. No more morning count. I had finally broke free and because I tore it down and built my life anew, I still had a life to live, seas to travel and oceans to cross. I had no house, no husband, no job but I did have time, freedom and no regrets. I mattered to me. There was only one thing I needed: a cowboy hat and a pair of heels. I had a moment that needed capturing. *This is me roaring.*

Epilogue

The sun burns a brilliant pink across my horizon. My legs lie stretched before me—tan, toned, now smooth minus the Ping-Pong ball lump and leisurely crossed in the warm rays of a setting sun. All I can hear is the distant call of a heron, the occasional dolphin's breath and the soft tapping of my fingers on the keys. I am working. I smile at the irony, because it's a Monday—which feels like a Saturday, like a Tuesday—and I am sitting on the deck of our beautiful boat, admiring the sunset and sipping a cool glass of wine while working. This is my new office, my new practice, my new kingdom.

Phillip and I made memories in the Keys that will make me laugh and sigh when I'm eighty, assuming I make it that long. The jewel-toned waters of the Dry Tortugas still come back to me, just as bright and shimmering, every time I close my eyes to conjure them. While it was simply the first of many breathtaking places we intend to sail to, I will always remember the Keys with unique clarity because it was our first planned destination on the boat and, for me personally, because we made the trip during such a tumultuous period in my life.

I was so uprooted at the time, everything was in chaos, but my pursuits and passions were clicked in to a point of focus I never thought achievable before. I have never wanted so little in my life yet wanted it so much. The Keys trip did exactly what we were hoping it would. It showed Phillip and I that we are well-suited for cruising. That we love to sail and travel and maintain our boat in exotic places but, more importantly, it showed me we really don't have to go that far to enjoy this lifestyle. There is no set definition of a "cruiser." It's not like you have to cross an ocean to get the title. There is no title, no certificate to hang on the wall, no official, organized group. They are just people who own a boat and like to travel to new and old places. Phillip and I now know: we are those people.

While the trip to the Keys did allow us to explore and discover many new places, it also showed us what pristine, unique cruising grounds we have right here in Pensacola. We have a big, deep bay filled with fish, dolphins and plenty of fetch for sailing. Our shores are lined with sugar-white beaches that serve as fantastic grounds for kitesurfing. While we haven't sailed the crystal green waters of the Exumas or dropped anchor near colorful Caribbean villages, our local anchorages here offer some of the most serene, breathtaking sunsets I have ever seen.

The best part, though, is that we are well on our way to sailing and cruising to all of those exotic places, just as we do here. We can go there, come back, stay, leave again. We can go or stay wherever we'd like because we are both as free as we have ever been. While I hate to say it was the money that scared me the most, if you already have your boat and health it is really the only other undeniable necessity for cruising. But just as I had believed it would—if I only found the courage to bust through—it all worked out.

When we returned from the Keys, I began working just as hard as I had in my lawyer days to build a new career around my writing, which required a lot of trial and error, many failed attempts, many rejections and many hard lessons learned in new skills such as editing, publishing, marketing, media and design. But it has been a rewarding and fortuitous journey. I am proud to say now, between my professional and pleasure writing, I make half as much as I used to as a high-stakes, hotshot attorney but I require a mere fraction. And I have no need for the the big, nice house with all the big, nice stuff in it. I simply don't need that stuff. I love the work and I can do it anywhere. My office goes with me everywhere and the possibilities for my continued employment are as vast and endless as the internet, because that is all I need. My new life is refreshingly nomadic.

It is not perfect though. It is not always cocktails and sunsets. It's a lot of hard work. I find myself often cramped up in a greasy engine room sweating and cursing, cringing as our bow crashes into another seemingly brick-wall wave and sinking with the receipt of another rejection when my words have failed to set the right scene and transport the reader in the way I know they can if I just keep trying. It is challenging, unpredictable yet totally life ratifying. Many people asked me when I turned and walked away from everything I had built—my seemingly very secure and comfortable life: "How much money do you have?" "What are you planning to do?" "Aren't you worried you won't be able to come back?"

And the question I seemed to face again and again: "Annie, aren't you afraid?"

My answer—although they do not want to hear it simply because they care about me—is this: "Not enough to not do it."

I feared more the regret I would face if I didn't chase my dreams simply because I was afraid. And I am so grateful. Now that I suffered and survived it and came out on the other side of the wall a stronger, steelier person. I am no longer confined. I cracked and crumbled the cinder blocks of my self-made cell because I refused to accept the absence of what I knew my future would not hold. But I also hurt people on the way out. I disappointed them, broke promises to them and had to bear the consequence of choosing my needs over theirs.

Some may find my decisions selfish, risky, and unorthodox because I own no property, no paintings, and no furniture. I have no children, no pets, no husband, no dependents. No one is expected to remember or mourn me when I'm gone. I am just here, in every moment, with no net beneath me and no secure future ahead. I sail on a boat to new and old places and I get by on a meager, never-predictable stream of income that trickles in from my toilings as an aspiring writer. It's a practice I have found to be far less lucrative, but infinitely more challenging and rewarding than the profession I initially chose and the degree I am still paying for.

I kitesurf in twenty-knot winds and chest-high waves. I climb, ski, dive and hang precariously from sheets of knotted silk, but those activities bring me only as much joy as the moments when I finally string together the perfect series of words that can imprint upon a person's soul. Or when I sit on the deck of our boat—basking in streaks of pink from a burning sun—and breathe heaving sighs of gratitude that I am alive and able, experiencing and struggling through it all.

I live my life the way that I do, because I remember when I almost lost it. I remember that night—my paralyzing, prison-break moment—and I remember my decision and the path I chose. I love to hear or read stories of how others have done it—took a stand, changed the things about themselves and their lives that they were unhappy with and made their life what they wanted it to be. It's inspiring.

In case my story inspires some other wayward soul out there trying to pick out a different path, I chose to share. And it doesn't have to be anything as bold or dangerous as sailing, skydiving, kitesurfing, any of that. By "adventure" I mean anything you want in life—be it a business venture, travel, the accomplishment of a physical or intellectual feat. Whatever it is you want most to do but that you have yet to do because you are afraid, or you worry it might disappoint others or you feel like all of the excuses you have woven around it are too thick to be unraveled. *That* is what I hope to inspire you to. Know that it is going to be challenging. It's going to frighten and change you. That's what makes the choice to embark anyway courageous, the experience rich and the people who do it rare. I hope you find it awakens you, perhaps revives you or—like me—saves you.

About the Author

In a former life, Annie Dike was a trial attorney. Six years in the practice taught her two very important things: 1) she loves to write, but 2) she hates to do it in a fluorescent-lit office. At twenty-nine, Annie stepped away with the clear mindset to travel, to sail, to live a different day every day and write about all of it. Annie now writes full-time and spends the majority of her days with the Captain cruising their 35-foot Niagara sailboat around Florida's west coast. Her debut non-fiction piece, Salt of a Sailor, was an Amazon #1 bestseller in sailing books. Annie has also written and published several practice guides, a novel and has more humorous and dramatic pieces in the works.

Check out Annie's other books on Amazon and Kindle and follow her many (mis)adventures via her blog posts, photos, Facebook posts and YouTube videos at HaveWindWillTravel.com.